Blood Read

John Digby

Blood Read

The Vampire as Metaphor in
Contemporary Culture

Edited by
JOAN GORDON and VERONICA HOLLINGER

Foreword by Brian Aldiss

PENN

University of Pennsylvania Press
Philadelphia

10 9 8 7 6 5 4 3 2 1

Published by
University of Pennsylvania Press
Philadelphia, Pennsylvania 19104-4011

Library of Congress Cataloging-in-Publication Data

Blood read : the vampire as metaphor in contemporary culture / edited
by Joan Gordon and Veronica Hollinger; foreword by Brian Aldiss.
    p.   cm.
    Includes bibliographical references (p.   ) and index.
    ISBN 0-8122-3419-7 (cloth, alk. paper). — ISBN 0-8122-1628-8 (pbk,
alk. paper)
    1. Horror tales, American—History and criticism. 2. Vampires
in literature. 3. American fiction—20th century—History and
criticism. 4. Popular culture—History—20th century. 5. Vampire
films—History and criticism. 6. Metaphor. I. Gordon, Joan,
1947–   . II. Hollinger, Veronica.
PS374.V35B58 1997
813'.0873808375—dc21   97-25079
                                              CIP

Frontispiece: Sweet Appetites, by John M. Digby.
Part openings, Death's-Head Hawkmoth, by John M. Digby.

For Wynne Francis
and for June Rosenbaum
with love and thanks

Contents

Foreword:
Vampires—The Ancient Fear

The vampire has come to the city. It was a country-dweller. Now it lives among the great urban masses and, like them, is inclined to take on the mantle of civilization.

Cities, with all their shortcomings, have proved irresistible to the human species that once knew no settled habitation, no building grander than a cave. Gradually, lands are becoming drained of their former populations, whether in sparsely tenanted countries like South America or in higher density ones of Asia. As the land empties, the cities fill up—to provide enormous blood banks for those who seek blood. No wonder ambulances wail like banshees.

In our cities, the taste for blood and horror is shared by the human inhabitants, on page and screen and in life. This volume pays tribute to some such phantasms. Perhaps death has become more terrible, now that it can strike when we are among strangers, now that it is no longer hedged about with ritual and poetry, now that those who die may not be missed from any community—as was the case when the world was smaller.

Nowadays, the capital cities of the Third World are the ones that contain record populations. Jakarta, Manila, Calcutta, Cairo, Shanghai, Teheran, Mexico City—these are the winners in this uncomfortable expansion race. Conversely, old urban centers such as New York, London, Paris, and Amsterdam show a tendency to shrink; their cores are empty and echoing by night, when their vast multi-story car parks become deserted by their gleaming daytime occupants. This sinister environment is the haunt of a vampire who once knew only mountains and valleys or perhaps a remote castle, that precursor of the concrete multi-story.

The linkage of ancient and modern was never better conveyed than in one of the most haunting of vampire/supernatural stories, Jack Williamson's "Darker Than You Think." Williamson's darkly puissant figures employ a magic whose roots lie back in the Stone Age. A recent learned book, Dorothy Carrington's *The Dream-Hunters of Corsica* (1995), lends weight to Williamson's story. Carrington, investigating the harsh and mountain-ous interior of the eponymous island, found there evidence of the survi-val of an old Megalithic faith, whose beliefs carried foreknowledge of death. The terrible shadowy whispering of that faith, dating perhaps from 3000 BC, may still sound in our ears. Certainly we fear the spirits of the dead, just as people did then. Vampires are part of that vision. The living and the dead still sleep in the same dormitories.

The vampire holds one great attraction for modern readers, apart from his or her polymorphously perverse sexual activities. It is ancient; its roots go back into distant time.

To the dwellers in present-day cities, whose grandparents probably lived in a shack among fields and who toiled as part of a landscape rather than a multi-national, what is ancient is to be revered or feared. In *The Golden Bough*, Sir James Frazer names the Slavonic people as those preyed on by "vampyres"; perhaps the last syllable of this spelling suggests the means by which the predators were warded off—fire. The "need-fires," Frazer suggests, may have been the originals of many ceremonial fires.

Such fires were needed to protect both people and cattle. Now that we obtain our meat from supermarkets, human beings are, at least in fic-tion, the vampire's sole prey. But, as in Suzy McKee Charnas's excellent *The Vampire Tapestry*, the predator too now suffers from big city blues.

Bram Stoker's famous novel begins, you will recall, with the words "Left Munich . . ." Immediately, the city is to be exchanged for the wil-derness of Transylvania, the delights of countries with Ordnance Survey maps for uncharted territories, and the modern for all that molders. Jona-than Harker's train is abandoned for an uncomfortable coach that sways "like a boat tossed on a stormy sea."

But, in this great transitional novel, we are not to remain among ancient things, whose distance brings comfort along with terror. The strength of Stoker's novel is that his evil Count, for all the world like a disease that cannot be checked, arrives in London. A barrier has been crossed; the infection has entered the modern vein.

London was the world's greatest city a century ago, and Stoker surely took a leaf from Charles Dickens's novels. Dickens is the first novelist of the lonely crowd, caught among choked thoroughfares and fogged alley-ways where Fagin, another sort of bloodsucker, is at large in the labyrinths of the metropolis.

There was a time—I remember it as a boy—when the movies *Frank-enstein* and *Dracula* were shown together on a double bill, with a nurse in attendance in the foyer of the cinema, just to put the wind up possible patrons. There is a similarity between the two myth-making stories, both telling of the undead and standing at either end of the nineteenth century like a couple of tombstones. Stoker, to make his horrors more real, adopts the method of Mary Shelley in her novel, by having multiple narrators tell the ghastly tale. "They can't all be lying," thinks the reader.

Are the writers under observation in this volume also lying? Are they simply trying to scare us?

Although I once wrote a Dracula novel myself, I confess to finding a vulgarity in general about vampires and vampire stories. Vulgar is an old-fashioned word, denoting a certain lack of delicacy; it implies something vaguely infantile, something reminiscent of the baby at the mother's breast, deriving its lifeblood through milk.

Nor can I summon belief in vampires. Carrington, in her Corsica book, speaks of mothers who claimed that their babies died during the night from the kiss of the vampire. She suggests that when there were too many children and food was scarce, vampirism could provide a convenient cover for infanticide.

However, the strength of the legend of vampirism cannot be denied; the Count has many progeny. The death of organized religion frees the mind to dwell on many horrors, of which perhaps this notion of life after death is the nastiest. As the editors emphasize, vampirism has become for post-modern writers a ready metaphor for the sickness of our society. Perhaps dealing with the subject should be considered a healthy sign, and the stories considered sufficient to elevate us to a mythic, if dark realm.

Carl Jung in his book *Memories, Dreams, Reflections* reports the case of a young woman of seventeen, a victim of incest, who dreamed of a vampire. In her catatonic state, she believed she lived on the Moon. The vampire, the dominant father-figure, terrorized people there. She never saw his face. Resolving to kill him, she went after him with a long sacrificial knife.

The vampire spread his wings. She saw before her a man of unearthly beauty. He lifted the girl up and flew off with her.

Are we all sick, "desolate and sick of an old passion," as the poet has it? Or will we all in time learn to fly, and be beautiful?

— BRIAN W. ALDISS

Acknowledgments

We would like to express our gratitude to the members of the International Association for the Fantastic in the Arts at whose annual Conference we met several years ago while presenting—quite appropriately—papers in the same session on vampires. Over the years, the Conference has provided us with much intellectual stimulation and many fine colleagues, not least the members of IAFA's vampire caucus, the Lord Ruthven Assembly. In addition, separately and together we would like to thank Brian Attebery for his wise advice along the way, Joseph Andriano for his suggestions about final revisions, John Digby for our cover and other illustrations, John Scheckter for our title, John Scheckter and Stuart Chamberlain for their moral support, Nassau Community College for its encouragement of scholarship through granting a much-needed sabbatical, and colleagues and students at Trent University for their intellectual companionship. Not least, we would like to offer a special thanks to Patricia Smith, our editor at the University of Pennsylvania Press, whose interest and encouragement made the completion of this project possible.

Nina Auerbach's "My Vampire, My Friend: The Intimacy Dracula Destroyed" is excerpted from *Our Vampires, Ourselves* (University of Chicago Press, 1995); Sandra Tomc's "Dieting and Damnation: Anne Rice's *Interview with the Vampire*" originally appeared in *English Studies in Canada* 22 (Dec. 1996), 441–60; Jewelle Gomez's "Rewriting the Mythology: Writing Vampire Fiction" is based on an interview that appeared in *HOT WIRE: The Journal of Women's Music and Culture* (Nov. 1987), 42–43, 60. We are grateful to the University of Chicago Press, *English Studies in Canada*, and *HOT WIRE: The Journal of Women's Music and Culture* for permission to reprint this material in our collection, as well as to Warner Bros. for permission to use the film stills in Rob Latham's "Consuming Youth: The Lost Boys Cruise Mallworld."

And these acknowledgments would not be complete without an expression of our sincere appreciation to the writers and scholars who participated in *Blood Read*. It's been wonderful working with you. Let's do it again sometime.

The vampire of subjectivity sees the play of identity from the metalevel, sees the fragrant possibilities of multiple voice and subject position, the endless refraction of desire, with a visual apparatus that has become irreducibly and fatally different. Once one receives this Dark Gift, there is no way back to a simpler and less problematic time. The gaze of the vampire, once achieved, cannot be repudiated; it changes vision forever.

—Allucquère Rosanne Stone,
The War of Desire and Technology at the
Close of the Mechanical Age

1

Introduction:
The Shape of Vampires

JOAN GORDON AND VERONICA HOLLINGER

> Very little about the underlying structure of horror images
> really changes, though our cultural uses for them are as shape-
> changing as Dracula himself.
> —David J. Skal, *The Monster Show* 23

> . . . perhaps we live in a continuing crisis . . . that sometimes
> takes the shape of vampires.
> —Nina Auerbach, *Our Vampires, Ourselves* 117

An ambiguously coded figure, a source of both erotic anxiety and corrupt desire, the literary vampire is one of the most powerful archetypes
bequeathed to us from the imagination of the nineteenth century. Vampire
tales have been and, in some cases, continue to be "grisly nightmares that
touch on the basic fears that make us all vulnerable" (Dickstein 67). More
relevant to the aims of this present collection, however, is Nina Auerbach's elegantly simple observation that "every age embraces the vampire
it needs" (145). *Blood Read* aims to examine some aspects of the vampire as
late twentieth-century cultural necessity.

Even as "grisly nightmare," the vampire has tended to be a graciously
well-groomed horror. Until quite recently, the quintessential vampire was
a direct descendent of Bram Stoker's Dracula as embodied in Bela Lugosi's
suave Eastern European Count. Since the mid-1970s, however, most particularly since the publication of the first and most influential of Anne
Rice's *Vampire Chronicles, Interview with the Vampire* (1976),[1] the figure of
the vampire has undergone a variety of fascinating transformations in response, at least in part, to ongoing transformations in the broader cultural
and political mise-en-scène.

One of the most interesting and significant metamorphoses in the conventional figure of the literary (and cinematic) vampire has to do with what several of the writers in this present collection refer to as its "domestication." Whether we mourn or celebrate these changes, the contemporary vampire is no longer only that figure of relatively uncomplicated evil so famously represented by Count Dracula, that fatal silence at the heart of Stoker's novel.[2]

In large part, the domestication of the vampire has come about through a shift in the perspective from which the horror tale has conventionally been told. Following Mary Shelley's unusual narrative technique in *Frankenstein* (1818), although adapting it to their own purposes, many writers now narrate their horror stories from the inside, as it were, filtering them through the consciousness of the horrors that inhabit them. Not surprisingly, the impact of this shift from human to "other" perspective works to invite sympathy for the monstrous outsider at the same time as it serves to diminish the terror generated by what remains outside our frame of the familiar and the knowable.[3] A seemingly unending stream of stories, novels, and films continue to be produced in which the vampire enacts its familiar role as life-consuming threat—films like *Buffy the Vampire Slayer* (1992) come to mind here, as well as *The Lost Boys* (1987). There are, nevertheless, an increasing number of cases in which the vampire, if not completely sympathetic—as in Rice's novels or those of Chelsea Quinn Yarbro—is, at the least, portrayed with an empathy that would have been unthinkable in earlier decades.

As an inevitable result of the shifting ideological development of the vampire, its metaphorical charge has also been transformed, often in very complex ways. While it is obvious that the power of the vampire is at once immediate and direct—the grisly nightmares it can evoke are visceral, not rational—it is also true that any treatment of the figure of the Other is an ideological moment that can usefully be interpreted for political and cultural significance. Indeed, the work of metaphor is crucial to the construction of all fantastic narratives, since, as Rosemary Jackson notes, the realm of the fantastic is precisely composed of "all that is not said, all that is unsayable, through realistic forms" (26). A study of the vampire as metaphor, then, will go some way towards revealing the investments of contemporary fantasy. In the terms introduced by Fredric Jameson in *The Political Unconscious,* "the production of aesthetic or narrative form is to be seen as an ideological act in its own right, with the function of inventing imaginary or formal 'solutions' to unresolvable social contradictions" (79).

The essays and articles in *Blood Read* read the vampire from a variety of critical perspectives and in a variety of texts, but all reflect a common aim: they consider differing manifestations of the contemporary vampire from the perspective of their metaphorical roles. And, contrary to the old legends that tell us that vampires have no reflection, we do indeed see many diverse reflections—of ourselves—as the vampire stands before us cloaked in metaphor. Indeed, it is the rich metaphorical usefulness of the vampire which, we believe, helps to explain its continuing "undeath" in contemporary popular culture, its powerful grip on our imaginations.[4] Just as our own self-representations are constructions that are transformed over time—as Michel Foucault, for one, has demonstrated in his "archeological" studies—so are the constructions and representations of our monsters transformed over time. Such transformations deserve serious critical attention.

The figure of the vampire, as metaphor, can tell us about sexuality, of course, and about power; it can also inscribe more specific contemporary concerns, such as relations of power and alienation, attitudes toward illness, and the definition of evil at the end of an unprecedentedly secular century. And it can help to clarify the nature of the fantastic realities that seem occasionally to overwhelm the empirical. In recent decades, the vampire has re-affirmed its power as an icon of popular culture—for example, in the incredible popularity of Rice's *Vampire Chronicles* (1976–1994), in the appearance of *Forever Knight* (1992–) as a regular TV series, in the success of films like *Near Dark* (1987), *The Lost Boys,* Francis Ford Coppola's *Bram Stoker's Dracula* (1992), and Jordan's version of *Interview with the Vampire* (1994), in new revisions of *Dracula* by authors such as Fred Saberhagen (*The Dracula Tape,* 1975) and Brian Aldiss (*Dracula Unbound,* 1991), and in the proliferation of vampire literature that continues to spread throughout the horror sections of book shops and comic book stores. So familiar a part of our everyday culture has the vampire become that, most appropriately, it provided the subject of director Mel Brooks's most recent parody of popular taste, *Dracula: Dead and Loving It* (1995).

Given all this, it is perhaps surprising that so few recent examinations approach the vampire other than as a literal manifestation of some of our "grisly nightmares," one of a collection of grim figures from our history of horror. In Radu Florescu and Raymond McNally's volumes on the historical figure of Vlad Dracula (for example, *Dracula, Prince of Many Faces: His Life and Times,* 1989); in interviews with would-be vampires (reported, for example, in Olga Hoyt's *Lust for Blood,* 1984), in lush pictorials such as

Manuela Dunn Mascetti's *Vampire: The Complete Guide to the World of the Undead* (1992), we see a strange blurring of myth and reality, a longing, perhaps, to transform the vampire into the inhabitant of a world more glamorous than our own. The vampire even has its own encyclopedia now, J. Gordon Melton's huge *Vampire Book* (1994), which oscillates, entry by entry, for 852 pages, between the skeptical and the ingenuous, seldom employing what one might think of as a scholarly distance from the sensational potential of its subject/object.[5]

Yet succumbing to the vampire's charm by inviting it into the mundane world risks trivializing its image, tarnishing its glamor, and casting those so occupied among the superstitious subjects of another category of works about the vampire, works of cultural anthropology such as Paul Barber's *Vampires, Burial, and Death* (1988). Barber's anthropological history demonstrates how powerful the vampire's grip has been throughout history and across cultures and reminds us that the myths and legends surrounding the vampire do not describe an actual physical being, but something much more powerful, a creature who can take on the allegorical weight of changing times and collective psyches.

While it is as metaphor that the vampire has been least acknowledged, there nevertheless exists a growing body of critical studies in this area. Margaret L. Carter's collection, *Dracula: The Vampire and the Critics* (1988) and James B. Twitchell's *The Living Dead: A Study of the Vampire in Romantic Literature* (1981) focus on pre-twentieth-century works. David J. Skal explores the vampire's introduction into the twentieth-century popular imagination in his superb cultural history of horror, *The Monster Show* (1993). Most recently, Nina Auerbach's *Our Vampires, Ourselves* (1995) presents a history of the past two centuries that develops around the changing figure of the vampire and the cycle of political/cultural values which its transformations can help to interpret (Auerbach's essay in this present collection is excerpted from her longer study). A number of valuable but uncollected scholarly essays have also addressed this subject and their contributions are noted in many of the essays in this present collection.[6]

*   *   *

Blood Read is the first collection of articles and essays to focus specifically on the role of the vampire as metaphor in contemporary culture, exploring this aspect of the conventional horror figure in recent fiction and film and, glancingly, on television and in comics as well. This collection approaches the vampire not as the literal horror in some "night of the living dead" reconstruction, but as a metaphor for various aspects of contemporary life.

At this present postmodern moment, it seems that even our monsters have become transformed, as the boundaries between "human" and "monstrous" become increasingly problematized in contemporary vampire narratives. For this is one of the functions of our monsters: to help us construct our own humanity, to provide guidelines against which we can define ourselves. Even the stock horror vampire, one of the most prolific figures in popular culture, is never simply a vampire; the roles played out by this figure shift as our desires and anxieties adapt to particular cultural / political moments. In many ways, we are very far indeed from Stoker's Victorian world of 1897.

Blood Read presents a rather unconventional range of writing for an academically-oriented collection by combining essays by writers of vampire fiction with scholarly studies of fiction and film. This parallels the ongoing conversation among the artists and scholars who devote their time to various aspects of fantastic cultural production. Similarly, the diverse nature of the writings here parallels the increasingly disparate nature of the contemporary vampire. We trust that the various pieces of the dialogue that forms this collection will prove as stimulating to its readers as it has been to its writers and editors.

Having invited the subject in through this introduction, we open our study proper by looking back to the vampires of the nineteenth century, acknowledging the heritage of today's vampire and suggesting continuity in the metaphoric tradition. Nina Auerbach sees in J. Sheridan Le Fanu's classic novella, *Carmilla* (1872), a metaphor for intimacy in friendship, a metaphor that gives way by the time of *Dracula* to intimacy as conquest, so that in the twentieth century the vampire films inspired by *Carmilla* destroy the Victorian ideal of friendship. Jules Zanger's essay expresses a different nostalgia, for Dracula as metaphoric Anti-Christ, situated against the diminishment, in this century's fiction and film, of the vampire to metonymic "social deviant." Margaret Carter's essay points us forward in a broad survey of the vampire novel since 1970, which she sees as expressing a range of "cultural attitudes toward the outsider, the alien other." Joan Gordon's essay looks back to the mother figures of *Carmilla* and Coleridge's earlier "Christabel" (1797) to see how the maternal metaphor returns to haunt the cultural productions of several decades of the twentieth century. In the process, she offers a discussion of several rarely examined vampire fictions, including Theodore Sturgeon's moving *Some of Your Blood* (1961) and Tanith Lee's science-fictional *Sabella, or The Blood Stone* (1980).

Our next section reads the vampire from the vantage point of the fiction writer. Suzy McKee Charnas, author of the now-classic *The Vampire Tapestry* (1980), explains how her vampire evolved from her determination not to romanticize evil but to "tell the story of a simple and relentless predator." Brian Stableford's *The Empire of Fear* (1988) and *Young Blood* (1992) are lively and erudite vampire novels that deserve to be more widely known; his equally lively and erudite discussion on the alienness and eroticism in these novels will, we hope, encourage a wider readership. Finally, Jewelle Gomez explains how she came to write her *Gilda Stories* (1991) as a way to "create a mythology to express who I am as a black lesbian feminist." All three writers remind us that, while the vampire's popularity may sometimes result in trivialization, that same popularity recognizes how rich a subject the vampire provides for any writer strong enough to control it.

Our next group of essays reads the vampire as a metaphor for consumption. In the nineteenth century, to look back again, the vampire functioned as a natural metaphor for the symptoms of tuberculosis: consider its associations with wasting, with paleness, with the flow of blood from the mouth, night restlessness, alternate burning and chills, even with the victim's rumored sexual energy. In the post-antibiotic and post-Veblen twentieth century, however, consumption has taken on a new significance while remaining an apt locus for vampiric activity. Sandra Tomc proposes the vampire as a metaphor for "successful dieting," for the obsessions to curtail the consumption of food and the resulting "promised dissolution of female secondary sex characteristics"; she supports her proposal through an analysis of Rice's *Interview with the Vampire*. Nicola Nixon explores the vampire film's reflection of the Reagan era, offering a critique of its avoidance of the AIDS crisis and its emphasis on nebulously idealized family values; Nixon looks at the yuppie consumption of Tony Scott's film of *The Hunger* (1983), as well as at the good family/bad family dichotomies of *Near Dark* and *The Lost Boys*. In contrast, Rob Latham's essay applies Marx's equation of vampirism with consumer capital accumulation—as "dead labour which, vampire-like, lives only by sucking living labour"—to a reading of the vampire's current role as youth consumer in *The Lost Boys*.

The final section of *Blood Read* comprises four essays that embed the vampire-as-metaphor in its present postmodern context. Miriam Jones applies feminist and post-structuralist literary theory to a reading of Jewelle Gomez's *The Gilda Stories* in her exploration of the vampire as marginal other in a post-colonial world. Trevor Holmes works within the complex framework of queer theory to develop his introduction to some of the intersections of gay male vampire fiction and goth punk sensibility. His essay explores a wide range of cultural forums, including popular music, film and fiction, erotica, and electronic discussion groups. Mari Kotani's view of the other arises from her own unique position as reader of contemporary Japanese culture; she examines several Japanese works as attempts to "import and familiarize . . . western cultural commodities." In the fictions Kotani discusses, the western tradition represents the Other to be assimilated as the vampire makes the transfer from west to east. Finally, Veronica Hollinger discusses the vampire as "in itself an inherently deconstructive figure," supremely adapted to play a role in both postmodern fiction and theory; her paradigmatic instance is Angela Carter's short story, "The Lady of the House of Love."

The selection of articles and essays in this collection can only begin to suggest the scope of its subject. For this reason, we offer *Blood Read* not as a definitive reading of contemporary vampire culture but as a disparate series of glances at various aspects of that culture. (In fact, while the range of topics included here demonstrates the heterogeneity of the influence of the vampire-as-metaphor, it does not dispel a certain homogeneity in the form of recurring citations of works that have already begun to form a kind of "canon" of contemporary vampire texts.) The essays in *Blood Read* move usefully along paths of hegemony and disenfranchisement, economy and ecology, socialization and separation. Such themes suggest our current anxieties about the dissolution of boundaries between the private and the public, the individual and society, one social group or nation and another, ourselves and our environment. How apt that the vampire reflects such border anxieties, since it penetrates boundaries by its very nature—between life and death, between love and fear, between power and persecution. And how apt that it thrives in this postmodern milieu of dissolving borders, between the virtual and the real, between private and public personae, in the breaking down of cultural and national boundaries, while a plague transmitted by the penetration of bodily boundaries—and often through blood—sweeps the world.

Part One

READING

HISTORY

2

My Vampire, My Friend:
The Intimacy Dracula Destroyed

NINA AUERBACH

"I have never had a friend—shall I find one now?" croons J. Sheridan Le Fanu's Carmilla in 1872 when she confronts her beloved prey (87). Until the coming of the impersonal, imperial Dracula in 1897, this friend-seeking vampire dominated the nineteenth century, although only Carmilla, a female vampire, could fully realize these anti-social desires. Byron and Polidori's Lord Ruthven had lured his schoolmate into uncharted eastern countries with the seductive promise of "intimacy, or friendship," but everything male vampires seem to promise, Carmilla performs: she arouses, she pervades, she offers a sharing self. This female vampire is licensed to realize the homosexual, interpenetrative implications of the friendship male vampires aroused and denied.

Through dreams and tricks, Carmilla invades the lonely life of Laura, quickly supplanting her foolish father's authority. Looking back on Carmilla after a team of male experts have staked her, Laura tells with lyrical vividness the story of her one friend, whose attacks contain no Stokeresque blood or fangs, only homely and familiar sensations.

For Carmilla and Laura understand each other, sharing a life even before Carmilla murmurs, "I live in your warm life and you shall die—die, sweetly die—into mine . . . you and I are one for ever" (89–90). Both have lost their mothers and their countries; each suffuses the image of the other's absent mother. In the shared childhood dream in which they first encounter each other, each perceives the other as a "beautiful young lady," not another child. Like Laura's dead mother, Carmilla is a Karnstein, a vibrant remnant of an apparently extinct family. When Laura's mother breaks protectively into a vampire reverie, her message is so ambiguous that Laura misconstrues it, turning herself into Carmilla and her own mother into her friend's. Hearing a simultaneously sweet and terrible warning, "Your mother warns you to beware of the assassin," seeing Carmilla bathed in blood at the foot of her bed, Laura fuses self, killer, and mother: "I wakened with a shriek, possessed with the one idea that Carmilla was being murdered" (106). In the flow of female dreams, murderer and murdered, mother and lover, are one; women in *Carmilla* merge into a union which the men who watch over them never see.

In a genre that simultaneously expressed and inhibited its century's dream of homoerotic friendship, Carmilla speaks for the warier male vampires who came before her. Her vampirism, like theirs, is an interchange, a sharing, an identification, that breaks down the boundaries of familial roles and the sanctioned hierarchy of marriage. But the 1890s bequeathed new taboos to our own century. Oscar Wilde in 1895, on trial, stripped of freedom and audacity, and the hygienically heterosexual Dracula in 1897, transformed a tradition of intimacy to one of conquest. *Carmilla* lives on in a succession of twentieth-century films, but none is true to its vision of forbidden friendship; each, in the idiom of its decade, discards the intimacy of Le Fanu's dream tale, turning vampirism into a pageant orchestrated by an implied male viewer and leader.

Carl Dreyer's stately *Vampyr* (1932) is the first canonical vampire film not based on Dracula; it claims to be, instead, a loose adaptation of *Carmilla*. Despite its source, however, *Vampyr* scrupulously avoids not only erotic intimacy but all relationships; it is so solemn and its key images involve a solitude so intense that it is scarcely a vampire film at all. Its fastidious distance from its source guarantees its artistry for many critics: according to Pauline Kael, "most vampire movies are so silly that this film by Carl Dreyer—a great vampire film—hardly belongs to the genre" (812). To achieve art status, a director must drain away his vampires.

Dreyer's protagonist is neither Carmilla, here a blind old crone less visible than her diabolical male henchmen, nor Laura, whose character is split into two sisters: the stricken Léone, who spends most of the movie in bed, sobbing and shuddering over her own damnation, and the beleaguered Gisèle, whom the hero rescues at the end. The center of the film is the man who sees them. The opening title decrees the primacy of a male watcher: "This story is about the strange adventures of young Alan Gray. His studies of devil worship and vampire terror of earlier centuries have made him a dreamer, for whom the boundary between the real and the unreal has become dim." Like the dreamer/director Carl Dreyer, this poetic spectator retains full control over the mysterious world he projects.[1]

The story is indeed "about" Alan Gray's oblique experience of vampirism. We watch him watching the interplay between Satanic shadows and human characters; compulsively reading experts' accounts—as have less exalted vampire-watchers from Boucicault's melodramas through Hammer films; dreaming of his own burial alive, which he observes from his coffin in horror; sailing into mist with Gisèle once the crone has been staked. Vampirism here is Alan Gray's experience, his dream, or his creation. The viewer is barred from participating in it; we watch only Alan watching.

Vampirism is purged of sharing or interchange. The crone and Léone are scarcely together. When they are, the physical contrast between the massive blind woman and the frail girl is so striking that vampirism comes to resemble self-hypnosis rather than affinity. In one dream-like sequence, Léone wanders into the garden, where Alan and the spectators find her sprawled on a rock with the crone leaning over her. The scene freezes into a tableau that realizes Fuseli's famous painting, *The Nightmare*; its stopped motion deflects attention from active physical interchange toward a poetic spectator who appreciates cinematic painting.

Other scenes among women are similarly purged of affinity. Large close-ups of Léone or Gisèle with sorrowing or stern older women—the old servant, the austere nursing sister—force the women's visual incompatibility on the viewer: old and young, imposing and thin, dark and blonde seem to inhabit different physical universes. These insistent contrasts replace the amorphous maternal spirit of Carmilla, who both protects against and embodies the vampire. When Léone, half-transformed, bares her teeth, Gisèle shrinks away into the nun's arms, expressing no empathy with her beloved sister. Later, we hear from behind a closed door a woman's seductive plea, "Come with me! We will be one soul, one body! Death is waiting," but we see neither speaker nor hearer. *Vampyr* is that rarity in the vampire canon, a work that forecloses the possibility of intimacy.

The film's two most famous sequences have little to do with vampires: in both, men experience the claustrophobic solitude of burial alive. In a vision, Alan Gray observes his own funeral, watching the grave close over him through a glass partition in his coffin; at the end, the sinister doctor Marcis is trapped in a flour mill, flailing helplessly as a blizzard of whiteness covers him. These splendid sequences throw the focus away from vampirism, women, or any emotional interchange; the men who helplessly, silently watch themselves sink recapitulate the director's lonely terror at his own submergence in images. The one acknowledged masterpiece inspired by *Carmilla* announces implicitly that female vampires are incompatible with art's mastery.

One would expect feminist chic to radicalize more recent vampires, and in one sense it has: they have become success symbols. Somewhere between the self-obsessed, almost airless cinematic art of the 1930s and teasing spectacles of the 1960s like Roger Vadim's *Blood and Roses* (1961) or Roy Ward Baker's *The Vampire Lovers* (1970) is the Carmilla of the affluent 1980s, Miriam Blaylock in *The Hunger* (1983). Neither Scott's film nor the Whitley Strieber novel on which it is based acknowledges Le Fanu directly, but Miriam's seduction of Sarah, the scientist trying to study her, is at the center of *The Hunger*. Unlike Dreyer's sleepwalkers, Miriam and Sarah almost manage to be friends; they do talk to each other, unlike most women in vampire movies, but their creator's conventions come between them.

Tony Scott fractures Strieber's exactingly intelligent myth of "another species, living right here all along, an identical twin" of humanity (152). Strieber's Miriam is a dominant, superior consciousness who may be the last of her race; she has survived centuries of arrogant imperial persecution. Scott's is a creature of the 1980s, subordinate to seductive objects: jewelry, furniture, lavish houses in glamorous cities, leather clothes. Miriam, like the success stories of the consuming 1980s, lives through her things. She kills not with her teeth but with her jewelry, an ankh that hides a knife. She preserves her desiccated former lovers, who age eternally once their vampirism wears off, as carefully as she does her paintings and clothes. These things, along with the music and the cityscapes over which she presides, make us envy Miriam's accouterments instead of her immortality. Vampires in *The Hunger* are not their powers, but their assets.

The movie reduces Miriam not only by subordinating her to her props but by appropriating the staccato visual techniques of MTV. The characters, like the look of the film, are fractured. Miriam loses not only the memories that, in Strieber's novel, take her back to the beginning of western civilization, but also her controlling consciousness. Strieber's Miriam was a figure of lonely integrity throughout the waste of empires; Scott's becomes an icon of glamorous discontinuity.

Dreyer's vampire women shrank to stylized figments of a male poet's dream. Scott turns his characters into parts of themselves. Mouths predominate, often crosscut with the giant grimace of a laboratory monkey, but Scott also cuts between disjointed eyes, hands, nipples, teeth, throats, blood, and—in the love scene between Miriam and Sarah—legs and breasts, fetishizing fragments until the audience scarcely knows what eye or hand belongs to which man or woman, or—in the love and murder scenes—who is doing what to whom. Although Catherine Deneuve's soft blonde Miriam and Susan Sarandon's dark edgy Sarah are contrasting visual types whose rhythms evoke different centuries, Scott's slashing camera makes them effectively indistinguishable in key scenes. Postmodern cinema aligns itself with 1930s high art and 1960s soft porn, creating a collusion between director and viewer that dwarfs personality and overpowers the chief gift of Victorian vampires: their friendship.

Moreover, while Le Fanu's Laura became Carmilla by remembering her at the end, Sarandon's Sarah becomes Miriam by dismembering her: after flexing her new vampirism by butchering her male lover, Sarah defies and displaces Miriam. The movie ends with an opaque shot of Sarah and a female lover, looking down over another city; her distinctive style, her rhythm, her decor, all have replaced Miriam's. The vampirism that meant sharing in the 1870s adapts to the competitive business ethos that reigned over America in the 1980s. There is room for only one at the top.

From the 1930s to the 1980s, film directors have attributed all sorts of dangers to hungry women, but their central danger—their gift for friendship and empathy—was understood only by supposedly repressed Victorians. Memories of the real Carmilla do occasionally surface beyond the commercial and aesthetic canon. An ingenious Showtime TV Movie of *Carmilla* (1989, dir. Gabrielle Beaumont) is the only adaptation I have seen that is true to Victorian intensities of friendship. Jonathan Furst's script transposes the action to the ante-bellum American south, rife with furtive voodoo rites even before Carmilla enters. Carmilla seduces Laura— here called Marie—Byronically, with promises of travel, adventure, rebellion against her father's pathological possessiveness. "I can take you to worlds beyond your dreams," she whispers as she playfully dematerializes. Marie's father is not Le Fanu's cloudy, laughing obstruction, but a neurotic tyrant who madly sequesters his daughter "like one of his paintings" and lusts after Carmilla while Marie pleads: "Let me have a friend; that's all I'm asking." Marie's mother has not died but run away from her husband—to become a vampire in league with Carmilla, we learn at the end. The script equates vampirism not with lurid sex but with women's friendship as a rebellion against paternal control. As in Le Fanu's story, Marie finally overcomes the dead Carmilla—by becoming her.

This modernization of Le Fanu is shrewdly true to his essence. Beaumont's abandonment of mediating male observers captures the intensity and exhilaration, as well as the danger to family ties, of Victorian erotic friendship. Unfortunately Beaumont's shrewd dramatization has never reached theaters; compressed into an hour time slot, it played only in the obscurity of cable television. Reviving through the prism of contemporary feminism Le Fanu's Victorian dream of vampire friendship, Beaumont's *Carmilla* is still too frightening to find a place in our horror market.

3

Metaphor into Metonymy:
The Vampire Next Door

JULES ZANGER

The emergence of the "new" vampire as a popular mass culture figure during the 1970s and 1980s suggests a number of possible directions for inquiry concerning the effects of extensive multi-media presentation on a popular icon. In pursuing such an inquiry, there is room for a range of speculations, from the formally academic to the determinedly trivial, since a mass culture "myth" frequently resonates at every level of that culture, even if only unequally and fitfully. My premise in what follows is that the construction and popularity of the "new" vampire represent a demoticizing of the metaphoric vampire from Anti-Christ, from magical, metaphysical "other," toward the metonymic vampire as social deviant (from Count Dracula to Ted Bundy), eroding in that process of transformation many of the qualities that generated its original appeal.

To speak of the "new" vampire, however, demands that we first distinguish this creature from the "old" one, Bram Stoker's Dracula, who still retains much of his popularity and against whom all changes may be measured. Although the vampire myth had appeared in literature in a variety of forms from the beginning of the nineteenth century, it was Stoker's vampire that caught and dominated the popular imagination, first in the novel, then on the stage, and later in Bela Lugosi's definitive film version. In the last two decades, however, we have seen the commercial proliferation of new vampire images in a variety of media, from popular novels, to numerous films, to television serials and animated cartoons, to illustrated books for children "ages four and up." This multi-media proliferation is designed to appeal to an audience of readers and viewers of more widely diverse ages, levels of literacy, and education than Stoker could comfortably assume for his novel. In addition, this media proliferation demands that each particular image of the vampire differentiate itself—for legal and commercial as well as dramatic and aesthetic reasons—from previous images, accelerating and distorting the normal processes of what Northrop Frye called mythic displacement. All this results in a kind of entropic reductivism, a dialogue of attrition and subtraction, softening and smoothing over the hard-edged definitions of the vampire provided for us by Stoker's *Dracula*.

One characteristic that immediately distinguishes the new vampire from the old is that the new one tends to be communal, rather than solitary as was Dracula. Though Dracula does have a "family" in those three wickedly alluring ladies we are permitted too briefly to see in the opening of the novel, they are for narrative purposes completely functionless, dismissed after their first tantalizing appearance, and have no role at all in the subsequent development of the action. They are, in other words, proper Victorian ladies, remaining properly at home while the master of the house goes forth to do solitary battle against the forces of virtue. The new vampire, on the other hand, is often presented to us as multiple, communal, and familial, living with and relating to other vampires, as in Anne Rice's *Vampire Chronicles* or in films like *The Hunger* (1981), *The Lost Boys* (1987), or *Near Dark* (1987); or even in *Little Dracula Goes to School* (1992) in which Little Dracula's mother daily brings him "a glass of blood before bed" (Waddell 17).

Equally representative is the change in the metaphysical status of the vampire. In Stoker's novel, Dracula is presented to the reader as the earthly embodiment of supernal Evil, as the "arrow in the side of Him who died for man." Van Helsing exhorts his Army of Light: "Thus are we ministers of God's own wish: that the world and men for whom His Son died, will not be given over to monsters, whose very existence would defame him" (Stoker 265, 354–55). Dracula, for Stoker and for Stoker's readers, is the Anti-Christ. To emphasize Dracula's metaphysical status, Stoker, when having Renfield speak of him, employs capital letters, precisely as "God" is conventionally capitalized: "So when He came tonight, I was ready for Him . . . when I tried to cling to Him, He raised me up and flung me down" (311).

The "new" vampire possesses very little of that metaphysical, anti-Christian dimension, and his or her evil acts are expressions of individual personality and condition, not of any cosmic conflict between God and Satan. Consequently, the vampire's absolutely evil nature as objectified in *Dracula* becomes increasingly compromised, permitting the existence of "good" vampires as well as bad ones. Recently, as a case in point, we have had a television series, *Forever Knight*, the hero of which is a reformed vampire turned police detective. In P. N. Elrod's novel *Bloodlist* (1990), the hero is a vampire/crime reporter who conveniently lives near the Chicago Stockyards so he can feed, more or less innocently, on the doomed cattle in the pens. In Fred Saberhagen's series of vampire novels—*The Dracula Tape, The Holmes-Dracula File*, and *An Old Friend of the Family*—Dracula is the benevolent protector of his human friends.

With the loss of vampires' metaphysical and religious status, there is a parallel loss of many of their folkloric attributes. Though still possessing preternatural strength and shunning the light, most contemporary vampires have lost their mutability, which is the essence of all magic. They can no longer transform themselves into bats or mist or wolves or puffs of smoke; in addition, they need no longer wait to be invited over a threshold, and mirrors and crucifixes appear to have relatively little effect on them. When Louis, the vampire who narrates Rice's *Interview with the Vampire* (1976), is asked about his magical powers, he responds: "That is, how would you say today . . . bullshit?" (22).

Taken together, these shifts—from solitary to multiple and communal, from metaphoric Anti-Christ to secular sinner, from magical to mundane—demythologize the vampire, transform it from Satan's agent on Earth into someone who more nearly resembles a member of a secret society or a subversive political association, perhaps the Masons or the Ku Klux Klan. No longer embodying metaphysical evil, no longer a damned soul, the new vampire has become, in our concerned awareness for multiculturalism, merely ethnic, a victim of heredity, like being Sicilian or Jewish. Or, alternatively, vampirism can be understood, as it is in Barbara Hambly's novel *Those Who Hunt the Night* (1988), as a kind of viral infection, possibly like AIDS, without any necessary moral weight. It should be noted, however, that the new vampire, although "ethnic" in one special sense, does not come to us like Dracula from some mysterious foreign clime, preferably Eastern, but is resolutely American, appearing as a Louisiana plantation owner in *Interview with the Vampire*, a rural redneck in Kathryn Bigelow's film *Near Dark* (1987), a New England Brahmin in the television series *Dark Shadows* (1966–1971), or a California teenager in Joel Schumacher's film *The Lost Boys* (1987). This new, demystified vampire might well be our next door neighbor, as Dracula, by origin, appearance, caste, and speech, could never pretend to be.

These transformations of Dracula have particular implications. If we employ what have come to be accepted as the conventional distinctions made between metaphor and metonymy, the changes in the vampire suggest a shift from the metaphoric vampire to the metonymic one. David Sapir makes this rhetorical distinction in his essay "The Anatomy of Metaphor," in which he defines metaphor as stating "an equivalence between terms taken from separate semantic domains," while metonymy "replaces or juxtaposes contiguous terms that occupy a distinct or separate place within what is considered a single semantic or perceptual domain" (Sapir 4). Thus, for example, when we say "the woman is an angel," we are producing a metaphor, since in Western thought "woman" and "angel" belong to different semantic fields, one natural, the other supernatural. When, however, we say "the lady is a tramp," our construction is metonymic, since "lady" and "tramp" belong to a single human semantic category. It seems clear that with each demythologizing transformation, the new vampire moves more firmly in the direction of that single perceptual domain we call the "human," into greater contiguity with us as readers.

It is useful here to return to the rhetorical function of the new vampire as metaphor sliding into metonymy. Normally we think of metaphor and metonymy as devices whose function is to reveal, underline, emphasize those characteristics of the subject most significant to the author's intentions. Jean-Jacques Weber, in his essay "The Foreground-Background Distinction: A Survey of Its Definitions and Distinctions," describes foregrounding as a device by which meanings are called to the reader's attention through the use of figurative language—of metaphor and metonymy (Weber 5). What is significant here is that metaphor and metonymy can be used to obscure as well as to highlight, to background as well as to foreground. Roman Jakobson, in his *Fundamentals of Language*, suggests that metaphor and metonymy work by substitution, but also by subordination and suppression (53–82). Like the brilliant spotlight illuminating the circus aerialist in her pink tights while in the surrounding darkness the invisible roustabouts bring in the tigers' cage, the metonymy screens as it reveals. One function of the new vampire's contiguity is not so much to make clear as it is to conceal, to obscure, to misdirect our attention from his most salient characteristic as murderer, while at the same time retaining that characteristic for its essential, defining function.

Though the new vampire becomes more human with each modification of Stoker's original conception, relationships with actual humanity become increasingly attenuated and marginal. The Judeo-Christian monotheistic tradition permits the solitary God walking alone in the Garden to relate only to human beings, to us; our God's worshipers are jealous worshipers. On the other hand, the "pagan" pantheons—Greek, Roman, Norse, Hindu—permitted their multiple Gods to relate to each other in marriages, rivalries, infidelities, as fathers and mothers and children and lovers; human beings play relatively minor roles in the drama of their lives. The transformations of the vampire I have described might be understood analogically as a shift from a monotheistic, moralistic structure to a pagan hegemony of power and pleasure.

As a result of this shift, the role of human beings as victims becomes increasingly trivialized and marginal. To see this, one need only compare the relative proportion of space and attention given by Stoker to Dracula and to Mina, Lucy, Van Helsing, and the other human characters in his *Dracula* with the character development devoted to the vampires and human victims in Rice's *Vampire Chronicles*, in which almost all essential relationships are between vampire and vampire, and where the victims are as indistinguishable from each other as McDonald's hamburgers—and serve much the same function.

This decentering of the vampire-human relationship has as an additional consequence the diminishing of the vampire as well as the victim. In *Near Dark*, for example, the vampire commune capriciously stops its van in front of a small-town tavern and proceeds to massacre the occupants in an enthusiastic blood bath that reduces its victims to slaughtered sheep and, perhaps more significantly, reduces the vampires to rabid animals. Unlike those relationships in *Dracula* where the vampire's victims were selected, intended, and particularly pursued, the new victims become incidental, happenstance byproducts of time, place, and opportunity. The personal drama of Dracula's pursuit of Lucy and Mina becomes for these new vampires simply a lethal gang mugging, and the vampires themselves emerge as sadistic psychopaths.

A particularly important effect of this diminishing of the role of the human victim is that the sympathies of the reader or viewer no longer have a human locus to which they can attach themselves, no human character with whom to identify. Lacking a Van Helsing for whom to root, or a Mina for whom to fear, the contemporary audience must identify with the lesser of evils provided for it—the "good" vampire, the reluctant killer, the self-doubting murderer. The result is a further greying down of the moral dimensions of the narrative.

At the same time, however, the new communal role provided for vampires, though diminishing them metaphysically, permits them a greater

degree of social complexity. The solitary Dracula could, like the Old Tes-
tament God, only relate to humans and only within a very narrow range of
interlocking emotions: in Dracula's case, hunger, hate, bitterness, contempt. The new communal vampire can now experience tensions, love af-
fairs, elective affinities, rivalries, betrayals—of vampire with vampire, of
vampire with self—in the process mimicking human relationships. The
new vampire has become socialized and humanized, as well as secularized.
The narrow range of emotions permitted Dracula confined him to a narrow range of activities—to kill and to plan to kill. The new vampires can
be art lovers or rock stars or even police detectives, and this communal
condition permits them to love, to regret, to doubt, to question themselves, to experience interior conflicts and cross-impulses—to lose, in other
words, that monolithic force possessed by Dracula, his unalterable volition.

Here, in this new capacity for self-examination, for self-judgment,
even for self-loathing, appears the most significant aspect of the new vampire: his or her flawed volition as it is expressed in the desire and capacity
for change. By surrendering the absolute timeless condition of Dracula,
the new vampire moves into time and history, moves into the world of
mirrors whose essential function is to record change, aging, and mortality.[1]

Angela Carter's "The Lady of the House of Love" (1979) offers us a
kind of paradigm of the shift I have been describing. Here "the Queen of
the Vampires . . . the last bud of the poison tree that sprang from the loins
of Vlad the Impaler" is, we are told, "queen of night, queen of terror—
except [for] her horrible reluctance for the role" (94–95). Feeding on rab-
bits, small furry things, and an occasional peasant boy, she is finally delivered from her fate, made fully human, by the kiss of a touring English
bicyclist—at which point she immediately expires.

Whatever is lost, however, these new vampires gain by the transformation a kind of social space around the bloody central drive that insists
on our seeing them as somehow less "other."[2] That social space is usually
depicted as specially privileged. Although there are exceptions, the contemporary vampire, like Dracula, is often presented as wealthy, or at least
possessing secret sources of wealth, as sexually attractive, as sophisticated.
But this world of privilege is only given weight by the bloody central act of
murder it revolves around. Dracula, embodying metaphysical evil, represented a higher carnivorous form in the Great Food Chain of Being; the
new humanized vampire runs the risk of becoming simply a serial killer,
performing repeatedly what Angela Carter describes as cannibalism, "the
most elementary act of exploitation, that of turning the other directly into

a comestible; of seeing the other in the most primitive terms of use" (*The Sadeian Woman* 140). Dracula, traveling from East to West, was a kind of inverted Crusader in the service of transcendent evil. The new vampires murder simply for "human" reasons, for personal survival or personal pleasure, and to the degree that they become more humanized, the murders become less dramatically significant. As the lover whose embrace kills, as the host who murders his guest, as the guest who murders his host, Dracula, to underline his inhuman nature, violates every traditional human bond. The new vampire, however, embracing all those possibilities for betrayal, extends them beyond hunger to kill indiscriminately, casually, and, finally, banally. In Tony Scott's film *The Hunger* (1983), for example, David Bowie and Catherine Deneuve, playing two very elegant, civilized, and sophisticated vampire lovers, pick up three nameless, grungy young people at a disco for what will presumably be an evening of kinky sex. Instead, what occurs is a bloody slaughter that splashes all over the cheap hotel room and the screen. Beyond its excess—three victims for only two vampires!—one cannot help but notice the contrast between the languid elegance—recalling as it does Lugosi's Old World courtliness—of the vampires preceding and following the slasher killings and the unchecked ferocious self-indulgence of the actual murders, more reminiscent of Jack the Ripper's atrocities than of Dracula's dignified, sensual, and ritualized bloodlettings.

Unlike the werewolf, whose role as a killer is an expression of the temporary, uncontrollable dominance of a bestial nature, the new vampire is eminently contemporary—and divided, a citizen of our time, murdering rationally, or wantonly, or sadistically, out of self-interest, out of calculation, out of hysterical bloodlust, or out of all of them together. The intention to transform the vampire from an objectification of metaphysical evil into simply another image of ourselves seen in a distorting mirror is revealed most clearly in the novels of Anne Rice, who is probably the most successful of the producers of the new genre. In an interview published in *Lear's Magazine*, she states that "*Interview with the Vampire* is about grief, guilt, and the search for salvation even though one is in the eyes of the world and one's own eyes a total outcast! . . . When vampires search for their past trying to figure out who they are, where they come from, if they have a purpose, that's me asking the same questions about human beings" (88).

In regard to the question of the humanizing social dimension provided for the new vampire, it is illuminating to compare the recent popularity of this figure with the parallel emergence in the last two decades of another contemporary "mythic" hero, the Mafia Don. Under the impact of media proliferation, the gangster saga had been a staple of mass culture since Prohibition, and it flourished, especially in films, during the 1930s. It was not until the decade of the '60s, however, that the Mafia emerged to dominate the popular imagination, replacing those older, individualistic entrepreneurs of crime like James Cagney's "Public Enemy" or the real-life John Dillinger with a new corporate, communal, familial image of the criminal. The interest in the Mafia, like that in the vampire, was precipitated by a wide range of media images, from televised Senate hearings to a number of more or less serious studies like G. E. Schiavo's *The Truth About the Mafia* (1962), Michele Pantaleone's *The Mafia and Politics* (1966), and Peter Maas's *The Valachi Papers* (1968), all purporting to expose the operations of the Sicilian criminal "families" which, like Dracula, had imported their evil means and ends from Europe to the innocent West.

The most widely read and influential of these works was Mario Puzo's novel *The Godfather* (1969), which was followed by an extremely popular series of "epic" *Godfather* films in 1972 and 1974, by a marathon television version in 1977, and, most recently, by a *Godfather III* film in 1991; all these spawned in turn dozens of imitative novels, films, and television dramas, revealing to us the Mafia in shirtsleeves, in love, at table, at church. We attend their business meetings, their weddings, their beddings; we meet their fathers and mothers, their priests, their childhood sweethearts; we share their joy at the birth of healthy babies. In the center of all of this, however, they remain ruthless, self-serving, bloody murderers; without that *frisson* which their killing provides, they would be merely acquisitive ethnic businessmen playing out the American Dream, and finally neither more nor less interesting than ourselves.

The mafioso and the new vampire parallel each other in a number of additional ways. Like the new vampire, the mafioso's essential relationships are with other mafiosi, not with his nameless, faceless victims. Like the new vampire, the mafioso has become the civilized, socialized killer, capable of self-doubt, of regret, of loving flowers, success, and music. Seen in the context of the redemptory social space provided for him by the popular myth, the mafioso, like the new vampire, permits us to approach him on a kind of neutral turf on which the murderous activities that make his existence possible become shifted to the periphery where their moral enormity becomes obscured. There they remain, necessarily visible, but decently decentralized.

They are decentralized because the presence of significant victims would impede the flow of involvement, sympathy, and identification with the killers that both these motifs elicit. They remain necessarily visible, these murders, because without them the lives of these analogs of each other have neither meaning nor interest for the audience upon which their continued existence depends. By providing a comprehensible, domestic, even enviable dimension to the killers' lives, the fictions that embody them make possible a cognate theatrical experience in which we, as readers or viewers, can, vampire-like, feed on their bloody vitality, not voyeuristically, as in the case of *Dracula*, but as conjoiners and communicants.

It was this bloody vitality of the undead, this single-minded volition for evil, this metaphysical weight that gave Dracula his original appeal. In the Victorian world that created him, his absolute nature was an expression of the formally dichotomized structures of belief which, although crumbling, still dominated that world: religious, moral, political dichotomies that sharply distinguished good from evil for the mass culture, our side from their side. Dracula and the Children of the Night had for their formal counter-weight the Army of Light led by Van Helsing, precisely as the British Empire balanced itself against the "lesser breeds," as civilization balanced itself against savagery. In *No Place of Grace*, an analysis of the shifts undergone by modern mass culture in this century, Jackson Lears suggests that this equilibrium of opposites rapidly broke down under the impacts of bourgeois secularization, scientific determinism, and the whole cluster of social and cultural phenomena loosely labeled "modernism." As a result, he suggests, "spiritual confusion" replaced spiritual certainty, and "personal meaning had dissolved in comfort and complacency, where experience seemed weightless and death a euphemism" (123). Lears's use of the metaphor of weightlessness comes originally from Nietzsche and, more recently, Milan Kundera's *The Unbearable Lightness of Being* echoes that figure. The term implies a world of crumbled absolutes, of flaccid moral distinctions and religious or political commitments. Simon Reynolds, in an article in the *Manchester Guardian* that describes the "slack" inhabitants of such a world, writes that "they do envy those capable of action. They have a voyeuristic, vicarious fascination with assassins and mass murderers, perhaps because they offer a mesmerizing spectacle of pure volition" (Reynolds 26).

Certainly our new, diminished vampires continue to offer us in the acts of murder they perform the spectacle of such primal volition expressed in the revelatory shedding of all social pretenses, veneers, and disguises, of all conventional codes and values. Vampires, old or new, are cannibals feeding on the world around them, acting out in their own persons the bloody support system that sustains our lives—my shoes made by sweated labor in Brazil, my meat from castrated and constrained animals. In acting out the metaphor of vampirism, the vampire de-metaphorizes it and achieves a kind of momentary authenticity we must momentarily envy.

In *The Hunger*, Catherine Deneuve's beautiful mouth grimacing to reveal her growing incisors discloses to us one true face of the Other; that double shift, from hypocrisy to authenticity on the part of the vampire, from illusion to knowledge on the part of the victim, remains an essential appeal of the vampire legend, old or new. Dracula, of course, offered exactly such a spectacle, but he did so in a context of clear moral certainties that has in our time become increasingly muddied. His absolute evil implied and depended on the existence of an absolute good. His ultimate violence was done not to the temporal bodies but to the eternal souls of his victims. Lacking such an option, our new secularized, metonymic, increasingly contiguous vampires must content themselves with bloodier and bloodier slasher killings, and lose with each additional murder some of their original mythic integrity, so that finally they threaten to merge indistinguishably with all the other nightmare monsters and murderers haunting and splattering our popular culture.

4

The Vampire as Alien
in Contemporary Fiction

MARGARET L. CARTER

$\mathfrak{B}$etween the archetypal nineteenth-century image of the literary vampire, especially as embodied in Bram Stoker's Count Dracula, and the vampire as portrayed in much of the fiction of the past two decades, one overriding difference stands out. Although the vampire in a Victorian novel might exercise a magnetic attraction or even inspire sympathy, the implied author of such a novel always took it for granted that vampirism as such was evil. A fictional vampire aroused positive emotions in spite of, not because of, his or her "curse." In novels and stories published in the United States since 1970, on the other hand, the vampire often appears as an attractive figure precisely *because* he or she is a vampire. Frequently the vampire serves as the viewpoint character or even the narrator. This shift in fictional characterization reflects a change in cultural attitudes toward the outsider, the alien other.

Anne Rice, commenting on her *Interview with the Vampire* (1976) and its sequels, asserts that the vampire is "a metaphor for the outsider" (Anya Martin 38). She made Lestat a rock star in *The Vampire Lestat* (1984), she says, because "rock singers are symbolic outsiders" who are "expected to be completely wild, completely unpredictable, and completely themselves, and they are rewarded for that" (38). Contemporary American society, in glorifying and—at least to some extent—rewarding the outsider, differs from the cultural milieu that engendered the literary vampire.

The logic behind this identification of the vampire with the outsider is supported by Tobin Siebers's theory of superstition as "a symbolic activity, in which individuals of the same group mark one another as different"; singling out non-conforming neighbors as witches, for instance, is "a form of accusation that effects social differentiation" (Siebers 34). Superstition can function as a device for social control. Siebers observes that "the Enlightenment's critique of superstition originated in part from the observation that supernaturalism was an excuse for persecuting people of different religions and opinions" (26). Belief in the supernatural "represents individuals and groups as different from others in order to stratify violence and to create social hierarchies" (12). Historically, this view of supernaturalism is borne out by the fact that the upsurge in supposedly authentic cases of vampirism in the seventeenth century—also the peak of the witchcraft persecutions—coincided with territorial conflict among different branches of Christianity in Europe. On the individual level, many folklore traditions stigmatize redheads as likely vampires, no doubt simply because of the relative rarity of that hair color. "Superstition always represents identities as differences," according to Siebers: "The group represents individuals or other groups as different for the purpose of creating a stable center around which to achieve unanimity. . . . Such false differences create a structure of exclusion" (40–41).

Artists involved in the Romantic movement, on the other hand, often embraced the status of persecuted victim, employing a "strategy of self-expulsion" (Siebers 29). Part of this strategy, of course, includes the use of supernatural motifs in poetry and fiction. Siebers maintains that "the Romantics chose to regard themselves as alien rather than risk the violence that creates alien categories" (28). Today, creators of fictional vampires often choose the Romantic path of identification with the "alien" supernatural being rather than with the superstitious majority bent on excluding and destroying him or her.

That the vampire's status as outsider constitutes both its threat and its attraction is implied in John Allen Stevenson's essay on sexuality in *Dracula*. Contrary to earlier theories that *Dracula*'s subtext centers on symbolic incest, Stevenson suggests that Count Dracula's "sexual threat" consists of "a sin we can term excessive exogamy" (139). The Count is an outsider, a foreigner, who cannot perform the vampiric version of sexual intercourse—sucking blood—with his own kind, but must seduce as-yet-untransformed women. Guilty of "interracial sexual competition" (130), the vampire is dangerous because he corrupts and steals "our" women, releasing their sexuality in demonic ways. With his "omnivorous appetite for difference, for novelty" (139), Count Dracula gives his victims sexual experiences which the male heroes of the novel cannot match. Concerning the scene in *Dracula* in which the Count feeds on Mina and then forces her to drink his blood, Stevenson remarks, "What is going on? Fellatio? Lactation? It seems the vampire is sexually capable of everything" (146).

To the Victorian reader, this image reinforces the horror of vampirism. The late twentieth-century reader is apt to view the erotically omnicompetent vampire more favorably. And the enforced "exogamy" constitutes an essential part of the attraction.

Rosemary Jackson, like many other critics, also sees ambivalence toward Dracula's sexual prowess as central to the novel. In her view, Stoker objectifies forbidden desires in the vampires—Dracula and his female disciples—in order to assert the conservative values of established society by exterminating the vampires and, with them, the "subversive" drives that threaten to break free. By having his heroes stake Lucy and Dracula's three "wives," "Stoker reinforces social, class, racial, and sexual prejudices" (Jackson 121). Jackson also notes that "By defeating these [forbidden sexual] desires, the narrative reasserts a prohibition on exogamy" (119). Like Stevenson, she sees the vampire as an alien whose sexuality exerts such a powerful appeal that it must be suppressed at all costs: "With each penetration and 'return' to the unity of the imaginary, a new vampire is produced: further objects of desire are endlessly generated, creating an 'other' order of beings, for whom desire never dies and whose desire prevents them from dying" (120–21). Somewhat like Siebers, Jackson suggests that the representatives of society's order can maintain that order only by excluding the "alien," by framing the vampire as wholly other. "In what we could call a supernatural economy," she observes, "otherness is transcendent, marvellously different from the human" (23).

Where the vampire's otherness posed a terrifying threat for the original readers of *Dracula*, however, today that same alien quality is often perceived as an attraction. As rebellious outsider, as persecuted minority, as endangered species, and as member of a different "race" that legend portrays as sexually omnicompetent, the vampire makes a fitting hero for late twentieth-century popular fiction. Carol Senf observes that many contemporary novelists "use the vampire motif to explore sexual roles and human identity" (7). These authors frequently present the vampire as admirable for his or her "romantic independence" and "refusal to conform to arbitrary social standards" (7). She notes that in our time "changing attitudes toward authority and toward rebellion against that authority have . . . led to a more sympathetic treatment of the vampire" (150). Moreover, the vampiric eroticism—especially in female characters—that inspired horror and drew punishment in Victorian fiction is framed as positive rather than negative in today's fiction. Senf also suggests that a decreased respect for institutionalized religion contributes to many authors' abandonment of the diabolic image of the vampire. She concludes that recent "writers who have featured the vampire have focused on the individual's right to choose a different kind of existence. . . . Thus there has been increased emphasis on the positive aspects of the vampire's eroticism and on his or her right to rebel against the stultifying constraints of society and a decreasing emphasis on the vampire's quarrel with traditional religious beliefs" (163). In short, contemporary writers present vampires as admirable because of the very traits for which nineteenth-century authors vilified them.

This shift of emphasis from the threat of the other to the allure of the other is illuminated in James Tiptree's story, "And I Awoke and Found Me Here on the Cold Hill's Side" (1971). Although not a literal vampire story, it delivers a message that the narrator, listening to an embittered acquaintance in the familiar spaceport bar of classic science fiction, hears as "Never love an alien" (Tiptree 14). The old space-hand attempting to warn him, however, has a more profound message to convey. The yearning to know aliens, says the stranger, drains Earth of resources both physical and spiritual, just as the Polynesians lost their own culture in yearning after European technology. "Our soul is leaking out," says the stranger. "We're bleeding to death!" (16). He explains the surrender to this metaphorical vampirism in terms of "supernormal stimulus," a cause similar to that which drives some birds to reject their own eggs in favor of larger, more colorful substitutes: "Man is exogamous—all our history is one long drive to find and impregnate the stranger. Or get impregnated by him. . . . That's a drive, y'know, it's built in. Because it works fine as long as the stranger is human. For millions of years that kept the genes circulating. But now we've met aliens we can't screw, and we're about to die trying" (16). This drive is more than sexual; it springs from some "cargo cult of the soul. We're built to dream outwards" (17). The narrator, of course, hears the stranger's tirade without listening. In the final paragraph he catches "a glimpse of two sleek scarlet shapes" and, obliviously eager to have his soul drained, leaps up to hurry in pursuit of his "first real aliens" (17).

The human drive to "dream outwards" finds expression in numerous contemporary vampire tales. Anne Rice's *Interview with the Vampire* portrays the lure of the other through the boy interviewer to whom the vampire Louis chooses to reveal his past. Despite the boy's terror when he realizes Louis's true nature, he stays because he desperately wants this revelation. At the end, when Louis prepares to send him away, the boy repudiates the vampire's despair. Although Louis's story abounds in pain, grief, and horror, the boy begs to be made a vampire: "Don't you see how you made it sound? It was an adventure like I'll never know in my whole life! You talk about passion, you talk about longing! You talk about things that millions of us won't ever taste or come to understand" (343). Bitterly refusing the boy's plea, Louis punishes him with a non-fatal attack. Yet even that experience of pain and fear does not discourage the boy. As soon as he recovers, he rushes out to search for Lestat, who, he hopes, will grant his wish. Like the narrator of Tiptree's story, Rice's character cannot be deterred from seeking the embrace of the alien.

Unlike nineteenth-century vampire fiction, in which transformation into a vampire is always a disaster, some contemporary vampire tales present such transformation as a happy ending—or, sometimes, the inauspicious beginning of an altered life that proves, after all, to be happy. But not all vampire stories use the traditional supernatural motif and feature vampires who are transformed human beings, whether threatening or alluring. The theme of vampire as alien other is most clearly foregrounded by stories in which the vampire is a literal alien, not supernatural but a member of a separate species sharing our world with us.

Jacqueline Lichtenberg, author of a series featuring the quasi-vampiric Simes, as well as several more nearly traditional vampire tales, comments on the difference between the supernatural vampire and the science-fiction vampire: "In horror, the Unknown is a menace which is a menace because it's a menace. In sf, the Unknown is a menace because we don't understand it yet. . . . In horror, no amount of understanding can help. In sf, understanding, either intellectual or emotion [sic], or maybe both, is the key to the solution of the problem" ("Vampire with Muddy Boots" 4). As we shall see, Lichtenberg's own vampire fiction aims at understanding the needs, motives, and problems of these human-yet-alien creatures. Her goal in writing about her vampire species is "to step sideways into another universe and become another person for awhile" (5). She points out that "a supernatural vampire who can turn into a mist or a bat at will, doesn't get mud on his/her boots! A true supernatural force doesn't suffer the inconvenience of slogging through cold wet mud. And as a result, such an entity doesn't grow spiritually, in character or relationships" (5). On the other hand, her non-supernatural vampires, though they "display all the traits and attributes of the supernatural vampire," are naturally evolved creatures "who are just as REAL as you or I but who are caught in a situation that would crush you or me" (5). Numerous modern science-fiction writers use this likeness-with-a-difference in their vampire stories to illuminate human interrelationships and our species' role in the natural order.

Joan Gordon points out that portrayals of the vampire as a separate species foreground "cross-species responsibility with its implications about ecology and human relations" ("Rehabilitating Revenants" 231). In addition to the question of "how to behave when confronted with our first alien being," this motif also has connections "with ecology—the relationships among all the creatures on this planet—and by analogy, with human dynamics—the relationships between the sexes, among individuals, and among the many ethnic, racial, religious, and political groups of human beings" (231).

All these concerns are addressed on some level by one or more of the novels and stories I shall examine. Some authors convey an optimistic view of the probable results of inter-species co-existence, others a pessimistic view. Frequently vampires portrayed as alien but natural predators "become super-survivors instead of super-killers. To survive, they must live in harmony with their world, be flexible, adaptable, and possess stamina" (Gordon, "Rehabilitating Revenants" 230). Hence these fictional vampires, like Lichtenberg's "vampire with muddy boots," can grow, change, and thereby appeal to the reader's sympathy. As Gordon notes, it is more often female than male authors who choose to create sympathetic vampires. She suggests that this tendency reflects a "feminist rethinking of the traditional power structure" that draws on "female notions of power and strength" (230). The "feminist vision" perceives "power in the giver of nourishment as well as in the taker" (233). Thus the vampire, though a natural predator, need not be imagined as "greedy and rapacious," but may participate in a pattern of "exchange rather than hierarchy" (234).

One novel in particular presents a thorough and explicit analysis of the vampire as super-predator, with multifarious implications for cross-species as well as human relationships—Suzy McKee Charnas's *The Vampire Tapestry* (1981). Delivering a lecture in which he toys with his unwitting audience, the vampire anthropologist, Dr. Weyland, unfolds his answer to the question, "Now, how would nature design a vampire?" (25). All Weyland's speculations about the "corporeal vampire . . . the greatest of all predators, living as he would off the top of the food chain" (25), are, of course, factual descriptions of his own biology. Human beings are simply "the vampire's livestock," no more significant to him than cattle are to us (25). Since in pre-industrial times the vampire cannot travel far to find a fresh pool of unwary victims, he must periodically withdraw into extended hibernation: "A sleep several generations long would provide him with an untouched, ignorant population in the same location. He must be able to slow his metabolism, to induce in himself naturally a state of suspended animation" (26). Weyland suggests that this suspended animation, along with "minimal feeding," may contribute to the vampire's longevity, as research has shown to be the case with some animal species (26). The vampire's evolution favors long life over prolific breeding, for "the great predator would not wish to sire his own rivals" (26).

Rather than using fangs to draw blood, the natural vampire (as in Polish folklore) has "some sort of puncturing device, perhaps a needle in the tongue like a sting that would secrete an anticlotting device" (26); therefore the vampire need not endanger him- or herself by leaving conspicuous wounds or killing prey with copious blood loss. This vampire is not only the supreme predator but the supremely adaptive animal: "It may be that he responds to the stimuli in the environment by growing in his body as well as in his mind. Perhaps while awake his entire being exists at an intense level of inner activity and change" (28). In modern times, of course, as the complexity of human society and the rate of technological advance constantly increase, the vampire must adapt faster and more radically than ever before.

Weyland scorns traditional anti-vampire devices such as garlic and crucifixes as products of superstitious belief, which vampires themselves might have shared before they, like their human prey, advanced to a scientific world-view. The vampire's erotic fascination and "Satanic pride," according to Weyland, are literary fancies that have no relevance to the vampire as a creature of the natural world. He remarks sardonically that "a tiger who falls asleep in a jungle and on waking finds a thriving city overgrowing his lair has no energy to spare for displays of Satanic pride" (30).

Throughout the novel Weyland compares himself, and is compared by others, to animals. The one member of his audience who knows his true nature reflects that the other spectators perceive "nothing of his menace, only the beauty of his quick hawk-glance and his panther-playfulness" (28). In an interview, Charnas explains that, bored with the "garden variety vampire, based in this or that ethnic superstition complex," she decided to create a vampire who, instead of "a leftover historical human with puffed up social pretensions," is "a natural creature with a tiger's objectivity, just trying to get along and keep himself amused at the same time" (Margaret Carter, "Interview with Suzie McKee Charnas" 4). Commenting on human ecological wastefulness, she says, "I just decided that there would be something that preyed specifically on us, but in a much more rational manner than we prey on the rest of the world, putting us (I wish) to shame for our moronic clumsiness" (5). The result is Weyland, a creature with intelligence surpassing ours but with "the inner emotional life of the average housecat, a fact by the way of which he is well aware" (5).

This awareness, as we shall later see, leads Weyland into an emotional trap. He stands out as one of the few solitary alien vampires—others include Miriam in Whitley Strieber's *The Hunger* (1981) and the young vampire in a story I will consider in more detail below, Bob Leman's "The Pilgrimage of Clifford M." (1984). One attendee at Weyland's lecture comes away with a picture of "the vampire as a sort of leftover sabertooth tiger prowling the pavements, a truly endangered species" (31).

Whether solitary or part of a vampire subculture, the various alien vampires in contemporary fiction each deal in slightly different ways with the human majority among whom they must live. One characteristic many of them share, however, is an impulse toward self-disclosure. Like Rice's Louis and Lestat, they want to justify themselves to the human world. Weyland goes to a psychologist to get a certification of mental health in order to retain his professorship after his unexplained disappearance—the result of being shot by a vampire-hunter, a housekeeper at the college where he teaches—but finds himself revealing his true nature in therapy. The psychologist, Floria Landauer, remarks to Weyland that "beneath your various façades your true self suffers; like all true selves, it wants, needs to be honored as real and valuable through acceptance by another" (160). Joshua, the vampire hero of George R. R. Martin's *Fevre Dream* (1982), tells his life story to a Mississippi riverboat captain, Abner Marsh. On this unprecedented occasion, vampires and human "cattle" speak and listen honestly to each other. Bob Leman's Clifford is a vampire brought up by human foster parents, knowing nothing of his own heritage beyond what he can deduce from legend and ambiguous news reports of mysterious assaults. He leaves a final message to his human allies before he commits suicide in despair at what he has discovered about his true nature.

Despite the hazards of revealing themselves to their prey, many alien vampires in fiction yearn to reach out to human companions as strongly as the human characters yearn for knowledge of the alien other. And despite the reluctance of some, such as Weyland, to admit any kinship between themselves and their victims, the vampires' situation throws light on aspects of the human condition. Weyland considers his similarity to the human race, including his sexuality, to be no more than "detailed biological mimicry, a form of protective coloration" (138). Commenting on human ambition, he distances himself from such motives by emphasizing his own simplicity: "And people think of a vampire as arrogant! . . . This one wants to be President or Class Monitor or Department Chairman or Union Boss, another must be first to fly to the stars or to transplant the human brain, and on and on. As for me, I wish only to satisfy my appetite in peace" (157).

Floria, the psychologist, reflects on a former (human) patient whom she restored to functional health, only to have him go on to establish "a hellish 'home' for the aged" and "destroy the helpless for profit," a memory that makes her realize, "W. not my first predator, only most honest and direct" (158). The contrast between a vampire's modest depredations and the horrible behavior of human beings toward their own kind forms a recurrent theme in recent vampire fiction. Just as Weyland has an objective view of human ambitions and conflicts, he has a similar detached perspective on human sexual customs. He casually cuts to the heart of the historic position of women, stating that he finds men more accessible as prey "because women have been walled away like prizes or so physically impoverished by repeated childbearing as to be unhealthy prey for me" (132). With no erotic interest in human beings, either male or female, he prefers to hunt homosexual men because their fringe position in society makes them vulnerable. When a fellow professor introduces him to a lesbian couple, Weyland reflects, "Whether a person slept with partners of one sex or the other was one of those distinctions humans invented and then treated as a tablet of the law" (268).

Compared to the difference between human and vampire, culturally imposed differences among human beings appear trivial. Joshua, vampire hero of *Fevre Dream*, comments on the exclusion and destruction of human beings by their own kind in the name of superstition and prejudice: "I have seen your race burn old women because they were suspected of being one of us, and here in New Orleans I have witnessed the way you enslave your own kind, whip them and sell them like animals simply because of the darkness of their skin. The black people are closer to you, more kin, than ever my kind can be. You can even get children on their women, while no such interbreeding is possible between night and day" (162). Again, the image of a vampire race living among us places human differences in perspective. Because human society persecutes its own kind on the basis of superficial distinctions, Joshua knows it would not be safe for his race to come out of hiding; breaching their secrecy would invite extermination.

A series of novels for children, *Fifth Grade Monsters* by Mel Gilden, foregrounds the parallel between vampires and persecuted minorities in a lighter tone. Throughout the series, the value of accepting people who look different, perhaps at first sight even threatening, is emphasized. When four monster children—Howie Wolfner, an English werewolf, Frankie and Elisa Stein, from Germany, and C. D. Bitesky, a Transylvanian immigrant who wears evening clothes with a cape every day and carries a thermos of red liquid called Fluid of Life—join human protagonist Danny's fifth-grade class, he greets them with some nervousness. He soon discovers, however, that they make far better friends than Stevie, the (human) class bully.

In *There's a Batwing in My Lunchbox* (Hodgman 1988)—the one book in the series not written by Gilden—C. D. proves to be the only child in class with the courage to speak up when the teacher, Ms. Cosgrove, plans a traditional Thanksgiving feast. The vampire boy refuses to participate, because his ancestors had no connection with the Pilgrims, and turkey and pumpkin pie hold no cultural resonance for him. To his surprise, children of other ethnic backgrounds speak up to support him. Only Stevie, expressing his usual bigotry against the monsters, accuses C. D. of being "a complete unpatriot" (Hodgman 9) and threatens to have his father report C. D.'s rebellion to the school board. Ms. Cosgrove, recognizing her own ethnocentrism, decides instead to have a multi-cultural feast, with each student bringing a family recipe from his or her ancestral home, to "celebrate all the immigrants who have come to this country" (29). Howie the werewolf underscores the analogy between monsters and more mundane persecuted minorities with the remark, "The Pilgrims would probably have run my ancestors out of town—or burned them at the stake" (13). When C. D. presents his contribution to the Thanksgiving feast, a Potion of Friendliness, he tells the class that "my family has been persecuted there [Transylvania] for centuries. . . . In America, in England, in Transylvania—perhaps all over the world—no one likes people who are different" (64). The identification of vampires—and other victims of superstition—with human outsiders could hardly be more explicit.

In a later novel, *How to Be a Vampire in One Easy Lesson* (1990), C. D.'s famous relative, the Count, taking refuge in Brooklyn from old-country persecution, makes his home in the cellar of a grand old movie-theater. A benefit to save the theater from demolition leads Danny and his friends into a discussion of horror films. C. D. and the other little monsters dislike such movies because "they perpetuate a negative stereotype" (Gilden 7), a lighthearted allusion to similar problems with the portrayal of human ethnic minorities in the media.

Stevie, despite his dislike of the monster children, is fascinated by the showing of *Dracula* at the theater. He decides that he wants to become a vampire, not because he suddenly approves of monsters, but because he wants to become a more efficient bully by dominating others with the force of his will—this is, perhaps, analogous to Caucasians who try to appropriate Oriental and Native American modes of spirituality with impure motives and imperfect understanding. Unable to dissuade Stevie, C. D. turns the problem over to his parents, who introduce Stevie to the Count. After his ordeal with the Count in the catacombs beneath the theater, Stevie is convinced he has become a vampire. When the "transformation" proves to be a hoax, C. D. reminds him, "Before we began I told you that you are a vampire or you are not. . . . It is like having red hair and freckles" (90). Gilden's vampires, rather than supernatural beings spawned by the Devil, are simply an unusual ethnic group, to be accepted on their own merits as individuals, not stigmatized en masse as "monsters."

In *How to Be a Vampire in One Easy Lesson* even the bigoted Stevie feels the magnetic allure of vampirism. In adult novels about vampires as aliens, these creatures of the night attract human beings for a variety of reasons. Dr. Weyland becomes the target of Alan Reese, a Satanist who wants to augment his own power by dominating the "demonic" vampire; yet Reese, like Stevie, also reveals a suppressed desire to become a vampire himself. When Weyland, helpless from a nearly fatal gunshot wound, becomes a prisoner in an opportunistic New Yorker's apartment, his "host's" friend Reese arranges private exhibitions of the "monster" for his fellow cultists, to "display the antagonist he means to subdue" (92). Weyland explains to his captor's teenage nephew: "In reality, I can give Reese nothing—but he can take from me. He 'builds me up,' . . . in order to stand higher himself when he has cast me down. He presents me as some mystical and powerful being which he alone, the leader, the master, can conquer and destroy" (92).

As in Siebers's theory of superstition, Reese uses the exclusion of Weyland as a "demon" to enhance his own status. But at the novel's climax, when Reese tracks Weyland to his new home in Albuquerque, it turns out that appropriating the vampire's power by subduing him is no longer enough for Reese. Reese projects his own concept of power, his "dream of secret superiority" (286), upon the alien. Recognizing this subliminal motive, Weyland encourages it with seductive remarks such as, "I know that even in your childhood something cruel lived in you, not simple childish brutality but a core of ice for the sake of which you held yourself aloof"

(286). Having studied the dreams and myths of his prey, Weyland recognizes and evokes in Reese the archetypes of a child raised by wolves who "becomes the leader of a mythic pack ranging the forest forever" or a misfit who is told by a messenger from the stars, "Come, you are not one of these wretched little mammals, this has all been a mistake. You are one of us, mighty, wise, and immortal" (286). Once the Satanist's guard has been breached by the awakening of his desire to become what he ostensibly hates, Weyland is able to destroy him.

Other people project their own emotions upon the vampire in more benign ways. A female student at Weyland's lecture about the vampire as supreme predator asks, "Wouldn't he be lonely?" with "her posture eloquent of the desire to comfort that loneliness" (29). Weyland retorts, "Predators in nature do not indulge in the sort of romantic mooning that humans impute to them" (29). After the lecture, the woman who later shoots Weyland in self-defense muses, "For overcivilized people to experience the approach of such a predator as sexually attractive was not strange" (31). Floria, Weyland's therapist, in the midst of her own life's confusion, finds him attractive as a result of "the single, stark, primary condition: he is a predator who subsists on human blood," he possesses "[h]armony, strength, clarity, magnificence—all from that basic animal integrity" (160). She also feels attracted by his essential otherness. Prompted by her in a therapy session, he puts her desire—as he perceives it—into words: "As to the unicorn, out of your own legends—'Unicorn, come lay your head in my lap while the hunters close in. You are a wonder, and for love of wonder I will tame you'" (161). Floria realizes that because her work as a psychologist is "designed to make humans more human," she may be endangering his essential selfhood (161). When, at their final meeting, they share sexual intimacy for the first and only time—the only occasion when Weyland engages in sex for a motive other than predation—she does not wish to reform, dominate, or exploit him. Instead, she experiences "unlike closing with unlike across whatever likeness may be found" (178).

Several treatments of the vampire as alien emphasize the creature's erotic fascination. (In two notable exceptions, Leman's "The Pilgrimage of Clifford M." and Martin's *Fevre Dream*, the vampires belong to species that cannot interbreed with human beings and feel no sexual desire for their prey.) Elaine Bergstrom's vampire clan, the Austras, exert an irresistible magnetism over human beings, an involuntary phenomenon that operates, unless they consciously suppress it, especially when the vampires hunger for blood. Also, because—like many fictional vampires—they possess telepathy, they can shape their behavior to satisfy the human partner's inmost desires. In *Shattered Glass* (1989), the first victim of the renegade, homicidal vampire, Charles, finds that he pleasures her "[p]erfectly—as she would herself" (3). Under his touch, "a passion such as she had never known began to build in her. . . . Her fears, her needs, her life were forgotten as she shuddered in a fulfillment of glorious intensity" (3). Moreover, beyond sexual union, the Austras use telepathy to satisfy the human yearning to know the alien other. While drinking a human donor's blood—and sometimes without blood-sharing—the vampire can share his or her memories with the donor in a reenactment so vivid it seems actually to be happening.

Jacqueline Lichtenberg's vampires in *Those of My Blood* (1988), the *luren*, also use a form of telepathy, which they call Influence. Through Influence, the vampire can manufacture illusions and make an unwary human victim accept any distortion of reality as fact. Partly because of Influence and partly through the innate magnetism which Lichtenberg's vampires project when hungry, they, too, are sexually irresistible. The protagonist Titus's human lover asks him, "Is it especially good with—vampires? Or is that a myth, too?" He tells her, "I'll make it like nothing you've ever known" (95). He keeps that promise, using his power to coax her body's energy to its highest pitch before seeking satisfaction, acting out the feminine fantasy of the perfectly attentive lover whose fulfillment depends on his partner's.

In Susan Petrey's *Gifts of Blood* (1992), the Varkela, a blood-drinking tribe of the Russian steppes who earn their modest monthly ration of human blood by selling their skills as horsetamers and shamanistic healers, demonstrate similar sexual prowess. They possess the ability to "bewitch" women with the hypnotic song they use to calm patients during healing, but the Varkela physician Vaylance needs no such power when he lies with Myrna, a woman he meets in a "dreamwalk" across time to modern America. Somewhat like Bergstrom's vampires, he shares visions with her and tries to teach her to dreamwalk. The vampiric telepathy or empathy imagined by Lichtenberg, Bergstrom, and Petrey bridges the gulf between sexes, races, and species in a mode and with a completeness impossible—so far as we know—in real life. Myrna finds Vaylance to be "the most sensitive lover she had ever known" (126). Perhaps the fictional convention of alien vampires' sexual fascination may be read as analogous to the real-world myth among some Caucasians that Black people, the forbidden other race, have especially passionate natures and exaggerated potency.

If human characters in these stories are fascinated with the vampire's erotic magnetism and alluring otherness, vampires, from a variety of motives, are also irresistibly drawn to human beings. In *Fevre Dream* Joshua's race has no culture of its own, aside from the myth of a vampire kingdom that perished in a remote prehistoric age; they borrow everything from humanity, even language. Yet their bond with the human species consists of more than cultural parasitism and thirst for blood. Joshua reflects, "We killed you easily, and took joy in it, for we found beauty in you, and always my people had been drawn to beauty. Perhaps it was your likeness to us we found so captivating" (159). This fascination exists apart from the need for blood, since only after inventing an artificial blood-substitute which frees himself and his followers from the compulsion to kill once a month, does Joshua seek alliance and ultimately friendship with the riverboat captain, Abner Marsh.

Lichtenberg's *luren* need human beings because blood in itself does not provide true nourishment; the "ectoplasm," the human life energy, within it makes blood satisfying. Pledged not to feed on living people, subsisting on cloned blood, Titus cannot truly enjoy his "lifeless" drink until his human lover suffuses it with her psychic essence, her ectoplasm. The supreme satisfaction, he discovers, requires "total commitment, both from the luren and from the human," rather than exploitation of prey by predator (*Those of My Blood* 156). The *luren* mate with human partners, producing offspring who may inherit the potential to become vampires themselves. Bergstrom's vampires gravitate toward human lovers and, most of the time, feel little sexual attraction toward their own kind. When an Austra male and a human female mutually exchange blood—an intimacy that is taboo yet strangely alluring for the vampires—fertile mating can occur. Offspring or descendants of these rare unions, like Lichtenberg's human-*luren* hybrids, can become true vampires, given the right conditions. In Petrey's series, male Varkela—apparently a subspecies of Homo sapiens rather than a separate species—often mate with ordinary women, for Varkela females frequently die at puberty and are therefore scarce. For a male Varkela "to impregnate a human female was regarded as a sign of especial virility" (Petrey 39). Clearly, the sexual fascination of the alien other works in both directions.

Miriam, the solitary vampire of Whitley Strieber's *The Hunger*, is fascinated by humanity for more than sexual reasons. Like Weyland, she is the last survivor of her species, although, unlike him, she remembers others of her kind. And Miriam's attitude toward her prey contrasts with Weyland's contempt for the human race. While he scorns the "romantic" notion of the vampire's loneliness, Miriam "was lonely, and human beings gave her the love that pets give" (Strieber 64). Weyland wants nothing from his prey but their blood and resents even that much dependence on them; Miriam, on the other hand, takes one human companion after another, obsessed with futile attempts to transform her victims into creatures like herself. Despite the temporary illusion of success, these attempts always fail. Miriam sees her fascination with humanity, self-centered though it is, as a form of love. She attributes the decline of her species to the dangerous seductiveness of humankind: "If one loved human beings, how could one also kill them and still be happy enough with oneself to love one's own kind, and bear young?" (189). She enjoys sexual liaisons with human partners and, like most vampires, exercises erotic magnetism over both men and women. In *The Hunger* she becomes attached to a brilliant young scientist, Sarah, whose research holds the promise of transmitting Miriam's immortality to ordinary people. Once again Miriam's hopes are crushed, however, and at the end of the novel she takes a new lover, knowing she will "dream her dream of his immortality and tell herself that here at last was her eternal companion" (246). But she also knows that in time "nature would come and shatter her dream" (246). She has at last learned her lesson: "No matter how her loneliness tempted her to find one who would last forever, she resolved never to attempt the transformation of another Sarah, not this time or the next time, or for all time" (246). In Miriam's world the attraction between human and alien proves deadly to both.

The vampire in Leman's "The Pilgrimage of Clifford M." has no desire to transform human beings into vampires; instead, he originally thinks of himself as human. Ironically, Clifford has less chance of fitting into the human world than any other alien vampire. His kind begin life as voracious, den-dwelling carnivores with fur and shark-like teeth. After a decades-long childhood, they mature into outwardly human but completely nocturnal creatures who feed solely on blood. Accidentally separated from his parents, Clifford is brought up by a human family and thinks himself human. When he realizes that his biology is too radically different for him to be a human mutation, he undertakes a quest for his origins. Leading the life of a wealthy recluse, he feeds circumspectly, never killing or seriously harming his prey, and devotes his time and money to the search for other vampires. One motive for the quest is "simple lust; but lust for whom, for what? Not any woman that he had ever met; not any man or child or beast. This most urgent drive was toward a female of his own kind" (Leman 18). Cross-species eroticism plays no part in Leman's story; instead, Clifford wins the reader's sympathy through his loneliness and his search for self-knowledge.

At last he finds what are probably the last three living vampires in North America, two of them most likely his own parents. He discovers that with age, adult vampires, though human in appearance, become nearly mindless predators, "diurnally lying comatose in a muddy burrow, awakening only to prey disgustingly upon human beings" (27). Since he cannot stomach the thought of mating with the female, his sexual and social isolation becomes complete. He directs his human vampire-hunting allies—unaware, until the end, of his true nature—to the vampires' den, where he himself also waits to be killed. In his suicide letter—yet another instance of vampiric self-disclosure—he explains that he had visualized vampires as "cultivated humans who possessed—as it happened—certain nocturnal proclivities, and who required a somewhat specialized diet" (30). Aware that he himself must inevitably degenerate into one of these "dangerous and disgusting vermin," he falls into despair, for he realizes that "It would be quite impossible for me to live among such creatures; I would rather live with hyenas" (30). In preparation for his death, he dresses in evening clothes, somewhat to his own bewilderment. "I suppose," he speculates, "it is a final effort to show that although I am indubitably one of these creatures, yet still I am different—and better. And there is no doubt some sort of wry satisfaction, or even amusement, in knowing that I will be dressed like Count Dracula when I receive the stake" (30).

Clifford has acquired his erroneous image of vampires from human cultural stereotypes. His well-meaning foster parents and teachers, unwittingly attempting to make an alien into a human being, instead render him unfit for either world. He explains in his written apologia, "I was born a creature not human, and inhuman I am; but I was reared as a human, and human I am in my thoughts and attitudes. . . . I would like to be human" (29). The vampire becomes a symbol for any member of a minority group who loses his own identity but cannot be assimilated into the dominant culture. As Clifford realizes, "I cannot be a human being. I will not live as what I am" (30). Leman, like Strieber, shows human-alien interaction as destructive.

In contrast to Clifford, Weyland, rather than wishing to become human, views the prospect with repugnance. Yet living in the midst of human society alters him, too. Since he has to pose as a human being to hunt his prey—a necessity he resents—he faces the danger of becoming what he imitates. He tells Floria, "The seductiveness, the distraction of our—human contact worries me. I fear for the ruthlessness that keeps me alive" (Charnas 161). One symptom of his growing similarity to his victims is his love for ballet, a quirk he finds puzzling; why should he be emotionally stirred by the creations of inferior beings? At a production of *Tosca* in Santa Fe, the opera moves him so violently that it throws him into a temporary fugue, a reenactment of a moment from an earlier lifetime. Afterward, he speculates: "Where did it come from, this perilous new pattern of recognizing aspects of himself in the creations of his human livestock? . . . Had he been somehow irrevocably opened to the power of their art? He recoiled violently from such possibilities; he wanted nothing more from them than that which he already, relentlessly required: their blood" (226). Weyland, however, cannot turn back and renounce what he has gained. He can lose his new awareness only by retreating into the long sleep. He speculates that he has worked through this process many times before, in his forgotten past lives, and one purpose of his extended coma, he suspects, is to free him from the weight of unmanageable awareness and unbearable memories.

Despite his resistance to the process, he does reveal his true self to Floria and finds the experience valuable. In a letter written to her but never sent, he says of their single sexual encounter, "Perhaps I desired, there at the last, to repossess a part of myself I had unwittingly given you. At other times I think I wanted to touch a part of you that our speaking together had revealed to me" (252). In the end, though, he refuses the invitation to become human. He sees himself as "afflicted [not blessed] by attachment" (293), when he realizes he has begun to care for some of his human associates. "His life had been broken into, anyone might enter" (293). He even comes to understand—although he still hates the man—the drives and needs of his enemy, Reese. As Joan Gordon suggests, "the vampire's sentience makes him aware of the suffering of his prey, and of its existence not just as a species but as an individual. Such awareness is a kind of love" ("Rehabilitating Revenants" 232). Recognizing the threat such "love" poses to his identity as a predator, Weyland resolves, "I am not the monster who falls in love and is destroyed by his human feelings. I am the monster who stays true" (293).

Other alien vampires manage to remain true to their essential natures while coexisting with, even loving, human associates. Joshua in *Fevre Dream* devotes his life to learning not to kill, destroys a vampire rival who wants to maintain the old, savage ways, and makes a true friend of his human ally, Captain Marsh. The importance of this relationship to Joshua is demonstrated by his eventually placing an elaborate tombstone on Marsh's grave and visiting the site regularly for decades thereafter.

In Elaine Bergstrom's novels, the inter-species love is symbiotic. The Austras not only take blood from human prey, they also need the human race to revitalize their own gene pool. Similar to Petrey's Varkela females, who often die at puberty, Austra females usually die in childbirth. Helen, the human-vampire hybrid of *Shattered Glass*, offers the promise of birth without the inevitable sacrifice of the mother. Yet the Austras do not take from humanity without giving. Symbiotes rather than parasites, they contribute the products of their genius through AustraGlass, whose creations in stained glass have adorned human architecture since the Middle Ages.

The more optimistic of the vampire-as-alien novels reflect a positive vision of human relationships with other kinds of human beings and with nonhuman life. Bergstrom, Petrey, Lichtenberg, and Gilden model mutual exchange and sharing between "our kind" and the alien other. Charnas illustrates the importance of respecting the integrity and uniqueness of the other, instead of trying to distort him or her into a copy of ourselves. As Lichtenberg suggests, these novels invite us "to step sideways into another universe and become another person for awhile." In Tiptree's phrase, we are encouraged to "dream outwards." Through this exercise of entering the mind of the alien, we may become freer to understand the frightening yet attractive "other" sexes, races, and species that share our planet with us.

5

Sharper Than a Serpent's Tooth:
The Vampire in Search of Its Mother

JOAN GORDON

How sharper than a serpent's tooth it is
To have a thankless child.
— *King Lear* I.iv.312

Among the Poles of Upper Silesia and the Kashubes, a child
born with teeth is predisposed to become a vampire.
—Barber, *Vampires, Burial, and Death* 30

When we envision the vampire feeding, we see victim and predator, seduced and seducer: why not Madonna and child? Is the vampire's lust for blood an extension of a more natural desire for sustenance and Is Its quest for victims and for others of its kind really a search for mother and family? From Coleridge's "Christabel" (1797), through Sheridan Le Fanu's *Carmilla* (1871), to Jewelle Gomez's *The Gilda Stories* (1991) and Poppy Z. Brite's *Lost Souls* (1992), vampire children have been searching for their mothers with little success.

Coleridge's narrative poem "Christabel," charged as it is with sexuality, is also a tale of parental abandonment. Christabel, whose mother died in giving her birth, seems to find a mother surrogate in the lovely woman she finds by a "huge, broad-breasted, old oak tree" (26). However, Geraldine proves to be a vampiric travesty of motherhood, with "bosom old" and "bosom cold" (37), who battles over Christabel's soul with her mother's "guardian spirit," so she can, as false mother, join with Christabel's father in abandoning the daughter. The daughter in her abandonment takes on the reptilian aspect of the vampiric Geraldine.

Almost a century later, Sheridan Le Fanu's *Carmilla* again shows a motherless girl, Laura, finding companionship both nurturing and sexual in a vampiric mother-figure. Le Fanu makes Laura and her vampiric companion mirrors of one another: Carmilla, left at Laura's home, is seemingly abandoned by her own mother, and she reports a childhood dream of seeing Laura in her adult form lie down next to her like a mother with a child. The dream is identical to Laura's remembered childhood dream except, of course, that Laura sees Carmilla as the motherly companion.[1] Laura loses Carmilla, Carmilla loses her mother; but unlike Christabel, Laura gets to keep her father.

Now another hundred years have passed and the anxieties of the twentieth century are reflected in the motherless vampires' quests. Consider the episodic questing structure of Jewelle Gomez's *The Gilda Stories*, for example, in which Gilda, a lesbian vampire of color, searches for a family that has room for her unconventionality. We first meet Gilda in her human form, as an escaped motherless slave known only as the Girl, but under the motherly ministrations of the vampires who adopt her, she becomes a capable, nurturing vampire herself, traveling across the country and into the future, gathering family to her.

Consider, too, the alienated youth of Poppy Z. Brite's *Lost Souls*, abandoning or abandoned by their families and middle-class lives to search for an anarchic ideal. These vampire teens leave their soulless broken homes, traveling from callow suburban Washington, D.C. through the aptly named Missing Mile, North Carolina to steamy New Orleans, searching for kindred vampire spirits: other black-garbed, hollow-eyed, amoral, abandoned teens, vampiric here in fact, as so many are by wish and by fashion in our world. Brite's parentless waifs, like *Peanuts* gone punk, mirror in an operatically gory vampire novel the disaffection of deathrock and gothic style that cast a modish but poignant pall over high school and college campuses.

"Christabel" is the product of a prominent Romantic poet, *Carmilla* a scion of the vampiric literary canon, *Lost Souls* and *The Gilda Stories* popular newcomers. While the pattern is widespread, this essay focuses on three less well known works, two that have withstood the test of time, and one which may, but all of which are neglected in the vampiric canon and therefore need a bit of mothering themselves. Theodore Sturgeon's *Some of Your Blood* (1961) reflects its time's Freudian anxiety about parent/child sexuality. In a later, more politicized era, Tanith Lee's *Sabella, or the Blood Stone* (1980) mirrors feminist concerns over motherhood and power. In our present post-modern, post-Freudian, post-feminist decade, our anxiety to reconstruct the deconstructed family finds its image in Annette Curtis Klause's *The Silver Kiss* (1990).

Several critics have speculated about the vampiric mother/child relationship. For James Twitchell, "Christabel" is "in part, at least, an enactment of a sexual desire of the son for his mother" (44). Through some gender-juggling, Twitchell makes Christabel "the poet himself, displaced in dream life across sexual lines, to make representable a tabooed act" (44). Twitchell sees an Oedipal relationship between Christabel and the mother-substitute, emphasizing the sexual over the nurturant aspects of the relationship, although in his exploration of the poem's repeated breast imagery, Twitchell observes that Geraldine's breast, withered before she lies with Christabel, seems full afterward, "almost as if the mammary gland had been stimulated" (47). This interpretation, inevitable if Christabel represents an oedipal Coleridge, means that the vampire (Geraldine) is nursing the victim (Christabel).

Camille Paglia calls vampirism "a kind of drain of male energy by female fullness" (13). For her, "woman's latent vampirism is not a social aberration but a development of her maternal function" (13). Agreeing with Twitchell, Paglia describes Geraldine as "a classic vampire of great age, her breast withered only when she hungers. After she has sated herself, her breasts recover sensual fullness" (336). Unlike Twitchell, however, Paglia emphasizes the lesbian relationship between Geraldine and Christabel.

Janice Doane and Devon Hodges, discussing Anne Rice's *The Vampire Lestat*, reverse the suction: "with this new focus on the mother . . . comes an increased emphasis on the vampire's attachment to the preoedipal pleasures of sucking, biting, and symbiosis" (423). This preoedipal interpretation, applied to Christabel, would have Geraldine, the vampire, being nursed by her victim and filling her breast with Christabel's energy.[2] To see the vampire as the needy child puts an odd spin on Geraldine but acknowledges Christabel's own reptilian transformation. This view certainly recognizes the kindred spirituality of Laura and Carmilla.

Twitchell's and Paglia's male-centered but contradictory interpretations of the mother as sexual object or fecund threat, and the more convincing emphasis on preoedipal pleasures of Doane and Hodges, interpret a relationship for which the vampire often searches in vain. Childbirth throughout most of history has been a deadly enterprise, and one associated with vampires. In Malaysia "a penangglan, or vampire . . . is especially feared in houses where a birth has taken place" (Wright 4). And, although in folklore "vampires are far more often male than female, the exceptions to the rule are commonly mothers who have died in childbirth" (Barber 36), like the mothers of Christabel and Carmilla, to name two literary figures who predate modern birthing procedures and antibiotics. But mothers still die and families disintegrate now more than ever.

Theodore Sturgeon's *Some of Your Blood* certainly acknowledges these facts. This brief (143-page) novel may be seen as the early harbinger of the more recent wave of sympathetic vampire novels.[3] *Some of Your Blood* is an ignored masterpiece which, without making any use of fabulation, cuts to the metaphorical heart of the vampire, and does so with Sturgeon's characteristic grace, economy, and compassion. The current project to reissue Sturgeon's work has made *Some of Your Blood* available again, so it may gain the attention it deserves. The novel is a psychological mystery, its detective a psychologist searching for the cause and nature of his patient's disturbance; it borrows a bit from Shelley's *Frankenstein* in form, with its outside frame and its inner core of the tale told by the monster. As in *Frankenstein*, the monster reveals himself to be an innately good being, trapped by cruelty and neglect in an infantile state.

George Smith, Sturgeon's monster, is the son of desperately poor rural Kentucky parents, his father an amoral alcoholic brute and his mother a physically and emotionally weak victim. For George, reform school and army life represent ease and plenty, but he is sent summarily to a mental hospital from his army post, classified a violent psychopath on the basis of a mysterious vanished letter. The psychologist must discover whether George, now orphaned, is unjustly accused, and whether he is dangerous. Through hypnosis, George's own written account, an interview with George's lover, and the letter's reemergence on the novel's penultimate page, we learn that George is indeed a multiple murderer and a drinker of blood.

When the infant George sucked at his mother's breast, he tasted blood as well as milk, a fact of which she often reminded him. We are meant at first to believe that the lust for blood engendered by his nursing was oedipal, sexual, and that he gains sexual release from it. George seems to support this theory, not only in his responses to psychological tests but in his explanation of sexual appetite: "Everything that is alive in the whole world keeps taking things in and then working them over and then throwing out what it could not use. Taking in is why it goes and why it grows and how it grows too. No matter how good it feels . . . you can't duck the one thing, that sex is part two not part one. . . . The first part, taking-in, gives you

Satisfaction and the second part, throwing-out, gives you Relief. There is a whole lot of people in the world . . . [who] go all around looking for relief and then they get upset when it don't satisfy" (42).

But we eventually understand that George's development was arrested before any sexual awakening at all. His desire for blood-letting doesn't bring Relief; it brings Satisfaction. His relationship with his girlfriend Anna brought him, not sexual Relief, but infantile Satisfaction. The psychologist explains: "His blood-drinking is not like the bottled-up, raging pressures which drive the true sexual psychopath; it is much more like the demanding vacuum inside a suckling babe" (27–28). What seemed to be unfolding in the standard psychosexual Freudian manner becomes quite different by the end of the novel.

Sturgeon thus acknowledges the age of anxiety over sexual deviance, letting us interpret George's story as an oedipal conflict turned homicidal. And since this is Sturgeon writing, we find ourselves sympathizing with the deviant, which allows us to share what one character calls the "Kinsey Boon," the acceptance of many sexual practices as within a normal range (134). We eventually realize, however, that George's deviance is not sexual, but pre-sexual. As Doane and Hodges say of *The Vampire Lestat*, this behavior is really about "the preoedipal pleasures of sucking, biting, and symbiosis."

In Sturgeon's vision, however, the symbiosis is largely forgotten. Having made the comparison between George, the blood-drinking vampire of the novel, and a "suckling babe," he enlarges on it in the person of his psychologist detective: "The analogy . . . bears on the question in so many ways that it stops looking like an analogy and becomes, very nearly, an analysis. A hungry baby wants what it want [sic] with an insensate, unreasoning demand . . . . It is quite fair to describe a baby's emotional nexus as insane . . . maniacal . . . obsessive" (128). George's emotional needs are simple, like those of a baby—"to have your fill, to be safe with someone taking care, and just to quit thinking"—but when they are not met he seeks satisfaction by hunting small animals, occasionally by murdering human beings, and in only one relationship by symbiosis (62).

Anna gives him some of her blood, once a month, and he treats her gently and undemandingly in return; each satisfies the other.[4] We recognize the move from Freudian sexual anxiety to a more innocent if no less frightening impulse. In this symbiotic relationship, George has found his mother again, but healthier and more nurturing in this avatar. Anna fills him up so he doesn't feel the "demanding vacuum of the suckling babe."

And, while George loves Anna because she takes his mother's place, it is not an oedipal love. The comfort Sturgeon offers is not, however, that George has escaped the incest taboo in thought, word, and deed. After all, to be arrested at a preoedipal stage of development, and to murder for either relief or satisfaction, is still deeply disturbed. The comfort is Sturgeon's trademark one, that any act committed in love and without harm is good, and this is the comfort that transcends Freudian anxiety.

The social worker in *Some of Your Blood* asks, "can one reasonably suppose that a girl demands the breast any less because she is a girl?" (136). *Sabella* answers no, by showing a female vampire figure who gains sustenance, not sexuality, from her blood-sucking. However, in the twenty years between Sturgeon's novel and Tanith Lee's, the weight of the vampire metaphor has shifted from Freudianism to feminism.

Sabella is another small (157-page) but powerful novel and, with its richness of meter, description, metaphor, and symbol, well worth more attention than it has received. The novel takes place on an earth-colonized planet, Novo Mars, which had a (now extinct) native humanoid population: the work is science fiction rather than horror. Sabella, a human first-generation Novo Martian, takes on at puberty the traits of a vampire. Her mother dies—killed, Sabella believes, by the weight of her daughter's sins of sex and blood. When Sabella meets Jace, she discovers her match, and their confrontation brings the concluding revelations, among them that the transformation of Sabella and Jace into vampires is actually a transformation into indigenous Novo Martians and therefore natural rather than supernatural. The revelations, all of which concern issues of power, control, domination, and submission, clarify a number of metaphorical themes from post-colonialism through ecology, religion, and sado-masochism to symbiotic feminism.

As in *Some of Your Blood*, our first impression of the vampire's role is sexual, and, as in the other novel, that impression changes with late-page revelations. Sabella is a female vampire who sucks the blood of her exclusively male victims until they die, not from blood loss but from continuous orgasm. Her vamping seems to be a parody of feminism as its worst detractors fear it: here is the female as aggressor, hating men and destroying their manhood, embodying Camille Paglia's vision of the femme fatale. And the novel's denouement promises at first to be feminism's worst fear: the taming of the shrew. Here, indeed, are the anxieties of feminism laid bare. But Lee resolves them by drawing metaphorical parallels between sexuality and nurturing in a way that also speaks to issues of ecology, religion, and post-colonialism because she examines the nature of power in all these relationships.

The relationship between vampire and victim echoes that between the now-invisible, utterly assimilated, aboriginal Novo Martians, Sabella and Jace, and their human colonizers, which in turn echoes the demonizing of aboriginal peoples by their colonizers and of the colonizers by their victims.

The novel's energy-conserving vampirism, far from a wasteful blood-letting, is represented as an economical sharing: "Of the little water and the little food there was, one would eat and drink, and when he was strong, the other would take from him the vital element which food and drink had made—his blood" (155). Thus the vampire becomes a metaphor for the close guarding of the ecosystem: return to mother earth what you have bled from her. The revelation of this blood communion comes in a museum beneath a church and deliberately parallels Christian communion; the issues of domination and submission now take on a religious resonance. And while domination and submission may have religious application, they surely interrogate sexual relationships as well. In this application of the vampire metaphor to *Sabella*, we see an illustration of the importance of choice in any pleasurable sado-masochistic performance: one chooses to submit.

Finally, in this list of metaphorical themes, the vampire and her victim illustrate symbiotic feminism. The woman in power must learn to wield it fairly, the woman who nurtures must remember this, too, is power. Power does not mean parasitic predation or a reversal of the predator/prey relationship, but a symbiotic exchange. *Sabella*'s strong sado-masochistic component uses the metaphor of the vampire to illustrate the difference in a relationship of domination and submission between willing, controlled consent and an unwilling, uncontrolled arrangement. In both the feminist and anti-feminist nightmares with which the novel plays, one partner is unwilling and the other is uncontrolled; the unwilling party dies in spirit or in fact and the uncontrolled party devolves into a brute.

When in control of her vampiric feeding, Sabella, the black widow, the femme fatale, *la belle dame sans merci*, gives her willing victim the lay of his life, although she receives no sexual satisfaction herself; when she loses control, her victim loses his will and his life. When Jace becomes her victim, he teaches her a different role, that of submission. She describes her feelings in terms that echo George Smith's description of his needs: "A wonderful feeling washed through me. It wasn't only sex, which I'd never

truly felt before, it was a sensation of peace, of comfort almost. I couldn't
fight him. Neither could I fool him. Suddenly I understood I couldn't do
a single thing he couldn't handle; I couldn't take from him because he
would leave me no space to take, no room for any response but one. Nor
need I be ashamed, for I could commit no crime against him, only surrender, give in, let go" (146). And submitting, she finds sexual relief and satisfaction. But this is not because she has submitted to the woman's rightful
place, not because the shrew has been properly tamed. Even as she gives in
to Jace she is still the vampire, the aggressor, sucking his blood away. Vampire has not become victim: she remains the oppressor.

Instead, with Sabella's submission comes a re-examination of the roles
of domination and submission that applies at every level: "He has to dominate me, that's essential; for I take his life's blood. The victim must be
stronger than the oppressor—or he dies. He has to tell me when and how,
and where to walk, and if I may, and I obey him, but that's not for always.
I've wanted a discipline beyond myself, and needed it to show me how to
master myself, and I'm learning this too, he's teaching me. In the end,
maybe I shall be the one to say that this planet is where we return to and
where we remain" (156).

By shifting power from aggressor to victim, Lee revises the vampire
story. The vampire, the aggressor, loses itself to brutishness and sexual
emptiness to the extent that it dominates its victim. The victim loses its
identity and life to the extent that it invites its victimization. Be the aggressor a beautiful vampire or, speaking metaphorically, a greedy infant, a
colonizing empire, the myriad drains on an ecological system, a dominant
religion, or a dominant gender, it will destroy both itself and the lives
around it if it rules without check. By shifting power from aggressor to
victim, Lee shifts it from the feeding vampire to its nurturing victim, or
from child ("suckling babe") to mother figure. The role reversal is not then
a matter of which gender should dominate (does a girl demand the breast
any less?) but a question of whether power lies in greed and need or in
nourishing and giving. Sabella cautions the reader at the end of the story:
"Don't think me Jace's slave, for if you do, you miss all truth in what I've
told you, and you miss the promise that one day I may choose to make this
man the father to our planet's children. And on that day, or night, the last
shall be first" (157). If Sabella becomes a mother, she will be the nurturing
victim who must be stronger than the needy infant with its "demanding
vacuum."

Tanith Lee defuses the anxieties of feminism by showing how positions of domination and submission, relative weakness and relative strength, are dynamic, determined not by gender but by role. Any child can learn the strength of nurturing as well as the lesser strength of taking nourishment, learning both self-reliance and moderation. By learning these things, the child matures and, though it may have lost the mother and family it seeks, as Sabella did, it is now ready to form its own family, as Sabella will.

Annette Curtis Klause's *The Silver Kiss*, a young adult novel, reverses Sabella's movement from sexual aggression to forming a family. Here the child moves from the disintegration of family to sexual awakening. This novel, controlled and to some extent limited by its audience, is psychologically astute, gracefully written, both romantic and cynical about adolescent relationships. Its accurate placement as a young adult novel means that, despite its recognition within that category, it has received little attention elsewhere. Nevertheless, it demurely and less hysterically develops the same concerns over adolescent emptiness voiced in Brite's *Lost Souls*. Where Brite vividly showed the extremes of the teen-age wasteland in her drugged, violent, and lawless characters, Klause shows its presence in a more mundane setting, with tamer, more domestic protagonists.

Klause's appealing heroine Zoë is wasting away, not from vampiric predation but from sadness: her mother is dying of cancer, her father has little time for his daughter during this crisis, and her best friend Lorraine is moving away. Alienated from the people around her, she meets Simon, an ancient vampire eternally arrested in his adolescence. He is, inevitably, orphaned and isolated: when he tells his history to Zoë, there are many parallels. Simon, exercising control, need not kill when he feeds, but his brother Christopher, also a vampire, whose transformation arrested him as a much younger child, lacks that control; he kills wantonly and viciously and, tellingly, "killed his own mother [and Simon's] in the filthiest way" (101). Simon, in contrast, consummates his romantic relationship with Zoë with a less destructive, more pleasurable, and remarkably chaste vampiric kiss. Simon and Zoë together destroy Christopher, after which Simon commits suicide to free his soul and Zoë, having learned self-reliance, faces the world alone.

As sweet and romantic as this novel is, it offers an interesting version of the vampiric search for mother and a bleak response to this decade's anxiety about family disintegration. Simon and Zoë, vampire and human, both struggle to deal with the loss of their mothers. Where George Smith of *Some of Your Blood* searched for a substitute mother and Sabella searched for the control and power to become a mother herself, these adolescents search for a way to do without relationships at all. As Simon describes his mother's death, she abandons Simon to be seduced by Christopher, who savagely kills her. The Freudian connotations are clear. Beyond them lie others more resonant for today's youth. Simon watches his mother's affection and lively personality vanish as she mourns over Christopher's disappearance (he has been kidnapped—willingly—by a vampire). In other words, his family disintegrates in the wake of one child's prodigality. Only by punishing the prodigal son and destroying himself can the good son find peace; contrast this to the Bible's allegory in which the prodigal son is accepted enthusiastically back into the fold while the "good" son feels slighted. Simon finds the strength to punish Christopher only when he takes the integrating step of forming a relationship, sexual, romantic, and familial, with Zoë. But that relationship must be temporary; no permanent bond is formed.

Zoë feels abandoned by her parents, who in their suffering forget their protecting role. She finds, instead, someone who needs her, the vampire Simon. She tells him, "Lately, it seemed that you were the only one who knew I existed" (196). His need awakens her sexuality and he teaches her how to survive: "You have yourself. A good, kind, strong, brave self" (196). With her sexual awakening, then, comes a lonely self-reliance. As the novel ends, Zoë's mother lies close to death, her exhausted father sleeps through her dangerous adventures, her best friend has moved away, and her boyfriend has committed suicide. But the novel's last lines are upbeat: "It's up to me now, she thought. But somehow it wasn't scary anymore" (198). This offers incredibly bleak comfort. As today's disaffected youth watch their families splinter, they learn not to form new families as Poppy Brite's vampires do, but to live without any lasting connection: "Things changed, she realized. People grew, they moved, they died. Sometimes they withdrew into themselves, and sometimes they reached out after needing no one. . . . Why did it mean losing people you love?" (192–93). It is fair to say that the anxieties of our age are reflected in *The Silver Kiss*, but they are not resolved, merely confronted bravely.

If we consider these three novels, and virtually any vampire literature of the last two centuries, we find that they have much to say about motherhood and family which the dominant culture suppresses. *Some of Your Blood* reminds us that the preoedipal desire for nourishment can be more powerful and more dangerous to thwart than later oedipal lust. *Sabella* advances the discussion by exploring the power of such nourishment, thus reminding us that the mother's position is one of strength. And *The Silver Kiss* shows how the withdrawal of nourishment from a culture requires the child to take on some of that strength to mother itself.

By casting the seeker after mother and family beyond the pale, the author finds what Hawthorne called the freedom of the broken law. Sturgeon pushes beyond the acceptable modernist boundaries of Freud and Kinsey. Lee reverses the expectations of both sides in the gender wars. Klause shrugs off all sides in the family values debate by placing the heavy burden of self-reliance on the slender shoulders of anorexic youth.

How did Christabel and Carmilla raise up buried truths about nineteenth century notions of motherhood and family in their bloody searches? Perhaps, for a romantic outlaw such as Coleridge, to acknowledge fear of parental abandonment might be worse than to acknowledge the attraction of incest. Perhaps *Carmilla* exposes the subversive power of the mother in the Victorian household. Perhaps both works express the universal quest to find sustenance and family in an often hostile and indifferent world. Having examined some relatively obscure members of the literary vampire family, it would be valuable to consider more prominent members of the canon in a similar manner, unearthing a few truths that refuse to die.

Part Two

READING
THE
WRITERS

6

Meditations in Red:
On Writing *The Vampire Tapestry*

SUZY MCKEE CHARNAS

The vampire as a concept reflects the discovery that the monstrous is and always has been located primarily not outside us, in mythical creatures, but in our human neighbors on this planet; and sometimes in ourselves.

Our century bears witness, documented and widely known from Dachau to Dahmer to this human monstrosity. A twofold response appears in the treatment of the mythical monster in fiction as in psychology: we reassure ourselves that the monster isn't so bad when you get to know him— he's misunderstood and in fact is often less horrible than we are; or we demonize or deify the monster into an invincible figure with whom we then identify so that we can feel as powerful as he is. That way we can say: "Who, me, a victim? No way. I'm the baddest, I'm worse than Freddy the Slasher, so nobody dares mess with me."

Now since—I believe—we know in our guts that it is true that perfect love casts out fear, we often make the very crude translation into the formulation: "Take the monster to bed with you and he will turn into a fabulous lover, just as fabulous in love as he is fabulous in evil."

However vast the leap of love required to bring us into the monster's arms and him into ours, just so limitless is the reward for our courage, our steadfastness, our clarity of vision in making that leap. We will reap a reward of love and gratitude commensurate with the immense effort and risk of our approach to the monster with our arms open.

The subject becomes heroism. We moderns are not comfortable with heroism. But we are fascinated by sex and so these are the terms in which this story is told and retold over and over again. In these terms the story is accessible to everyone.

This is the source of the "sexiness" of our mythical monsters who in any halfway rational terms could hardly be less of a sexual turn-on, from

Frankenstein's patchwork of corpses to the grave-smelling parasite we know as the vampire. This latter creature, originating, in European legend at least, as a swollen, red-faced corpse of a peasant who feeds strictly on members of his own family, now comes decked in titles and loaded with treasure and castles and dinner jackets, all the class-derived symbols of power that we use to transform feared evil into something that has at least some positive aspect.

"If I must be somebody's dinner, make it not the grinning, slavering hyena [a much-maligned beast, actually], please God, but the tiger burning bright! Not the dumpy little torturer in the sweat-stained uniform but an ageless immortal in spotless linen!" Who wouldn't take Count Dracula over Dr. Joel Steinberg, say, as their contact with what we know in the world as evil?

In the world there is no such choice, but in our imaginations there is. So we create our seductive monsters of the imagination to amuse and comfort ourselves because, in reality, for those afflicted by pain and evil, the comforts and amusements are few.

When I set out to write *The Vampire Tapestry*, I deliberately tried to fly in the face of this desperate romanticizing of evil. The task I set myself was to tell the story of a simple and ruthless predator, a true tiger in human form with all his attributes logically accounted for within the terms of animal predation as we know it. No hypnosis, no fog, no wolves, no tombs, no coffins, no nonsense: let's observe the tiger, I thought. We will enter his mind and discover his view of us, without the softening effects of sentimentalism and snobbery.

So Dr. Weyland is not a Count or a Duke, or even a Captain of industry, but a professor; not rich but professional class, working for his living; not sufferingly lonely and longing for companionship through the ennui of the ages but focused on the present moment and its possibilities as a cat is focused; not supernatural but supremely natural, a creature of evolution—once you get past the initial jump of blood as sustenance and the extended lifespan; and not the center of some parodistic society of his comperes—a very common and well-worn trope of the genre these days—but unique in all the world and well content to be so.

I made him bright because a stupid vampire is not going to make it in any sort of comfort in our fast-paced and demanding world, and I made him physically attractive so that he could get close to a wide range of prey with minimal effort, again a matter of natural evolutionary advantage. To the best of my ability I made him the monster designed to the specs of

Nature rather than superstition. *The Vampire Tapestry* is in some respects an animal story, like *The Call of the Wild* or an inverse *Lassie Come Home*.

And damned if the whole thing didn't up and walk away with me. I was dragged kicking and screaming, and loving every minute of it, into the land of the romantic monster. Despite my intentions, Weyland turned into a sterling example of the oh-he's-not-so-bad-when-you-get-to-know-him school of vampire, complete with the irresistible seductiveness of that model and the inevitable conquest of his nature by various forms of love.

At the same time the world of humans surrounding him became the locus of the predatory instinct at its cruellest, so that my monster became a sort of *naif sauvage* struggling to keep his head above water. While adapting to his own basic needs the forms into which human predators fit their twisted appetites, he became himself the prey of rapacious humans like the cult leader Reese.

Set against human evil, Weyland's merely Darwinian ruthlessness shows up as a form of just trying to get along, with the rather endearing addition that he is at all times at a deep disadvantage: he is alien to the forms of social exploitation of which he makes use. They are inventions of ours, not his, and he has to teach himself how to use them.

As he is basically a wild animal, his subtlety is limited. The aloof, exploitative academic he mimics is a template created and made use of by human males, not by vampires. Numbers of readers have said to me, only half joking: "I know that guy—he was on my thesis committee!"

We are the subtle and inventive ones, continually devising new roles for ourselves as seductive parasites. Weyland merely pads along in the shadows among us, shifting as best he can to fit the paradigms we have come up with so that he can pass for one of us and so obtain his supper.

In fact, he becomes a mirror that throws back on us the evil that beings like him were designed to embody and contain. The monster shows up the monstrosity of true human evil, as well as calling forth to match that evil the full exercise of human virtue—the courage, compassion, and steadfastness of Mark, Katje, Floria, Irv, and Dorothea. That's a pretty impressive range of function; no wonder the vampire lives on!

Looming so much larger than we do in his stripped-down purity of purpose, he becomes beautiful. So much more modest in his complexity than we are, he rattles around inside his borrowed identity, not even able to enjoy all its human prerogatives because all he really wants is his food and his privacy. He becomes an object, at times, of almost pitying affection. We love him for embodying the exploitative role with its ugliest "real" features left dormant. He isn't driven to rape or torture, he just wants to get by.

So he allows us to relate to the seductive aspects of the role: the distant but dominant male, the alluring ice-King only awaiting the kiss of life to be rescued from what we insist on reading as his agonizing loneliness. We enjoy the presence of the monstrous in what seems, by comparison with the reality of the nightly news, say, to be blessed (if piquantly spiced) safety.

We are allowed to indulge in the victim's delusion: mine is the kiss that will wake him and release all his powers in positive ways (perfect love casteth out fear); and how can he help but adore me for liberating him in this way?—in imagination, without costly error or penalty. The monster is domesticated, the tiger walks in all his beauty and power tamely by our side, and we bask in our own glory and in his.

*   *   *

I find I keep writing about "him" not only because I have my own version of this character, Weyland, in mind, but because the predominant and successful predatory identity in human society is male. This is a pattern designed by men to allow them the illusion—and often the reality, through others' forced or willing consent—of power over everyone they fear, which is to say everything and everyone, from women and children and animals and earthquakes to other men. Male terror is the source of this mask of power.

The predator-male identity is endowed with romantic trappings by women to make life in the world that is run by and for this identity bearable—just as all people tend to romanticize our imaginary predators, our monsters.

Because of these gender-specific underpinnings of the predatory template in most of its forms, I think female vampire characters rarely pack the force of the male versions. It's been tried but seldom succeeds, because there is no widespread "real" socially and professionally dominant female identity to play off of with the fictional monster. Such real female power-roles as can be found come so heavily weighted with costs and penalties—not imposed on the old-cold-dominant-male-predator-identity—as to be largely unusable without either falsifying them or making them, not vampirism, the point of the study. .

The supposedly powerful and manipulative female parasite is almost invariably a fraud, as her supposed power is actually anchored in the real-world dominance of a male partner or sponsor (for example, the case of Imelda Marcos). She is more likely to be seen as ridiculous and contemptible than as awe-inspiring or erotic.

Of course as more real-world women fit themselves into man-made patterns of dominance and social predation (see Leona Helmsley and the "Queen Bee" model of female business executive), this situation may appear to change. In fact I would argue that such women have not, so far anyway, created original templates of "vampiric" behavior for an author to play with, but have simply stepped into the old templates created by and for males. Or else they fall into or are relegated to the narrow spectrum of the femme fatale stereotypes of noir fiction and film, also created by and for the interests of males.

The powerful female parasite, or vampire, is rare in fiction because, although vividly animate and dangerous in male fantasy (see *Fatal Attraction*, for example), she hardly exists in reality.

But academia shelters many pseudo-Weylands, including some women playing the men's game just as Weyland does in order to secure its advantages for themselves.

One way that my vampire became sympathetic in the novel was through the imposition on him—by me as author, for the fun of it and to see what happened—of the victim (or "feminine") role. In fact, this has led Joanna Russ, wearing her critic-hat, to declare that Weyland is as much feminine as he is masculine—perhaps even more so. He is wounded, imprisoned, controlled, pursued—to some extent "feminized"—which is how he learns to act not just as a predatory male but as a human being.

Similarly, I find that in my more specifically feminist work the only male characters who are worth a damn are those who have had their own security, supposed superiority, and arrogant assumptions of privilege shattered by experiences of powerlessness and victimization which are, unfortunately, quite normal for many women in the real world. The inference is that if you walk a mile in my high heels, you won't be so quick to trample me again with your societally-issued hobnailed men's boots afterward.

In other words, the only "good" male is a feminized male; or, the only male with any likelihood of behaving like a decent human being is a male who has been deprived of his automatic swagger-privileges and so has some insight into what it means to live in the world without them, that is, to live like a woman (or child or animal, etc.).

This idea is not often supported in reality. Most de-privileged men will do almost anything to distance themselves from women in the struggle to regain the superior position that is their "birthright." But one must find hope somewhere, or despair and die.

Still, the concept of the monster humanized by his monstrosity and reformed by love must seem a heartless mockery of the plight of women trapped in abusive situations, dissidents tormented by "special" police, children raped and exploited by those charged with protecting them, and the victims of psychotics like Charlie Manson. In the "real" world, real monstrosity rampages unhindered at every level of privilege or deprivation.

Fiction's solution to monstrosity, hope's solution—love, empathy, and compassion—seems in real-world terms impotent and overwhelmed. Even where love touches "evil" people, its effects tend to be so narrowly confined that their monstrous actions are barely affected. Josef Fouché, minister of police under everybody from Robespierre to the restored King of France, comes to mind; the Butcher of Lyons, a figure of repression and horror, was a fond family man at home. Modern history is full of Nazis and bloody-handed commissars of whom the same can be said.

And yet—and yet it's not a *lie*. The power of this pattern of the transformable beast goes beyond mere self-protective wishful thinking. There is some kind of irreduceable, palpable truth in that statement, "perfect love casteth out fear."

The problem is that perfect love is so very hard to come by.

*   *   *

I have had occasion to think a good deal about the vampire concept over a period of years (and my current "conclusions," stated above, are by no means set in concrete). One of the startling things about the vampire is his extraordinary hardiness: once roused up, he stays with you, dying back but continually reappearing, a perennial revenant.

I am speaking from on-going personal experience. Although I swore that *The Vampire Tapestry* would not become only the first of a series of books and stories about Edward Lewis Weyland, in the dozen or so years since publication I have returned repeatedly to this material, most often in a protracted effort to get a viable stage play out of it. The third chapter, "Unicorn Tapestry," has lent itself most easily to such treatment.

In fact I got into the playwrighting business, to the extent that I have actually done so, because strangers kept calling me up and asking for permission to make a stage script of this chapter—or to stage a script they had already created without benefit of such permission. Out of sheer self-defense, I finally decided to have a go at it myself.

The result, presently titled *Vampire Dreams*, has been performed in part at Cafe La Mama in New York, and at the Magic Theatre in San Francisco, both limited "workshop" style engagements which have not, to date, led to a permanent place in anybody's repertory (too bad, too). But I keep working on the script and sending it out, and it's always a pleasure to chew over the material again, discovering new flavors to be brought out, developing the recipe, as it were, toward new heights.

This script was also redesigned to be submitted to a comic-book company, where it has languished for years (not enough SPLAT, AAIIEEE!, I suspect). And I have done a collaborative story including Weyland as a major character for a vampire anthology, *Under the Fang* (1991), published under the auspices of the Horror Writers of America.[1] In my files as I write are the first thirty pages of another story about Weyland, although what length it may turn out to be if I ever finish it I can't now be sure.

In some ways the whole experience of coming up with this character, developing him, and continuing to mull over the implications of his nature and adventures has been an extended learning experience for me as an author and as a reflective person.

I had to go and learn a therapy system for "Unicorn Tapestry," never having been in therapy myself. Another section of the book, "A Musical Interlude," required trips to the Santa Fe Opera in winter with a camera to map the backstage layout and the surrounding landscape and to see how long it took to run from here to there, not to mention working out the precise timing of crucial events using three different recordings of *Tosca*.

And in the end, I decided that because my vampire was *not* a romantic figure but a brute predator, he would *not* be vanquished by—well, by love. He would prove his alienness from humanity, his truly "other" nature, by simply walking away from it all, shedding his Weyland identity just as he plans to do—but, in the event, does not do—in the final chapter. He was going to shuck off the human emotions he had acquired and the human connections he had made just as a snake sheds its skin, discarding his fatally compromised professorial identity because—not being human—he could.

Don't we all long to be able to do the same, at certain excruciating moments of our emotional lives? And, be it noted, our true human monsters of the Manson variety accomplish this very thing. It's because of this ability that they are able to move from murder to murder without a shred of remorse or any effect on themselves of what they have done. That's why we secretly envy and admire them, at the same time that we shudder and condemn. I was only trying to hold my vampire's story to the anti-romantic, "realistic" pattern I had begun with.

My editor, however, objected. It won't work, he said. To end with Weyland hitch-hiking north to a new identity without a backward glance or a further thought for all the people he has come so close to in the body of the novel betrays the emotional investment in those encounters that the reader has been led to make. It's not fair.

Please, he said; try it my way. Have him fold, have him give up and go back to sleep to escape the effects of all this human contact and interaction, so that his emotional investment is revealed to be similar to ours—so that we can care about what he finally manages to do about it.

I held out, I sulked, I muttered resentfully about "artistic integrity." Then I remembered that exactly what the editor was suggesting had been my own first impulse, rejected by me as too trite, too predictable. So how could I refuse to at least give it a try?

I gave it a try. To my amazement and chagrin the "trite" ending wrote itself, with enormous ease and speed, and read a whole hell of a lot better than what I had first written. What's more, in the writing of this new ending I suddenly found myself spelling out exactly what the previous chapters had meant to Weyland himself as a character, and how those events formed a coherent line of development leading inexorably to this place of defeat and withdrawal for my dangerously humanized monster.

So this tale that had begun as a short story and proceeded to extend itself episode by episode at last revealed itself as a unified narrative, a novel rather than a clutch of short stories pretending to be a novel. Against my best intentions, my better judgment, and everything else I could bring to bear, the "new," "romantic" ending was a lot more satisfying to me as both reader and writer than the old, more innovative and clever one had ever been.

Which proves—what, if anything? That romance is built into the vampire paradigm so firmly that it can't be excised without losing the power of the whole? That, on the contrary, this extractive surgery can be successfully performed, but not by me? That sex and monstrosity can never be parted because monstrosity is seen as powerful, and power in our culture always and everywhere is equated with sexuality?

Certainly a strong strain in our popular entertainment is that of the development of sexual bonds across chasms of difference—black/white, rich/poor, age/youth, one culture/another culture—which openly include or at least imply inherent power imbalances. The Prince and the peasant girl, the aesthete and his rough-trade lover, the gamekeeper and the lady—the patterns go on and on, and somehow the perceived power imbalances add a charge to the sexual bonds.

Similarly, the monster and the girl, from King Kong and Fay Wray to the gangster and his moll: everybody but the Mummy gets his romance—and Anne Rice fixes that by giving the old creature big baby blues and updating his wardrobe, and presto, he's the sexiest thing on the block![2] Dracula has not one bride, but a half dozen and still counting.

So when I write about a vampire who generally finds sex disgusting and is mostly impotent anyway, what happens? He cannot help but incline, ruinously for himself, toward those who have taken the enormous risk of putting themselves into his power knowingly and, in some sense, lovingly. With the courage of love, the longing of love, the hopefulness of love, they reach across the immense gap between species, and what is brave and needy and hopeful in him is awakened and responds.

It happens like that because I wrote it that way, and I wrote it that way because I know in my heart that love is stronger than fear, as in our deepest hearts—when we are not afraid to admit it—we all know, with a knowledge that comes from sources deeper than any creed, any book, any commandment. It comes from the part of us that refuses to exclude monstrosity but won't settle for it either; the part that aspires, that demands, that risks all to create more than bare, brute selfishness in others, and in ourselves as well.

We love and honor our monsters for bringing us to that place in ourselves, the place from which we continually create humanity in a brutal, fearful world.

7

Sang for Supper: Notes on the Metaphorical Use of Vampires in *The Empire of Fear* and *Young Blood*

BRIAN STABLEFORD

In Remy de Gourmont's brief Decadent fantasy "Le magnolia" (*Histoires magiques*, 1894), a young woman named Arabelle is about to be married to a dying man, in order to satisfy his final wish. She finds a symbolic parallel to her situation in the last remaining blossoms on a magnolia tree. One is already withered, but the other is still beautiful. The symbolism of the magnolia flower—a corolla of white petals surrounding a splash of vivid red—is explicitly stated: "la vie était signifiée dans la neige des corolles charnues par une goutte de sang" [life was signified in the snow of the fleshy corollas by a drop of blood]. Arabelle laments the fate of her husband-to-be, saying: "Il va mourir avec les secondes fleurs du magnolia, celui qui devait aviver d'une goutte de sang la fleur que je suis" [he will die with the second flowering of the magnolia, he who should quicken, with a spurt of blood—or, metaphorically, semen—the flower which I am].

Gourmont's second use of the phrase "goutte de sang" is, of course, euphemistic; the veiled reference is to semen rather than to blood. A translator attempting to render the story into English, having no parallel wordplay to exploit, would be forced to preserve the double meaning by recruiting some weak-kneed phrase like "vital fluid." This is a pity, because it adds an extra layer of confusion to what is already a curious pattern of equivalence. One consequence of this is that the French, in the context of language, are better-equipped than the English to understand the kind of vampire story in which the symbolism of blood and semen is inextricably entwined, so that the nourishment of blood becomes a partly-reversed mirror of sexual intercourse.

In the climax of "Le magnolia," of course, the husband achieves after death the defloration which he was unable to accomplish in life, although the result certainly does not warrant the use of a verb like "aviver." Arabelle is supernaturally drawn to the magnolia, where a shadow awaits her, and, when she goes to meet it, "l'ombre étendit les bras, des bras fluides et serpentins, puis les laissa tomber, telles deux vipères d'enfer, sur les épaules, où elles se tordirent en sifflant" [the shadow extended its arms, arms which were fluid and serpentine, then let them fall, like two hellish vipers, onto her shoulders, where they writhed and hissed]. In accordance with the iron law of narrative propriety, Arabelle is found—drained of her vital fluids by those "hellish vipers"—with a withered magnolia flower clutched in her dead hand.

* * *

In another fairly characteristic product of the French Decadent movement, "Le verre de sang" [The Glass of Blood] (*Buveurs d'âmes*, 1893) by Jean Lorrain, the reader discovers a woman waiting patiently in a hotel lobby, confronted by a symbolic display of flowers in a vase of Venetian glass. These flowers, unlike Gourmont's effetely effeminate magnolia, are possessed of "une dureté cruelle et suggestive" [a cruel and suggestive hardness]; the irises seem like "fers de hallebarde" [pike-heads] and the narcissi like shooting-stars "tombées d'un ciel de nuit d'hiver" [fallen from a night sky in winter].

Lorrain gradually and teasingly unfolds the explanation of why the woman is there. She has been a famous actress, renowned for her Nordic good looks and her immunity to romance, but she gave up her career in order to marry an Italian diplomat—not because she loved *him* but because she loved his young daughter. Having given up everything for her loved one, however, the unfortunate actress found that her inamorata slowly began to fade away. The doctors she has consulted agree that the tuberculosis which is killing the little girl was brought on by the actress' overabundant love for her, and that the only possible cure is for her to take a daily draught of fresh blood in the local abattoir. The actress, who finds the odor of the abattoir unbearable, always waits in the hotel while the girl takes her medicine—but when her loved one returns and kisses her on the lips, her instinctive revulsion to the taste of blood is miraculously transformed into its opposite.

Given that "Le verre de sang" is one of the very few tales of lesbian pedophilia ever penned, it is perhaps unsurprising that it proceeds in an unexpected and rather implausible direction, but it is worth noting that the doctors of fin-de-siècle Paris did have rather eccentric ideas about the causes of disease—Pasteur's theories had not yet driven out their rivals. Jean Lorrain was himself both homosexual and consumptive, and probably suspected—if he did not actually believe—that the two might be causally connected. The daily dose of fresh blood did indeed figure among the prescriptions he tried out—as did drinking ether, which also didn't work, although its hallucinatory effects inspired many of his most vivid horror stories. "Le verre de sang" thus qualifies as one of the few stories of non-supernatural vampirism based on actual experience, and there is no doubt that its complex network of metaphors was constructed with genuine feeling.

* * *

These two stories present interesting interminglings of the notions of vampirism and sexual perversity. (A marriage between a dying man and a young girl may not fall into any familiar category of "perversity," but it is a discomfiting notion nevertheless.) The former is more conventional, transmuting perversity into horror according to a familiar moral alchemy, but it should be noted that at the time he wrote "Le magnolia" Gourmont had not yet fallen victim to the disfiguring disease that wrecked his life as surely as tuberculosis wrecked Lorrain's. The disease in question was then known as "tubercular lupus," and the quacks who compounded Lorrain's misery with their lousy advice presumably viewed Gourmont's case in much the same light; it is hardly surprising that Gourmont's later fiction became increasingly obsessed with, and ironically sympathetic to, offbeat lust of various kinds. Lorrain's story, like all his work, is determinedly suspicious of the kind of moral judgment Gourmont's takes for granted; it is a horror story of sorts, but it also poses a calculated moral challenge, an invitation to the reader to examine his or her own idiosyncrasies, fantasies, and fascinations.

The symbolism of both these stories is entirely conscious and explicit, and they provide useful paradigm cases which allow us to perceive similar—although less conscious and less explicit—patterns of symbolism in other works. It is no coincidence that the era which produced "Le magnolia" and "Le verre de sang" also saw the publication of Richard Krafft-Ebing's *Psychopathia Sexualis* (1886). This was the work that helped popularize the notion of real-world vampirism *as* a form of sexual perversion, but the idea was hardly new, and the reductive "explanation" of vampirism as a peculiar form of fetishism did less justice to the complexity of human fascination with the idea of vampires than did the exploratory work done by earlier litterateurs. John Polidori's graphic representation of avid sexual appetite as vampiric lust in *The Vampyre* (1819) was undoubtedly based in hysterical spite against his one-time employer Lord Byron, but what it produced in the figure of Lord Ruthven was a peculiarly charismatic figure who retained a good deal of the sex-appeal which made Byron—in the words of the luckless Lady Caroline Lamb—so "dangerous to know."

The extraordinary power of unorthodox lust is admitted, if not exactly celebrated, by most of the nineteenth-century classics of vampire fiction. Théophile Gautier's novella *La morte amoureuse* (1836) is an exquisitely lurid account of a young priest's lust for a wicked and very beautiful parishioner, whose seduction of him cannot reach its climax until she is dead. He is saved from death by his superior, but Gautier raises the awkward question—which also crops up in the similar novella *Arria Marcella* (1852)—whether real life can possibly have anything to offer that is anywhere near as intensely intoxicating as the love of a sexy vampire. Outside France—which, being a Catholic country, was fertile ground for the nurture of Romantic and sentimental Satanists of all kinds—sympathy for vampires was inevitably more muted, but never entirely obliterated by the conscientious horror of its contemplation. An oft-reprinted story ostensibly translated from the German around 1810—usually falsely attributed to Ludwig Tieck—variously called "The Bride of the Grave" and "Wake Not the Dead!" takes a much dimmer view of the propriety of female vampirism, as does J. Sheridan Le Fanu's remarkable lesbian fantasy *Carmilla* (1872), but both stories are still vividly erotic.

Polidori's fascinated loathing is reproduced in numerous English stories of a similar kind, but becomes much more problematic in some. John Keats, in "Lamia" (1820), and Vernon Lee, in "Amour Dure" (1890) and "Prince Alberic and the Snake-Lady" (1896), were both able to perceive a measure of ironically life-enhancing potential in vampiric romance. This was presumably not unconnected with the facts that Keats was dying of tuberculosis—perhaps further complicated by hopeless passion—while Vernon Lee was a homosexual(woman)-in-exile, but this in no way diminishes the stature of their work. Bram Stoker—who might have been showing the earlier symptoms of syphilis at the time—was far too horror-stricken to take a sympathetic view of vampires in *Dracula* (1897), but Fred Saberhagen, reinterpreting the events of that novel in the light of sympathetic reason in *The Dracula Tape* (1975), might arguably be said to have revealed the remarkable extent to which Stoker belonged to the devil's party without knowing it.

*   *   *

It was not, of course, absolutely necessary to be the victim of a socially-stigmatized disease before one could become interested in vampires, even in the nineteenth century; nor was it a firm requirement that one should be uneasily aware of a certain unorthodoxy in one's sexual tastes or fantasies—but such circumstances obviously helped. Nowadays, of course, the significance of such predispositions has declined very markedly; we live in more enlightened times.

Modern ideas about disease are very different from those which burdened Jean Lorrain and Remy de Gourmont. Even the vilest of the multitudinous quacks who nowadays pose as exponents of "alternative medicine" is unlikely to suggest that tuberculosis is the result of sexual perversion, or that it might be cured by drinking daily doses of fresh blood. Not all of our neighbors have yet to become virtuous liberals, content to say that any and all routes to sexual fulfilment are unexceptionable provided only that they do not involve coercion, but they are getting there. The war that will end war by securing a final victory for understanding and tolerance is still going on, and there are many battles still to be fought against racism, sexism, and religious fundamentalism—to name but a few of our enemies—but the good guys are definitely winning.

One of the more eccentric of the very many ways in which this unfolding victory has been celebrated is the production of numerous modern stories in which good liberals display their tolerance by extending it, with retrospective apologies, to the real and imaginary scapegoats of past eras. The monstrousness of such figures is revealed by re-examination to have been the product of ignorance and folly, and our relative enlightenment is celebrated by a new willingness to look for the pathetic and the heroic in yesterday's demons. We all feel sorry for all the innocents who were tortured and burned—or hanged—by our forefathers as heretics and/or witches, and we take some pride in saying so. In much the same way, at least some of us are prepared to entertain the notion that Lord Ruthven, like his human model, might after all have been worthy of love—or, at least, sufficiently thrilling when on the job to make mere matters of worthiness irrelevant.

Modern vampires, like Count Kotor's family in Pierre Kast's *Les Vampires d'Alfama* (1975), can function as heroic symbols of philosophical enlightenment, scientific progress, and sexual liberation, while those who hunt them down can be portrayed as bigoted psychopaths. A child of the free-and-easy 1960s who met a vampire, as the one in Jane Gaskell's *The Shiny Narrow Grin* (1964) did, would have been far more likely to think "Groovy!" than "Aaaargh!" Unfortunate immortals who have internalized and long carried with them the awful burden of generations of hatred, like the heroes of Anne Rice's *Interview with the Vampire* (1976) and its sequels, are ripe for psychoanalytic redemption, and any right-on shrink of today who happens to run into a vampire, as the one in Suzy McKee Charnas's *The Vampire Tapestry* (1980) does, will naturally do her level best to help him feel good about himself—although, as Charnas scrupulously points out, it will not necessarily be to a vampire's advantage to find out that there is a lot of authentic heart-wringing humanity lurking in his predatory psyche. And when today's novelist looks back on the various phases of a vampire's career, as Chelsea Quinn Yarbro does in *Hotel Transylvania* (1978) and its sequels, she has the delicious option of being able to portray him as an infinitely superior version of Lord Byron: sane, good, and a pleasure to be laid by—a veritable lamb in rake's clothing!

* * *

It bears repeating that it is not necessary, in order to write works like the above-mentioned modern vampire stories, to be a literal social outsider in the way that Jean Lorrain always was and Remy de Gourmont unfortunately became. Modern writers of vampire stories are, for the most part, amiable and well-adjusted people. One of the benefits of living in a chaotically pluralistic society, however, is that almost everyone with an atom of imagination can very easily see himself or herself as an outsider of some sort.

Many of the words we have coined in order to describe this state of outsiderhood are vaguely pejorative—those old sociological favorites "alienation" and "anomie" are cardinal examples—but we still can, and should, think of the capacity to imagine oneself as an outsider as a *benefit*. Those unfortunate people who long for reconnection to some kind of quasi-organic social whole, whether it be on the scale of the nuclear family or the socialist Utopia, are suffering from a delusive disorder closely akin to other saccharine sicknesses like nostalgia and romantic infatuation. It is true that feeling like an alien is conducive to a certain paranoid unease, but it is surely time to recognize and admit that anyone in today's world who does not feel at least slightly paranoid is as mad as a hatter.

Given all this, it is not at all surprising that modern fictions whose purpose is the elaborate and fascinated study of the hypothetical existential predicament of the vampire should be popular.

Not all exercises in vampire fiction are consciously and elaborately based in a deep-seated sense of the author's own alienness, and one would naturally be wary of drawing such a conclusion in respect of an author who had never put such a conviction on the public record. In the case of Brian Stableford, however, there is no need to draw on privileged information in order to establish that this is the case. Readers interested in the particular evolution and precise form of this sensibility can find a tediously elaborate account of it in the autobiographical essay which Stableford wrote for the "Profession of Science Fiction" series in the journal *Foundation* (1990), which makes it obvious that a profoundly awkward sense of alienness colored Stableford's literary taste long before he was capable of analyzing it, and that it later became an important aspect of his various critical analyses of the history of the literary vampire—most notably the essay "Eroticism in Supernatural Literature" in *Survey of Modern Fantasy Literature* (1983). His two vampire novels, *The Empire of Fear* (1988) and *Young Blood* (1992) must be viewed as a kind of spinoff from this interested critical analysis.

*   *   *

The Empire of Fear (1988) grew out of a short story, "The Man Who Loved the Vampire Lady," written in 1986 but not published until 1988. The story develops a science-fictional version of vampirism, which roots the powers and predilections of its blood-dependent species in their physiology. These vampires are not fugitive predators forever in hiding; their peculiar superhumanity has given them the means to become an aristocracy ruling over the mass of "common men" throughout Europe and Asia.

The traditional image of the vampire must of necessity be altered if vampirism is to be made a matter of biology rather than being frankly supernatural. Those trappings which seem purely superstitious and logically incoherent—fear of crosses; the absence of reflections in mirrors; a necessity to sleep in coffins lined with native soil—have to be discarded. Stableford goes further than this in one vital respect; his vampires can walk abroad in daylight. The three indispensable characteristics of the vampire which he retains are 1) the necessity to feed on human blood; 2) longevity and relative invulnerability to injury; and 3) extraordinary sexual attractiveness. The first of these attributes is, of course, definitive; the second is merely traditional; the third lies at the heart of the purely literary functions of the motif.

The reconstruction of vampires as living beings rather than undead ones inevitably requires some rethinking in respect of the mechanism by which vampires make more vampires. Even writers working with more traditional vampires have been forced to make modifications of this kind when faced with the logical problems implicit in the population-explosion effect described by Stephen King in 'Salem's Lot (1975). Mindful of the claims made by certain critics that Dracula can be read as an allegory of syphilis, Stableford decided to make the biological vampirism of "The Man Who Loved the Vampire Lady" a form of sexually-transmitted disease; the real world had obligingly provided a topical exemplar. In the world of "The Man Who Loved the Vampire Lady," only male vampires can make more vampires, although they are themselves confused and misled by their own magical theories about how they accomplish that result. The rate at which they can "reproduce" is slowed by virtue of their suffering a diminution of virility proportional to their potential longevity. Thus the vampire aristocracy is slow to expand by comparison with the potential for growth which the population of common humanity retains.

One convenient corollary of this subsidiary hypothesis is that the activities of heterosexual vampires produce a disproportionate number of eternally young and unusually beautiful female vampires. (They are unusually beautiful partly by virtue of being disease-free, and partly by virtue of a mysterious luster which this species of vampirism confers on human skin.) The logic of the situation implies that these female vampires inevitably prefer common lovers—by reason of their virility—and that they set aesthetic standards with which common women cannot easily compete. This provides a supposedly rational basis for an assumption intrinsic to the vast majority of modern vampire stories: that supernatural lovers are intrinsically more attractive and exciting than common-or-garden partners could ever be.

"The Man Who Loved the Vampire Lady" is set in the seventeenth century of a Europe to which vampirism has been introduced in the distant past by Attila the Hun, thus altering the consequent history of the divided Roman Empire; the discovery of America has not taken place and Great Britain remains, in political terms, part of France. The seventeenth century is selected as the most appropriate time to display the hypothesis because it was the era in our own history in which the scientific method and the scientific imagination both took wing; the story attempts to exploit the melodrama inherent in the moment when ordinary human beings first begin to set aside their superstitious awe of the vampires and begin to think of vampirism as a gift of nature rather than magic.

The key image of "The Man Who Loved the Vampire Lady" is the microscope. The story turns on the hypothesis that the new kind of insight the microscope promises and symbolizes might be enough in itself—irrespective of whether anything relevant can actually be seen therein—to make the vampires fear for their empire and commoners confident that it might be overturned. In order to supply the story with a human dimension, it employs a central character, Edmund Cordery, who is in a crucially ambiguous position. He is a trusted lackey of the vampire aristocracy but is secretly a revolutionary working against them; his private emotions are equally ambivalent, for he has reached his position largely as a result of having been the lover of an influential vampire lady. It is she who is delegated by her own kind to be the agent of his destruction, and his reasons for attempting to be the agent of hers are appropriately mixed.

*   *   *

After writing "The Man Who Loved the Vampire Lady," the author began to collect other plotworthy corollaries of the central complex of ideas. Some of these emerged while he was listening to papers and discussions at the International Conference on the Fantastic in the Arts in Houston in 1987, including those in which the editors of the present volume took part—but they are not, of course, in any way to blame for the contents of the novel—or, for that matter, the contents of this paper.

Understandably, given that he was employed at the time as a teacher of sociology, offering courses in the philosophy of social science and the sociology of literature, Stableford became intrigued by the notion that different cultures might react quite differently to the introduction of his biologically-based vampirism, and that African tribal societies might more easily accommodate it into their religion than European societies, thus producing a very different kind of élite. It is not entirely surprising, given this and his constant predilection for inverting and subverting other people's plots, that the core of *The Empire of Fear* is an alternative-historical African lost-race adventure which sets out to pervert and overturn all the key images and imperialistic values of H. Rider Haggard's *She*.

In the interests of melodrama, *The Empire of Fear* also takes care to involve some well-known characters from our own history. Richard Lionheart replaces the "Girard" who was credited with being the ruler of "Grand Normandy" in "The Man Who Loved the Vampire Lady." Extensive off-stage roles are given to Francis Bacon and Kenelm Digby, and a less extensive—but subtly crucial—one to Simon Sturtevant.[1] Richard reappears to play a part in the big battle which eventually settles the fate of this alternative Europe once the central characters have returned from their African lost land with the secret of vampirism. In this part of the novel a quasi-Spanish Armada sets forth to destroy Malta, carrying an army of marines under the joint leadership of Richard and—how could any author have resisted the temptation?—Vlad the Impaler, alias Dracula—or, as his scribes more often signed his name, Dragulya. In order to replace the (dead) hero of the original novelette, and to reproduce his strangely mixed feelings about vampire ladies, *The Empire of Fear* also has a connecting episode in which Edmund Cordery's son Noell undergoes a crucially problematic sentimental education; this sequence also introduces the other major characters: the pirate Langoisse, his mistress Leilah, and the scholar-monk Quintus.

In order to make the plot work the author is forced to develop an element of vampire nature which he had not brought out in the novelette: it is necessary, in order that their secrets may not be obtained from them by torture, that these vampires have an immunity to *pain* as well as to injury. As a result of being required to make this move, the author became intrigued by certain hypotheses regarding the evolutionary and existential costs and benefits of pain, which gave rise to important sub-themes in some of his later works, most notably *The Angel of Pain* (1991).

The Empire of Fear ends with a coda set in the present day of the alternative world, whose events mirror—in cunningly distorted fashion—the events of the opening novelette, and which includes a full account of the biochemistry of the version of vampirism used in the book. This part of the story completes the process by which vampirism—which had at first been viewed by all the inhabitants of the alternative world as a kind of quasi-demonic magic—is ultimately domesticated by medicine and biotechnology, as would be inevitable with any matter of physiology.

The author was fully aware while designing this plot of the remarkably bad press which the idea of immortality has had in fantasy and sf—see, for instance, his entry on "Immortality" in the *Encyclopedia of Science Fiction* (1993)—and he set out deliberately to reverse a commonplace plotline by which an apparently-benevolent immortality turns into a curse. In *The Empire of Fear* an apparently-monstrous immortality—or, strictly speaking, "emortality"—turns out to be a great boon *even to those unlucky individuals who cannot attain it.* This supremely happy conclusion—surely the happiest imaginable!—reaffirms that the eponymous empire which is cast down in the story is *not* the imperium ruled by the vampires—which is only metaphorically an "empire of fear"—but the domination of human thought by superstitious dread, which is a perfectly literal "empire of fear."

*   *   *

The metaphorical links between the species of vampirism envisaged in *The Empire of Fear* and AIDS left some critics less than delighted. Rob Latham, in a review in *Necrofile*, went so far as to condemn the novel as "homophobic," although that was certainly not the author's intention. One of the main characters—Langoisse—is certainly homophobic, but it may be worth noting that the effect of his homophobia is twice to deny him the vampiric immortality that is his dearest desire, once when he rudely rejects Richard's advances to him and again when his desire to revenge himself for that "insult" results in his death. Noell Cordery's attitude to homosexuality is also rather fearful, but this is a mere corollary of his general attitude to sex, which is intrinsically tormented. Given that one of the subtexts of the novel is a commentary on the essential perversity of the sexual impulse, this is not entirely surprising. (It might also be noted that it is a marked idiosyncrasy of this particular author to use decidedly unheroic protagonists with whom it is often difficult to sympathize; whether this reflects some deep-seated self-dissatisfaction on the part of the author we can, of course, only speculate.)

The Empire of Fear sets before the reader an uncommonly straightforward version of the metaphorical equivalence of vampirism and sexual intercourse which we find in such stories as de Gourmont's "Le magnolia" and Lorrain's "Le verre de sang." The female vampires featured in the story habitually combine the taking of blood with sexual activity, and it is implied that this is commonplace. The female vampires can, in effect, use their sexual favors to "reward" common lovers for their donations of blood. The male vampires, however, are in a very different situation—the only reward they have to offer those whom they victimize is a remote possibility of recruitment to the vampire ranks. Although some male vampires, including Richard, do have "favorites" who serve as suppliers of blood, others—notably Dragulya—sneer at such sentimentalization and adopt a strictly pragmatic attitude to the routines of sanguinary predation.

This difference of attitude is reflected in the political ideas of the male vampires: Richard is a true believer in the divine right of kings and the (intrinsically hypocritical) chivalric ethos of feudalism, while Dragulya is the kind of cynical opportunist whose philosophies are so shrewdly analyzed in Machiavelli's classic study of *The Vampire Prince*. The political allegory in *The Empire of Fear*, although fully conscious, is, however, a subsidiary theme. The main effect of the differences in sexual physiology between the male and female vampires of this alternative world is dramatically to exaggerate the differences of attitude to matters of sexuality which exist between vampire lords and vampire ladies—and which inevitably have their effect on the attitudes of the common men and women who live, as it were, in their shadow. What relevance such a bizarre hypothetical situation might have to the differences of attitude to matters of sexuality which common men and women have in a vampire-less world it is not easy to judge, but if common men and women did not have an intense and intimate interest in the creation and contemplation of such hypothetical possibilities the sexual fantasies of common men and women would be far less rich and exotic than they probably are.

*   *   *

Young Blood is as different from *The Empire of Fear* as the author could contrive, although it similarly sets out, quite explicitly, to examine and exploit the sexual subtexts which underlie modern vampire fiction. It confronts the image and the role of the Byronic vampire in a much more straightforward fashion than its predecessor, and there is no ambiguity at all about the representation of blood-drinking as an intrinsically sexual experience.

The vampire in *Young Blood* is a dark-cloaked demon lover named Maldureve, who is conjured out of the shadowy borderlands of existence by a neurotic girl. He is at once protective and threatening, exotically compounded out of her contorted anxieties and repressed desires. He is more traditional in this aspect than the vampires of *The Empire of Fear*, but he too is modified so as to fit in more easily with a rational worldview. Like the vampires of *The Empire of Fear*, Maldureve—his name, as the text scrupulously points out, is a silly play on words—has no fangs. Such questions as his attitude to garlic and crosses, and his reflectability in mirrors, simply never arise—but he does eventually acquire the power to manifest himself by day.

The narrative of *Young Blood* is divided into three main parts, with a coda that throws the preceding events into a new perspective. Parts one and two show the fundamental situation—the visitation of the vampire—from two sharply contrasted points of view. Both are narrated in the first person, part one by Anne Charet, who assumes that Maldureve and the other apparitions which follow in his wake are objectively real, and part two by her human boyfriend Gil Molari, who takes it as axiomatic that any apparently-supernatural occurrence must be a subjective hallucination. Part three reverts to Anne's point of view, although she is now forced by circumstance gradually to modify her opinions, and the reader—having been presented with a dramatically different but strangely-concluded account of events in part two—is bound to regard the resumed discourse in a very different light.

*   *   *

There is, of course, a long tradition of horror stories and metaphysical fantasies that play with alternative explanations of apparently-supernatural events. Tzvetan Todorov has even taken the trouble to construct a "theory" which argues at great length and with altogether unwarranted ponderousness the brutally simple thesis that stories in which the contest between objective and subjective interpretations remains unresolved belong to a distinct genre (the "fantastic"). In a good deal of recent horror fiction, however, the question of whether the events experienced by the characters are "real" or "illusory" simply does not matter; this is no longer a question of any real narrative importance, and is certainly not a question whose answer could any longer provide a sense of *resolution*. "And then he woke up . . ." is not nowadays acceptable as a method of ending a story; by the same token, the central character's realization that he or she *isn't* dreaming cannot function as a conclusion either. A modern story that focuses on the question whether the events it describes are real or illusory has somehow to renew the sharpness of that question, and its resolution has to go beyond the simple choice of "yes," "no," or "I'm not going to tell you, so there." This is what *Young Blood* tries to do.

In order to sharpen the question of whether the vampire in *Young Blood* is real or not, the author equips the two central characters with very specific intellectual resources. Anne is a student of philosophy, who is therefore ready, willing, and able to debate with herself at some length and in some depth exactly what might be implied by acceptance of the "reality" of a vampire. Gil is a research student engaged in the study of psychotropic viruses, who can hardly help but interpret bizarre experiences according to the assumption that he has accidentally become infected by his own materials. The introduction of the notion of "psychotropic viruses" also opens up scope for a conclusion in which the subjective and the objective can be interestingly intertwined in such a way that their implied mutual exclusivity breaks down. Because of this, the eventual conclusion of the novel is not "fantastic" by default—which is what happens when an author simply abandons the reader to indecision regarding alternative readings of the events—but "fantastic" by *design*. There is in the coda a metaphysical readjustment of what have earlier been seen as alternative readings, which endeavors to bring them into an unanticipated harmony.

*   *   *

One of the most interesting things about this game of subjective/objective as played out in *Young Blood* is that the metaphysical issues which arise in connection with the question of whether Maldureve is a real vampire or a hallucination induced by a psychotropic virus are inevitably reflected in the blatantly sexual subtext. Thus, what starts out as a particular instance of perverse sexual fantasy eventually becomes extrapolated into something much more peculiar. The convoluted plot proceeds unerringly to the kind of climax specified by tradition—a final confrontation between the heroine (armed with a pointed stake) and the vampire (rendered helpless by circumstance)—but by the time that climactic moment arrives, the question of what, if anything, the staking of the vampire might symbolize or achieve is wide open.

There is a certain level of risk involved when any male writer attempts to tell a story from the viewpoint of a young girl—especially if he is a writer who has been accused by reviewers, as Stableford has on more than one occasion, of not being able to draw convincing female characters. The hazards are redoubled when the narrative's focal point is the sexuality of the character in question, and further increased when that sexuality is supposed to be so tormented by anxiety as to have become neurotic. Noell Cordery's peculiar attitude to vampire lovers, although unprecedented in matters of mere detail, can easily be likened to the attitudes of countless heroes of Gautieresque erotic fantasy, but Anne Charet's peculiar attitude to Maldureve and his various natural and supernatural "rivals" does not readily fall into any pre-existent literary category. The closest analogues— which the author undoubtedly had in mind while constructing his plot— are probably the allegories of female maturation wrought by the inversion of traditional fairy-tale themes by Angela Carter in *The Bloody Chamber* (1979).

Because of the intimacy of the narrative, *Young Blood* is much more obviously a sustained erotic fantasy than *The Empire of Fear*. It has no reconstructed history or political allegory to deflect attention away from the sexual allegory by means of which Anne's desires and fears are transmuted into extraordinary experience. The metaphysical issues which are raised as the two central characters strive to make sense of what is happening introduce a certain intellectual coolness into the ongoing orgy of exotic orgasms, but the characters continually turn their philosophically-informed points of view on their own processes of sexual and emotional development, re-emphasizing the erotic foundations of the narrative. The true irony of the coda is not what it reveals about the reality or otherwise of the events which have taken place in the course of the story but the fashion in which it cynically re-appraises the existential significance of sex as a biological phenomenon.

Despite what the narrative voice actually says in the final paragraphs, there will probably be few readers who will consider the ending to be an uplifting one; but *Young Blood*—like *The Empire of Fear*—is a science-fiction novel rather than a horror story, and it maintains a commitment, however perverse, to the idea and the ideal of progress. All of the author's recent fiction is dedicated to this ideal, although some of his rhetorical strategies are undeniably peculiar.

* * *

Young Blood borrows—as *The Empire of Fear* did in a more oblique fashion—from the ongoing critical analysis of vampire fiction which is a notable feature of the annual International Conference for the Fantastic in the Arts. The argument of a paper presented there in 1991 by Lloyd Worley is transplanted lock, stock, and barrel—with the original author's permission and blessing—into the mouth of one of the subsidiary characters. The argument in question suggests that our continued uneasy fascination with the vampire motif may be rooted in that experience of vampiric existence which we all have as a result of spending nine months in the womb and a further nine—or more—obtaining nourishment by suckling. Whether this is true or not remains a matter of conjecture, but it is a beautiful hypothesis not only because it seems so neat but also because it seems so disturbing. The popularity of vampires in modern fiction has nothing to do with any residuum of obsolete folkloristic beliefs and everything to do with the most intimate transactions imaginable by our anxious and desirous minds.

Just as the blue blood that courses in our veins is instantly transmuted by the alchemy of oxygenation to something richly and arterially red whenever it is shed, so something else which is secret and unseen is transformed by narrative expression into that red milk on which literary vampires feed. We know that it is a "vital fluid" of some kind, but we do not know exactly what, and symbolism is the only imaginative instrument we have with which to search, and probe, and draw hypotheses. Such hypotheses cannot be tested in the scientific sense, because the only jury to which we can deliver them for consideration is the wayward tribunal of the emotions, where horror and erotic excitement substitute for reason and the balance of probabilities. Nevertheless, the process has a ritual value not unakin to the ritual value which the operations of science and the law have, over and above their utilitarian functions.

Whatever faults *The Empire of Fear* and *Young Blood* may have, they may surely lay claim to a certain kind of intellectual seriousness. Like so many of the stories in whose footsteps they follow they are colorfully eccentric, wildly playful, and flirtatiously horrific, but they are not blunt instruments. Their narrative scalpels are aimed to uncover and display those nerves which they aspire, in their own calculatedly nasty-minded fashion, to twist.

8

Recasting the Mythology:
Writing Vampire Fiction

JEWELLE GOMEZ

One of the most important things in my writing career is to try to push boundaries outward for women, lesbians, and writers. Intensifying connections and pushing outward are the only ways I can write, the only ways I can live.

From the first time I saw a Dracula film when I was an adolescent, I thought the character (played then by Bela Lugosi) was fascinating, exciting, sensuous—although I'm sure I would not have articulated it quite that way at that time. The early films were clumsy and covert in their portrayal of sensuality, but the later Frank Langella version crystallized for me the idea of linking desire with the vampire's hungers.

In the earlier films, the sexual energy was more oblique. Dracula's pursuit of Mina and Lucy was always couched in the traditional male/female chase configuration. But perhaps because of lingering Victorian proscriptions or simply lack of imagination, films from Bela Lugosi's to Christopher Lee's only went so far before retreating into mindless bloodletting— as if the romantic pursuit that preceded the denouement were irrelevant. The sexual nature of the vampire's desire—the embrace, the kiss to the neck, the longing glances—are all as symptomatic of sexual desire as they are of bloodlust. That nature is relegated to the subtext during the climax of the narrative. Seeing Langella's *Dracula* and the comic version with George Hamilton (*Love at First Bite*, 1979), I understood that it is more than just the blood: it's desire. The Langella film designed his encounter with Lucy as a seduction and consummation complete with fireworks. In Sheridan Le Fanu's novella *Carmilla* the symptoms the young girl exhibits when she dreams of and finally meets Carmilla resemble what in the nineteenth century was called "the vapors." They also resemble the symptoms of love or desire.

I began writing a contemporary/gothic vampire novel, *A Dream of Angels*, which is still languishing under my desk. I did character sketches and vignettes to work out how I would incorporate vampire mythology into emotional situations; how contemporary life would be affected by the preternatural powers of vampirism; and how I would re-cast the mythology of vampirism to fit my own lesbian/feminist philosophy. *A Dream of Angels* may never see the light of day, but it did act as a catalyst for my thinking about the importance of mythology in women's lives, literature, and politics.

I developed the character Gilda in those vignettes, and decided to write stories just about her. I wrote a series—eight stories in all—taking place in different decades of U.S. history, each focusing on her attempt to know herself as a black woman and as a vampire. The episodes explore her passions, her need to recreate a family for herself, and her ways of survival. I then wrote more to fill in areas; the story that depicts her escape from slavery and shows how she became a vampire, for example, was written after many of the others. I began doing rewrites to link the stories, establish a stronger narrative, and refine the characterizations so that the collection could be sold as a novel. I worked on the stories over a ten-year period; the last two I spent on rewrites. I did a number of readings from the material around the United States at women's events and bookstores, before *The Gilda Stories* was finally published by the lesbian/feminist publisher, Firebrand Books, in 1991. Both prior to this and subsequently, chapters from the book have been published independently in a variety of anthologies: *Worlds Apart, Embracing the Dark, Disorderly Conduct,* and *Children of the Night.*[1] Each of these anthologies has, in its own way, been concerned with the question raised by my core premise: what happens to human nature when a single element is changed, putting a person at odds with the rest of humanity?

Creating New Mythology

My character, Gilda, is a lesbian because I'm a lesbian. Even though some lesbian-feminists have challenged my choice, suggesting it was too negative an idea to connect to lesbians, I feel I can remake mythology as well as anyone. These issues that Gilda deals with—power, isolation, recreating a family, fulfilling desire, maintaining honor, sharing—are the central themes of the work I am doing. As I write, I really want my work to appeal to the people I grew up with, the women and men who were my friends. Those people struggling on a day-to-day basis with bottom-line issues like food, housing, racism, sexism. They, like everyone else, want heroes. And if a hero can be created who can be respected, why not? The women's movement showed us how much we want heroic figures. And I wanted to show that we already had them—in our families—and with some creative thought they could be strategically placed within our culture.

When I began writing *The Gilda Stories* in the early 1980s, I had no idea women would be so excited by the idea of a lesbian vampire. Few women I knew, in or out of the lesbian community, ever expressed much interest in fantasy beyond the feminist utopian fictions. I underestimated the loyalty of vampire enthusiasts who seemed to be closeted quite liberally among lesbian feminists. While female vampires had often appeared in film, for example in *Daughters of Darkness*, a lesbian cult favorite, when I began my work, few if any books had been published that examined the connection between vampire mythology and lesbians. In fact, for quite some time I thought—just as we often do before coming out—I was the only one.

I was a bit embarrassed that vampire stories were too trivial, not literate or acceptable to the academy—and if the book had come out in the early 1980s rather than the early '90s I think that would have been the case. But in the years of working on the book, times changed, aesthetics, politics, culture grew and shifted. Somewhere in the late '80s the dark vision offered by vampires became of interest to more than the cultists I knew.

Despite my skepticism about others' response to my work, I began to read other vampire fiction and to do research. I saw how important the idea of the vampire—or, at least, of prolonged life—was to so many cultures. Many ancient societies had vampire mythology, although different from that which produced the Count. Rather, their emphases were on the animals and spirits and rituals that imply there are ways to escape death. In China, for example, the *kiang-si* (or *chiang-shih*) resembles the Western vampire. It sleeps during daylight hours and can be driven from the body of its victim by fire. In Africa there is the Adze, who, according to Ewe mythology, sucks blood and drinks coconut water and sits on the mouth of its victim using a sucking apparatus that resembles an elephant's trunk.

Naturally the mythology we've grown up on here in the United States is steeped in Christianity, hence the fear of the cross or the lack of the mirror reflection which indicates the absence of a Christian soul. The challenge for me was to create a *new* mythology, to strip away the dogma that has shaped the vampire figure within the rather narrow Western, Caucasian expectation, and to recreate a heroic figure within a broader, more ancient cultural frame of reference.

My vampires are less grounded in European cultural traditions than most. Gilda is an African-American. She carries a cross with her always because it was something given to her by her mother in slavery. It holds little religious import for her and it certainly doesn't repel her. The symbols that I've retained for my vampire mythology are connected to physical elements such as the danger of running water and the sun or the protective nature of native soil.

Other Vampires

Two women who have created memorable vampire characters in modern literature are Chelsea Quinn Yarbro and Anne Rice, although women characters remain peripheral to their work. Yarbro's impressive series of novels features the elegant and sensitive Count Saint-Germain, whose adventures span many centuries and countries. In each, the Count develops lasting relationships with strong women, some of whom become vampires as well. Yarbro's most spectacular character, Madeline, is an archaeologist who deserves a vampire series all her own.

Anne Rice's *Interview with the Vampire* and *The Vampire Lestat* have moved from cult status to the major motion picture screen in spite of their strong homoeroticism. Characters like Louis, Lestat, and Marius have powerful sensual connections. But Lestat's mother, Gabrielle, who in her vampire state revels in her intelligence and independence, remains a relatively minor character. The lustiness she displays in flashes becomes mere plot device. Despite her potential as a feminist vampire—or because of it— she disappears entirely from the film version of Rice's work.

I was very surprised as I read more and more vampire fiction to see that so little of it featured women vampires. Even the famous *Carmilla* is about a young girl rather than a motivated adult. A notable early exception was the science-fiction comedy, *I, Vampire* by Jody Scott (1984), in which a jaded 700-year-old vampire falls in love with an alien who has taken the form of Virginia Woolf. Scott creates a space where eternal life and female desire are symbiotic. Since then lesbian vampire fiction has proliferated. Victoria A. Brownworth's recent anthology, *Night Bites* (1996), features 16 women writing lesbian vampire stories.[2]

Prior to the 1990s, however, people of color and lesbians were rarely allowed to participate in these fantasies, either in fiction or in the movies.

Films like *Blacula* (1972) and the much more daring *Ganja and Hess* (1973) try to reinterpret the vampire myth for black culture, but they still adhere to the formulaic design: (black) woman as handmaiden or (black) woman as temptress/bait. *The Hunger* (1983), for instance, which features an adult (white) woman vampire in lesbian encounters, never elucidates the main character's needs as either a woman or a vampire. While the film is a visual delight, the structure of both the original novel and the film falls apart at the end so completely that little analysis can be made of the characters or the intent.

Vampire films have proliferated in the 1990s, but only occasionally does the story transcend the traditions; *Buffy the Vampire Slayer* (1992), a comic film about a cheerleader who battles the forces of evil, is more fully grounded in female power and sensuality than many vampire films. But in current films such as Eddie Murphy's *A Vampire in Brooklyn* (1994) or the earlier and very fine *The Lost Boys* (1987), women remain decorative rather than powerful.

Traditional vampire fiction, both black and white, has been just that—traditional. Women are victims or objects of desire. Typical male fiction naturally continues the mythology: desire equals destruction; men can have desires, women cannot; men desire women; men destroy women. I think it's pathetic that mainstream fantasy and science-fiction writers, who like to see themselves as our literary and social visionaries, remain so limited when reflecting race and gender in fantasy writing. There have always been a few exceptions, of course. Joanna Russ has always written from the perspective of a lesbian feminist and is one of the few being published in the mainstream. Samuel R. Delany is the most popular black science-fiction writer in the world, and he continues to challenge traditional thinking, especially in the area of sexuality. Octavia Butler, a black science-fiction writer with a cult following, saw her books go completely out of print for a decade, until she was rediscovered in the late 1980s. These writers—who have been toiling for twenty years—remain exceptions to the hundreds of other best-selling fantasy and science-fiction writers whose stories overflow the bookshelves with traditional narratives. While neither Yarbro nor Rice has adhered completely to orthodox conventions, only Yarbro has chosen to risk making a woman the center of her fiction. *A Flame in Byzantium* (1987) features Atta Olivia Clemens, longtime friend of Saint-Germain, the usual star of Yarbro's series. And like the Count, Olivia has a social conscience heightened by knowledge of her own power.

Then there's the economics of it all. Economics and politics shape both what gets considered for publication and what we write. Publishing is a business above everything else. Publishers and editors push the idea that only books with men as central characters will "sell big"—that is, big enough to make everyone who stands between the writer and the final printed page rich. So they discourage work featuring women or people of color. Unless it can be shown to be an extraordinary anomaly, like Alice Walker's *The Color Purple*, a highly literate novel written partially in black dialect by a straight woman about lesbianism and in which that dread word is never spoken, and which takes place in a foggy past. So consciously and subconsciously writers who want to be published commercially are affected by the narrow projection of what sells. Even James Baldwin claimed that Toni Morrison had finally come of age only when she wrote a novel with a male protagonist; this is a consummate insult to a writer who has created two of the most impressive women characters—Sula and Pilot—in American literature. And publishers suggest that black people don't read, so why bother writing about them!

Beyond Tradition

My political grounding as a lesbian/feminist makes it impossible for me to perpetuate the traditional mythology. It offers me a wonderful challenge to reshape it keeping the essential elements, the ideas that make vampires compelling and scary while introducing other elements more related to who I am and who my audience is.

Unfortunately, many women have understood "feminist" to mean that we interpret our lives through a utopian haze. So we don't deal with sex, power, need, strength in any direct or meaningful way, except to be against them. I like utopian romance as well as anyone, but not as a steady diet. Sex, power, needs, strength become distorted in fiction and in our lives when only viewed idealistically—either as totally positive or totally negative. They become either too important or not important enough. But all of these are elements of who we are as women. Most male writers don't have the feminist background to re-orient their interpretations, and others—who are not active feminists—may not think about re-orienting their perspective much beyond the effort of not making their male vampires misogynistic.

When a friend—a black lesbian feminist—protested to me that connecting vampirism with lesbianism was negative and destructive, I was shocked. I was certain I could create a mythology to express who I am as a black lesbian feminist and what I want. Traditional vampire mythology has exploited the male/female dyad perpetuated in society. The concept of predator/vampire is classically male and European. But in the larger perspective, ecologically, all life is interdependent and death is a natural part of life—not necessarily a separate horror. As a lesbian/feminist it was simple to recast the basic idea once I figured out that vampires don't have to kill to get blood. If people can donate a pint of blood to the Red Cross and live, they can give it to Gilda. And in order to enhance the process, in many cases for Gilda it is not simply a theft but an exchange. She doesn't batter people into submission; when she takes blood she leaves something in return. I don't perpetually equate sex with violence against women, and I felt that in exploring the sensual nature of vampires I could recast it in a less exploitative mode. That seemed fairly easy to do once I stripped away the Christian trappings and modern cultural assumptions.

Those who can see beyond the traditional idea can imagine the story being interpreted with no predator and no victim. In this way we can see into the real story about power and family. We need to be able to accept contradictions—such as the fact that women are both powerful and victimized—in order to visualize beyond our own immediate experience. A child suckling at its mother's breast is not called a predator or a leech, but might not someone from an alien planet see it that way? That experience is also a sensual one, despite all the social taboos which prevent discussion of it in those terms. By embracing the complications and contradictions of our emotional and sensual existence, we have a chance to imagine our lives as bigger than we may have imagined them in the past.

I've listened to many women who've been excited by *The Gilda Stories*. Often they've not only offered praise, but also taken issue with things they didn't feel comfortable with (such as feeling that Gilda should not turn people into vampires without their permission). Many of their thoughtful suggestions helped shape the story. Black women especially have responded enthusiastically to Gilda as a survivor and a hero. They identify with her power and her vulnerability. And all women recognize the connections I've tried to make with them. I figured who would better understand the blood cycle than a woman? From puberty we're used to feeling the changes in our bodies because of the menstrual cycle. We know the uneasy feeling of being totally in our bodies and also adapting to the chemical changes that make us feel alien to those bodies. We're inextricably in tune with nature on a regular basis, even when we feel we're outsiders in so many other ways.

My apprehension about the place of my black lesbian vampire novel in literature proved fully justified and at the same time pointless. Every major publisher, both literary and science fiction, turned down the manuscript. But feminist publishing has always made room for those pushing boundaries. After its publication in 1991, *The Gilda Stories* won the Lambda Literary Awards for both fiction and science fiction. It is currently in its fourth printing.

I have since adapted the novel for the stage as a commission for the New York-based dance company, Urban Bush Women. The company toured the show, entitled *Bones and Ash: A Gilda Story*, in the United States during its 1995–96 season.[3] My script was created in collaboration with the dancers themselves and incorporates original music by lesbian recording artist Toshi Reagon and choreography by the company's artistic director, Jawole Willa Jo Zollar. While the theater piece does not have the historic scope of the novel—it ranges over one hundred years rather than two—the character Gilda remains, as do the central themes: fulfillment of desire, the search for community, and an understanding of the uses of power. It has been deeply satisfying to see actors inhabiting the roles, to see actual black women on stage expressing their familial love, their desire for each other, and their control over their own destinies. Without eliminating the contradictions of a black lesbian's life, the mythic figure emerges from the story ordinary and extraordinary at the same time. Near the end of the play, Gilda asks her lover: "How do we hold anger and love at the same time?" On stage the physicalization deepens the sensual experience. The answer lies in the doing, not in words.

As the curtain rises, the uneasiness of audiences from Maine to Iowa to Seattle is often palpable. But early in the first act they usually overcome their resistance to a "vampire" story or a "lesbian" story or a "black" story and begin to see themselves in the characters. In question-and-answer periods after the performances, the audiences clearly reveal that they've responded to the emotional need we all have to connect with others, to find our own power.

Over the decade during which I developed *The Gilda Stories*, vampires became an acceptable vehicle to use in telling women's stories. Popular culture has begun to corrode the boundaries between "legitimate" and "illegitimate" modes of expression. In my exploration of a traditional form I hoped to contribute to a new, more feminist-grounded mythology. The vampire figure's identification with both sensuality and power proved to be an ideal way to re-examine a black lesbian feminist relationship to those two issues which are at the center of our liberation.

Part Three

READING
CONSUMPTION

9

Dieting and Damnation:
Anne Rice's *Interview with the Vampire*

SANDRA TOMC

At one point in Anne Rice's *Interview with the Vampire*, the vampires Louis and Claudia journey to Eastern Europe on a quest to find others like themselves. Elegant, intelligent, and beautiful, Louis and Claudia are shocked to find that the fabled vampires of Romania are little more than zombies, rotten half-eaten corpses who suffer the fate of being animated. "I had met the European vampire, the creature of the Old World," Louis pronounces as he kills the last of these. "He was dead" (192).

Although literally a comparison of monsters, Louis's words might just as well describe a generic as a narrative twist. In 1975, the year before Rice published *Interview with the Vampire*, Stephen King published his only vampire novel, *'Salem's Lot*, a novel that featured vampires who resembled, to a remarkable degree, the kind that would repulse Louis. King's vampires were, of course, the norm. They partook of an ancestry that threads its way from the works of Polidori, Le Fanu, and Stoker in the nineteenth century to those of Theodore Sturgeon, Robert Aickman, and Paul Morrissey in the twentieth, an ancestry whose members, even the most illustrious, are manifestly sub-human. They were clever, they might be attractive, but their bodies were too hairy, their sense of smell too acute. When the chic and beautiful Louis met the vampires of Eastern Europe, he was, as Rice well knew, meeting one hundred and fifty years of monster stereotype.

It was, of course, the pattern of Rice's chic vampire rather than Stephen King's bestial one that became the focus of such absorbed and wild popularity in the 1980s and 1990s. From Rice's own sequels, *The Vampire Lestat* (1985), *Queen of the Damned* (1988), *The Tale of the Body Thief* (1992), and *Memnoch the Devil* (1995), to such films as *The Lost Boys*, *Innocent Blood*, and Francis Ford Coppola's *Bram Stoker's Dracula*, the vampire of enviable looks and inspiring ambitions—not sub-human so much as ultra-human—reigned. But the vampire's transformation had its corollary in a process of domestication, a process that seemed to be cemented with the casting of Tom Cruise, a squeaky-clean icon of normative masculinity, in the role of the amoral, sexually ambiguous Lestat for the 1994 film version of *Interview with the Vampire*. Vampirism, says Joan Copjec, "presents us with a bodily double that we can neither make sense of nor recognize as our own" (128). But with Cruise playing Lestat—a piece of casting that Rice herself bitterly opposed and then enthusiastically supported[1]—the vampire had ceased to be unrecognizable. Once a menace to the conclaves of average America, he was now an honorary resident.

The journey of the vampire from monster to yuppie may not have been predicted in *Interview with the Vampire*, but it is, I would suggest, encoded there. In order to separate her own vampires from those indigenous to the genre, Rice borrowed heavily from 1970s discourses of gender mutability and bodily transformation, finding in the twin paradigms of androgyny and weight loss an articulation appropriate to her generically radical aims. But if the then-revolutionary potential of gender and corporeal metamorphosis liberated Rice's vampires from the stocks of their heritage, it also, I would suggest, facilitated their bland domestication. The following essay examines the mechanisms of that domestication, with, I might add, as much an eye to using Rice's text to read 1970s discourses of bodily alteration as the reverse. In the 1970s upheaval around bodies and weight, particularly women's bodies, we can trace the means by which the very process of becoming ultra-human—of becoming a new person, a new monster, a new woman—could realize itself in confinement and limitation.

When Rice set out to make the "animal" vampire a new person (Ramsland 149), she imagined the process as part of a larger program of what the 1970s called "liberation," whether sexual, gay, or women's. The icons of this program were already figures of ambiguous signification, bodied forth by the beautiful-boy stars of glam rock or the "unisex" fashions launched by designers like Rudi Gernreich. For Rice, trying to unsettle "clichés" (Ramsland 148) and to imagine her way out of the ossified categories of human and monster, self and other, gender uncertainty provided an exemplary metaphor. But what emerged as the sexual ambiguity of Rice's vampires was finally more than just a flouting of generic conventions. Rice told her biographer, "'I've always loved the images of androgyny . . . whether it's a beautiful woman in the opera dressed as a man or rock stars changing and shifting. . . . I see the androgynous figure as the ideal figure'" (Ramsland 148). That ideal was consonant with the egalitarian aims of 1970s' liberalism: Rice wanted to image "'erotic scenes . . . that take place between totally equally franchised human beings'" (148).

While perhaps startling to us today, it would have come as no surprise to anyone thinking about bodies in 1975 that Rice modeled the vampire's transformation on one of the most powerful narratives of gender meta-morphosis available to 1970s culture: the story of successful dieting. With its promised dissolution of female secondary sex characteristics, the story of successful dieting forcefully projected an androgynous body, one whose challenge to traditional gender roles would lie in its exclusion of their physical signifiers. The intersections of slimness, androgyny, and liberation are encapsulated in the (to many of us) memorable series of ads run by Virginia Slims. Tagged by the copy "You've come a long way, baby," these ads featured a sepia-tinted inset of "our grandmothers" laboring over some archaic domestic task. They were laced into late-Victorian S-shaped corsets, their bosoms and hips enormous, their figures patently maternal. Striding over the inset in full color, by contrast, was the modern Virginia Slims woman. Long-legged, flat, and hipless, the Virginia Slims woman had been unburdened of her woman's body—and, concomitantly, of her domestic chores. For American middle-class women of this period who were leaving behind nearly two decades of post-war domesticity and enter-ing the labor force in unprecedented numbers,[2] such icons articulated their abandonment of women's conventional nurturing and reproductive func-tions. By the same token, narratives of dieting provided for women au-thors an apt means of contemplating the socio-sexual alternatives available through corporeal alteration.

Now *Interview with the Vampire* incorporates the liberatory model of radical weight loss, but it does so in a striking and uncharacteristic way. Although the novel contains all the signal features of the diet narrative—its characters are preoccupied throughout with hunger and food and with the manipulation of their bodies[3]—it also contains no significant women characters. Rice's impulse here complements her utopian agenda in a par-ticularly extreme way. In its pursuit of a kind of pure and ultimate an-drogyny, *Interview with the Vampire* takes the Virginia Slims story to its ultimate conclusion by fantasizing a community of beings from which all signs of female sexuality and its traditional limitations have been erased. And here, curiously, is where the model of revised and liberated person-hood begins to break down. If the erasure of the female body is precisely what enables Rice to transform the monster vampire into a free and equal "franchised being," it is also, paradoxically, the gap around which her utopian project undoes itself.

Perhaps nowhere is Rice's dissociation of traditional woman and ideal being more evident than in the fact that her community of vampires is populated by men and children only. Theoretically, Rice's supernatural beings are not meant to be read as either men or children. Although the erotic interactions among the male vampires in this novel led many to praise Rice for her daring presentation of homosexuality, the sexuality of her vampires, in fact, bears little resemblance to the forms of gratification conventionally associated with the interactions of men's bodies. Rather, the vampire's body is something entirely new. It represents a type of polymorphousness and androgyny founded on the disappearance of the markers of sexual and reproductive difference. No matter what his or her residual sexual organs denote, both the vampire's experience of erotic pleasure and its ability to reproduce are located orally, not genitally; sucking blood is the vampire's way of feeding, of gratifying itself, and of making other vampires.[4] This "gender-free" ideal (Ramsland 148) does not of necessity exclude vampires who are residually women, but it is powerfully associated in the novel with an absence of women's characteristics. Not only are all Rice's central vampires residually male, her only significant female vampire, Claudia, is a little girl permanently arrested in her physical development at the age of five.

While Claudia's little-girlishness signals the exclusion of adult female sexuality from the vampire's body, the scene of her creation emphasizes the extent to which that exclusion predicates vampire existence generally. When Louis and Lestat make a vampire out of Claudia, they do so quite literally over her mother's dead body. Discovering the still-human little girl alone in a house and crying over the corpse of her mother, Louis is at first aware of some mysterious maternal power that emanates from the mother and challenges his own claims to Claudia. But this "natural" maternity is soon exposed as the inferior stuff of mortal frailty. In a fit of humor, Lestat grabs the mother's "stinking body" from the bed and dances with her while her decaying head "snaps" back and "black fluid" pours out of her mouth (75). This violent demystification of maternal power, centered as it is on the mother's body as something dead and obsolete, then opens the conceptual space for the alternative represented by vampire sexuality. Having traduced conventional motherhood, Lestat takes over the mother's role: "I want a child tonight," he tells Louis. "I am like a mother . . . I want a child!" (89). Claudia's birth in turn inaugurates an expansion of socio-sexual options for the vampires, who now play through an almost dizzying variety of roles. Louis is variously Claudia's lover, father, and mother; he is Lestat's wife and son, Armand's gay paramour, Madeleine's father and husband. And their radical diversity is what makes the vampires, as Louis says, all "equal."

That the demystification of traditional maternal power is the founding moment of this equality underlines Rice's reliance on the refusal of female sexuality to legitimate the alternatives her vampires represent. Yet, strangely enough, Rice's exclusion of the feminine body from her descriptions of vampire life and physiology seems to demand a similar, and less explicable, exclusion at the level of representation. Not only does Rice purge her vampire community of all signs of women's sexuality, she avoids representing women characters, even human women characters, in her novel. In part, this strategy operates as a metaphor for the anomaly that women represent in Rice's gender-free economy. Accordingly, when women characters do appear for brief moments—when the women vampires kiss Armand, for instance, and Louis is overcome with jealousy—they function metaphorically as a threat to the seamlessness of the androgyne order. However, more interesting than these metaphoric moments is the fact that Rice apparently *can't* introduce women characters as significant players in the drama without her own representation of androgyny showing signs of dismantling itself. Witness what happens, for example, when at the end of her novel she introduces the provocative and motherly Madeleine. Confronted with having to make Madeleine a vampire, which means enjoying her sexually, the till now thoroughly feminized Louis admits: "Desire her I did, more than she knew. . . . And with a *man's* pride I wanted to prove that to her" (270; my emphasis). Women characters, in other words, are not absent in this novel just to make a metaphoric point. They present a problem, and to avoid confronting that problem in ways that could compromise the gender-free ideal, Rice simply gets rid of them.

Now what is interesting about this lack of women characters is the way in which it replicates one of the central fantasies of dieting, albeit a fantasy that is not entirely compatible with dieting's projection of an androgynous body. On the one hand, dieting extremists, those with eating disorders like anorexia nervosa, wish for exactly the kind of body that Rice imagines, one that has been purged of the signs of being a woman. As one anorexic puts it, "I have a deep fear of having a womanly body, round and fully developed. I want to be tight and muscular and thin" (Bruch, *Golden Cage* 85); another asserts, "I want to stay slender because I look more like a man," while another, fantasizing a Claudia-like stasis, says: "not wanting to mature as a female body is a child's way of looking at it. I never wanted to grow up" (Bruch, *Conversations* 125, 122).[5] On the other hand, the absence of women characters in *Interview with the Vampire* illustrates how closely bound this revision of the body is to another related desire on the part of compulsive slimmers not just to revise the body but to disown it—to go the route of 1970s icon Karen Carpenter and diet until you disappear.[6] This is a fantasy Rice inadvertently expressed about her own body. Having gained a worrisome amount of weight just before she started writing *Interview with the Vampire*, Rice began to "defend" herself by telling friends "that the extra pounds weren't really her." She would "acknowledge only the parts from the wrist down and the neck up" (Ramsland 133). In other words, if *Interview with the Vampire* locates its revision of gender categories in an equally radical revision of gendered bodies, its lack of women characters also indicates how dependent this model is on a fantasy of "disownership." To assure the success of her radical bodily ideal, Rice premises its representation on the logical extreme of the diet narrative: that the ever-diminishing substance of the female body, far from producing a new kind of body, will simply conclude with the body vanishing.

To ascertain the effect of this disappearance it is useful to compare *Interview with the Vampire* to two novels also published in the mid-1970s but more overtly concerned with women and dieting: Margaret Atwood's *Lady Oracle* (1976) and Judith Krantz's *Scruples* (1978). Both novels recapitulate the narrative we saw in the Virginia Slims ad: the heroine begins the story as an overweight, unhappy individual and through rigorous dieting sheds her unwanted flesh and discovers both personal empowerment and an abrupt proliferation of social options.[7] But the crucial thing in both novels is that no matter how much weight the heroine loses her body never stops being a problem—either for the heroine, who must now contend with the bewildering pressures of being an object of male desire, or in the text itself as a problematic site of competing cultural values. Atwood's heroine Joan Foster may, like Rice, wish to end her dilemmas by turning "invisible" (141), and may indeed stage a series of "disappearances" by faking her own death, but that wish remains a fantasy; her woman's body, no matter how thin, remains a bulk to be reconciled with the ideal of its own disappearance. Indeed, Joan's and Krantz's heroine Billy's changing yet ever-present flesh forces an ongoing reevaluation in both texts of the female body's relationship as a material entity to the material conditions of its subordination.

In *Interview with the Vampire*, however, this is not the case. The disownership of a problematic womanhood may enable Rice to posit the purity of her androgynous vampires, but Rice's paradigm of disownership, while it fantasizes the absence of the feminine body, does not at the same time incorporate the logical terms for a dismantling of the feminine as a frame of gender reference. What *Interview with the Vampire* accentuates, rather, is that in the economy formulated by dieting the idea of the womanly body remains untouched in the imagination of the dieter where it resides as the symbolic focus of hunger. As such, its power is felt in a degree proportional to its negation. That is, the less you eat and the more thin and immaterial you become, the hungrier you get and the more you long for the state of feminine fullness and bodily plenitude that eating represents. Thus, while Rice effects the disappearance of women's bodies, according to the logic made legible in her text the hypothetical point at which the feminine body disappears completely is also, paradoxically, the point at which it reaches the height of its power and desirability over the hungering self—or in this case, over the hungering text.

One of the first things we notice about *Interview with the Vampire* is that, while the feminine body is effectively purged from the narrative, it is nevertheless systematically reinscribed in other areas of the text where it functions as a kind of disembodied counterpoint to its own erasure. So on the one hand we have the dead body of Claudia's mother, reviled, horrifying, a thing to be discarded and left behind, while on the other we have the eulogy to abstract motherhood that accompanies Louis's rebirth: he wanders through the forest enamored of his new condition, hearing the night "as if it were a chorus of whispering women, all beckoning me to their breasts" (21). During this same scene, while taking blood from Lestat, Louis rediscovers "for the first time since infancy the special pleasure of sucking nourishment" (19). Such metaphors not only re-present an erased maternal body through a complex of disembodied symbols, they also, through their conventional equation of the mother's body and food, obliquely identify femininity itself as an object of hunger, as a thing that fulfils.[8]

The synonymy of female bodies and food suggested here is even more pointedly manifested in the several spectacular scenes in this novel in which women literally form the meals on which the vampires feast. Memorable among these is Louis's visit to the Théâtre des Vampires where the vampire Armand, before an audience of rapt humans, feeds on a young woman of "heartbreaking beauty." Rice's description here highlights the special allure, the promise of the body being consumed: "And slowly he [Armand] drew the string from the loose gathers of her blouse. I could see the cloth falling, see the pale, flawless skin pulsing with her heart and the tiny nipples letting the cloth slip precariously, the vampire holding her right wrist tightly. . . . And now, turning her slowly to the side so that they [the audience] could all see her serene face, he was lifting her, her back arching as her naked breasts touched his buttons, her pale arms enfolded his neck. She stiffened, cried out as he sank his teeth . . . the nape of her neck as enticing as the small buttocks or the flawless skin of her long thighs" (223, 225). The erotic quality of this description modulates into an equally charged presentation of the girl as an object of gastronomic desire. Watching the performance, Louis says, "I felt weak, dazed, hunger rising in me, knotting my heart, my veins. . . . The air seemed fragrant with her salted skin, and close and hot and sweet. . . . I was sitting back in my chair, my mouth full of the taste of her, my veins in torment" (226). Unlike the scene with Claudia's dead mother, there is no attempt here to demystify the allure of the feminine body. On the contrary, when the show is over and the lights come up, Louis still "tastes" the girl on his lips (227). "It was as though on the smell of the rain came her perfume still, and in the empty theater I could hear the throb of her beating heart" (227). It is worth noting that the power of the girl resides in the fact that she doesn't last, that she is immediately dissolved into the amorphous rain and converted into the "emptiness" of the theater. Beginning as an unreachable, distant object of a hunger that Louis, sitting in the audience, is unable to satisfy, the girl's body exerts an attraction proportional to its unavailability, an attraction that reaches its crescendo at the moment the girl disappears as a physical entity.

The relevance of this scene to Rice's gender polemic, moreover, lies not only in its reinscription of the feminine as an object of desire but in its simultaneous staging of conventional heterosexual concourse—the "seduction" of the girl by Armand—a concourse the text is subsequently unable to challenge precisely because one of its terms, the feminine, has already been established as *not there*. Although this is surely one of the most striking scenes in the novel, it intrudes not at all on any of the events that follow. In the next scene the androgyne order is reestablished, the erotic concourse reasserted as an energy among residual males only. Yet the more conventional sexual possibilities implied in the scene with the girl, identified as they are with hunger, linger as something unsatisfied.

To the extent that Rice's vampires are the subjects on whose bodies is written the novel's excision of womanhood, they tend to behave in the same way that the text behaves, incorporating its agendas and, particularly in Louis's case, replicating its contradictions. Much like the text itself, Louis is preoccupied with the purity and freedom available to the body that refuses food. Ostensibly, Louis's refusal to eat is framed as a metaphysical and moral issue. Because for vampires eating involves killing people, Louis, who cannot discard his human moral sensibilities, who associates killing with damnation, is engaged in a constant struggle to keep his soul and his body morally pure. But that this desire for purity mirrors Rice's similar attempts to purify the gendered body is made evident by the fact that Louis's refusal of food is not simply described as a reluctance to commit murder. It resembles a constant vigil to keep from gaining weight. Subsisting for the most part on a diet of small animals—the vampiric counterpart, one supposes, of celery sticks and Rykrisp crackers—Louis describes over and over again how he is "Torn apart by the wish to take no action—to starve, to wither in thought on the one hand" or to give in to his "craving," his "vile insupportable hunger" on the other (73, 116). When Louis does break down and indulge his craving, he describes it as a "sin," an illicit gorging, like eating a whole chocolate cake. Coming upon Claudia when she is still a human child and he is in one of his fits of self-starvation, he says: "You must understand that by now I was burning with physical need to drink. I could not have made it through another day without feeding. But there were alternatives: rats abounded in the streets, and somewhere very near a dog was howling hopelessly. . . . But the question pounded in me: Am I damned? . . . If I am damned I must want to kill her, I must want to make her nothing but food for a cursed existence. . . . [A]nd I felt, yes, damned and this is hell, and in that instant I had bent down and driven hard into her soft, small neck. . . . For four years I had not savored a human; for four years I hadn't really known . . . the rich blood rushing too fast for me, the room reeling" (74–75).

If Louis is the anorexic produced in this novel's extremist association of freedom and physical attenuation, his problems with eating also reflect back on the apparatus that determines him. What is significant about the passage I just quoted is not Louis's understandable reluctance to commit murder but his attraction to the object of his self-denial, his choice of Claudia above the dog and the rats not because he needs humans to survive but because Claudia in his perception is more delicious; she exerts a power over him. The source of this power lies not in Claudia herself but in Louis's idea of his own body. Because Louis's sense of integrity is bound up with his

control over the needs of his body, with his affirmation of finer spirit over
base substance, his power over himself increases in proportion not only to
his hunger but to the allure of the food that he keeps refusing. The greater
his temptation, that is, the more pious and empowering his self-denial.
Such syllogisms invest food with a power that paradoxically intensifies as
Louis's control of his own body grows, for, of course, that control is always
predicated on a fairly equal contest between the power of food and the
power of self. Given that Rice's idea of the androgyne's freedom is founded
on a similar notion of conquest and manipulation, it contains the same
kind of paradox. In other words, it isn't that the text represses the feminine
body at the level of narrative only to have it inadvertently reinscribed elsewhere, but that its model of androgyny depends on that reinscription. It
depends on the desirability in abstract form of the body through whose
recurring conquest the dieting self acquires power and viability.

It is perhaps no surprise that this repetitive conquest, by which one's
power over body or soul diminishes as it increases, should finally end in the
self's dissolution. This is the fate of Rice's androgynes, all of whom by the
end of the novel are engaged in acts of self-destruction. Claudia, on whose
body is most radically written the absence of femininity, spends the novel
affirming her freedom by searching for the mother she lost and the mature
maternal body from which she has been barred. Like Louis's pursuit of self-
determination, Claudia's is articulated as hunger, her desire for the plenitude that both sustains and relentlessly undermines her identity: "I kill
humans every night. I seduce them, draw them close to me, with an insatiable hunger, a constant, never-ending search for something . . . something, I don't know what it is" (125). That this desire for satiation is
paradoxically both the fulfilment and the end of her freedom is underlined
by the fact that as soon as Claudia gets the mother she wants in the form
of Madeleine, she dies. Her death literalizes the identities among satiation,
womanhood, and vacancy. In a grisly echo of the paradigm of the vanishing
woman's body, nothing is left of Claudia when Louis finds her but her hair
and her empty clothes. The journeys of Louis, Lestat, and Armand, similarly self-destructive, are also similarly determined by the logic of attenuation. At the novel's end, the gormandizing Lestat, deprived of food for
his soul, ends his existence by starving himself on a diet of alleycats (329).
Armand, who tells Louis that when an old vampire "goes out to die"
he will leave nothing of his body—"He will vanish" (285)—finally performs this trick on himself and disappears. Although knowing that eating
"threaten[s] consciousness" (258), Louis eventually succumbs to his craving

for humans. But within the logic that equates plenitude with vacancy, the result of Louis's eating is not that he gets fuller but that the more he eats the emptier he feels until at last he thinks of himself as "nothing" (336).

By the end of *Interview with the Vampire*, the absence that was supposed to guarantee the success of Rice's radical gender alternative has assured its dissolution. With their androgyny in the first place anchored in their hunger for a lost womanhood, the vampires can only achieve their ideal status through an ongoing process of self-sabotage, becoming more radical only as their hunger for traditionalism intensifies. And yet for all that this novel's utopian agenda folds in on itself and finally collapses, it would be inaccurate to ascribe to its politics of hunger an inherent or inevitable conservatism. When Rice, almost ten years after she published *Interview with the Vampire*, returned to the topic of vampirism in a series of novels she called *The Vampire Chronicles*, she abandoned hunger as a central component of vampire life. These later novels feature the same characters we met in *Interview*, but they purport to tell a "truer" version of their story, one in which appetite, significantly, plays no part. For this purpose, Rice invents a new feature of vampire physiology: when vampires become ancient enough—as her protagonists quickly do—they no longer need nourishment to survive. Thus unburdened of their problematic desire for food, Louis, Lestat, and Armand return from nothingness to take their place in a bucolic "Great Family" of vampires, a circle of gender renegades whose members live their lives with precisely that grace and success that had eluded the vampires in *Interview*.

There is much to suggest, however, that ridding the vampire of his desire and self-deprivation is at the heart of his eventual domestication. In their continued pursuit of utopian alternatives, Rice's later novels do away with the equation of hunger and emancipation that had proved so debilitating in her first; but, as Janice Doane and Devon Hodges point out, Rice's later novels are also considerably more tentative in their critique of accepted norms: "In *Interview with the Vampire* . . . a decidedly angry woman [Claudia] does battle with men in her hopes to rewrite the script for femininity. She fails, though the precariousness of male bonds at the end of the novel suggests that patriarchy has been nonetheless weakened" (423). By the time we get to *Queen of the Damned*, the angry little girl has given way to the primal, "post-feminist" "good mother" (434), a figure who fights her battles not with patriarchy but with the man-hating Akasha, a woman turned "feminist monster" (433). In some sense, the differences between *Queen of the Damned* and *Interview* are a product of the time that separates them, a decade of "backlashing," "postfeminism," New Right agitation, and the rise of New Age women's cults. But it remains significant that the victory of the "good mother" in *Queen of the Damned* is secured through the recasting of women's relationship to food. Unlike the eternally tiny and voracious Claudia, the "good mother" Mekare is a figure in whom hunger and skinniness have given way to appeasement and expansion. In their roles as matriarchs, nurturers, primal origins, Mekare and her twin sister Maharet could well be the vanishing mother from *Interview* restored to her material embodiment.[9] The manner of her triumph is instructive. Mekare succeeds against the rabidly feminist Akasha by cannibalizing her, by literally gobbling up her heart and brain in order to appropriate her considerable powers (455). Whereas the absent mother in *Interview* left "precariousness" in her wake, the fully present "good mother" in *Queen of the Damned*, who consumes without guilt, is the means by which dissent is incorporated into a unitary anatomy.[10]

Rice's manipulation of appetite illuminates the trajectory of the vampire from tortured anorexic to guiltless consumer; but it also clarifies the complexity of the relationship between dieting and women's liberation in 1970s culture. On one level, that relationship is clearly recuperative. The massive entry of middle-class women into the North American labor force between 1970 and 1980 required a female body whose iconography would specify its productivity in the workplace rather than its traditional *re*productivity and nurturance in the home. But as the yearnings of Rice's vampires suggest, it was precisely by dissolving the material signifiers of women's domesticity that dieting withdrew an economically obsolete femininity from the "real" world of material relations in order to constitute it elsewhere as an object of fantasy. Organizing hunger around an untenable and disappearing womanhood, dieting effectively assured the continued centrality of traditional femininity psychically in an economy that had ceased to have need of it materially. It is this process of internalization that *Interview with the Vampire* inadvertently uncovers. Within the logic manifested in Rice's text, the starving away of archaic women's flesh results only in the displacement of traditional gender norms from their depiction on the body to their invisible operation on desire.

On another level, however, *Interview with the Vampire* also suggests how the displacement of femininity, even as it sabotages the meaningful realization of alternative gender standards, might simultaneously generate the conditions for a heightened political awareness. The key to this possibility is to be found in the richer, more fully individuated and fully aware self acquired by Louis as he fetishizes and refuses food. If traditional womanly plenitude is symbolically contained in the food the dieter desires, Louis's situation indicates that the very act of staying hungry, the choice of keeping gratification at bay, consolidates the self around acts of resistance, producing an expansion of consciousness that is proportional to the diminishment of the body. The stakes in this game of resistance are high. "Today," *Vogue* informed its readers in 1976, "many women are wondering if it is possible to be fully human and still remain feminine" (du Dubovay 100). For Rice the answer is no. The process of self-enrichment through starvation may finally annihilate both Claudia and Louis, but it also anchors their status as "equally franchised beings." As a direct result of their hunger, that is, both Louis and Claudia experience a dilation of consciousness that makes them, in the idiom of 1970s feminism, more "fully human"—and thus more fully deserving of their "human rights."

In Louis's case, his physical transformation from human being to vampire overtly marks the start of what the novel repeatedly refers to as his development of a richer "humanity." "My vampire nature has been for me the greatest adventure of my life," he tells Lestat. "[A]ll that went before was confused, clouded; I went through mortal life like a blind man groping from solid object to solid object. It was only when I became a vampire that I respected for the first time all of life. I never saw a living pulsing human being until I was a vampire; I never knew what life was until it ran out in a red gush over my lips, my hands!" (82). The continual war that Louis wages with the needs of his body in order to preserve life, precisely because it affirms the power of spirit over substance and respect over abuse, enhances his "soul," producing his exquisite moral sensibilities, his "passion," his "sense of justice" (236). From the "vicious egotism" (7) of his former self, Louis expands through self-denial to represent, despite his vampirism, what is best about "humanity." The other vampires, Armand tells him, "reflect the age in cynicism. . . . You reflect your age differently. You reflect its broken heart" (289). Louis's expansion, constituted as it is through his refusal of normative categories, produces not just a richer humanity but a political awareness of the inequity of his circumstances. It is while trying to convince Lestat, the "Father," of the value of self-starvation that Louis understands the true nature of their relationship: "I realized I'd been his slave all along" (84).

For Claudia, whose tiny body signifies her more fundamental resistance to womanly plenitude, the result of her famine is a kind of tragic over-development of the inner self. As Claudia gets hungrier and hungrier without ever getting physically "full," her soul keeps expanding until her minuscule shape harbors an "eerie and powerful seductress" and a mature "woman's" mind too ambitious for its girlish confines (102, 106). "To give me immortality in this hopeless guise," she cries to Louis, "this helpless form!" (264). Louis thinks of her as empty: cold, detached, devoid of the "humanity" he so cherishes in himself. But he discovers that her diminutive shape has filled her to the brim with "rage" and "pain" and "suffering," the very elements that constitute Louis's own claims to humanity (264, 268). As with Louis, the expansion of Claudia's self generates a radicalized consciousness—a more radicalized consciousness, since her hunger for plenitude is greater. In the process of her "growth," Claudia acquires an awareness of her own potential and integrity that culminates in the recognition that she has been "enslaved" by her "fathers" (123). As Louis tells Lestat, she "sees herself as equal to us now, and us as equal to each other" (107). Her decision to murder Lestat, which Doane and Hodges call "a protest against the kind of femininity offered to women in a patriarchal culture" (424), is also a radical decision to demand the father's power for herself: "Such blood, such power. Do you think I'll possess his power and my own power when I take him?" (125).[11]

Of course, the idea that dieting might generate the conditions for political awareness is radically at odds with what the vast majority of feminist scholars and researchers have concluded. For them dieting is inimical to feminist agendas because, by forcing women to concentrate so completely on their bodies, it diverts them from the more politically constructive cultivation of their minds. Susan Bordo says of anorexia: "Paradoxically—and often tragically—these pathologies of female 'protest' . . . actually function as if in collusion with the cultural conditions that produced them. . . . Women may feel themselves deeply attracted by the aura of freedom and independence suggested by the boyish body ideal of today. Yet, each hour, each minute that is spent in anxious pursuit of that ideal . . . is *in fact* time and energy diverted from inner development and social achievement. As a feminist protest, the obsession with slenderness is hopelessly counterproductive" (105). Similarly, Kim Chernin equates the starvation of women's bodies with the starvation of their "souls" and recommends as "food" for these souls a "reentry into the positive knowledge of women's experience," "our capacity to think, to act, to struggle, to cry out, to express" (*Obsession* 198, 199).

Worth noting, however, is that various discourses of dieting concur with Rice in emphasizing an expansion of the "soul" as a crucial consequence of slimming. Anorexics almost unanimously report on the increased feelings of independence, confidence, self-worth, pride, and power that accompany their compulsive weight-watching. Many equate their shrinkage with individuation. Hilda Bruch recalls one patient who "explained that losing weight was giving her power, that each pound lost was like a treasure that added to her power. This accumulation of power was giving her another kind of 'weight,' the right to be recognized as an individual" (*Golden Cage* 5). The theme of individuation, which features so centrally in the language of anorexia, appears with equal force in 1970s diet advice, which invariably insists on the power, independence, and self-esteem available to those who discipline their bodies. In a 1976 article explaining the function of metabolism, *Cosmopolitan* advised its readers: "Now consider again the girl who blames metabolism for her inability to lose weight. The truth is she probably wasn't *born* with a sluggish metabolism, but rather cultivated a lazy one. Consider all she can do to pep up her metabolism so calories are pressed into *service* rather than just turning into fat! Sweet to know *you're* the one in control, isn't it?" (Roddick 40).

For Judith Krantz, as for Rice, the result of such exercises of self-control is the self's consolidation. When her heroine Billy's new svelte figure gives her the confidence to speak aloud in French, her spirit expands: "It opened all the doors of Billy's mind, destroyed all her hesitations, vanquished her timidity" (71). As for Atwood's heroine Joan Foster, who after years of being overweight has trouble learning to *think* like a thin person, Billy's former "freakish" self stays with her, leaving her with "scars that no amount of outward physical change could ever erase" (329–30). But her resistance to this ghost, played out in her constant hunger, at once expands her soul and, by extension, sustains her rejection of traditional feminine roles. Following the abysmal end of her first love affair, Billy realizes, "She was thin and she was beautiful. . . . Those were the important things. The rest she would have to get for herself. She had no intention of dying for love of a man, like one of the nineteenth-century women in the books she had read. She was no Emma Bovary, no Anna Karenina, no Camille—no spineless, adoring, passive creature who would let a man take away her reason for living by taking away his love. The next time she loved, she promised herself, it would be on her terms" (82).

Claudia's evaporation, Louis's nothingness, Billy's hedgings and compromises, and the anorexic's hospitalization are less than salutary ends to their ecstatic burgeoning of selfhood. But in these individual manifestations of consciousness expansion and "raising" we can see how women's

diet fads might have encouraged the emancipatory energies they also cur-
tailed. The paradox of this process is illuminated by Michel Foucault's description of a not-dissimilar congruence of self-discipline and humanistic
self-enrichment that occurred in the evolution of the "soul" of modern
prisoners. In *Discipline and Punish* Foucault addresses the historical moment at which the state's punitive strategies shift focus from the prisoner's
body, which had earlier been the object of public spectacles of torture and
execution, to his inner conscience, "a punishment that acts in depth on the
heart, the thoughts, the will, the inclinations" (16). As Foucault sees it, this
shift of focus does not address a consciousness that already exists. Rather,
the new "technology of power over the body," the forms of supervision,
training, and moral correction that replace corporal punishment, themselves produce a "soul," a "psyche, subjectivity, personality, consciousness," on which reformed punitive methods can act (29–30). We could say,
in effect, that the development of more "humane" and "liberal" forms of
punishment produces a more "human" subject, one whose newly constituted "soul" is capable of fulfilling liberalist ideals of justice and reform.

While it would be misleading to map Foucault's explication wholesale
onto the synchrony of diet fads and women's liberation, his insights are
instructive.[12] As a significant change in the political technology of women's
bodies, dieting helped to generate the spirit of a modernized womanhood—savvy, political, sexually emancipated, and newly formed for what
Stuart Ewen calls a migration into "the social structures of industrial discipline" (*All-Consuming Images* 193).[13] Although women's thinness had
come into fashion in the 1960s, it is in the 1970s, the decade whose mid-
point is marked by the International Year of the Woman, that weight-
watching acquires the proportions of an obsession and the rigors of a
"technology." According to Roberta Pollack Seid, "Between 1968 and
1969, twenty-five diet articles were listed in the *Reader's Guide*. By 1978–
79, the number had leapt to eighty-eight—a deceptively low figure, since
the *Guide* did not include the diet columns that were now regular magazine features nor the myriad diets that routinely appeared in more popular
publications" (166). Hillel Schwartz reports that Weight Watchers' reve-
nues jumped from $8 million in 1970 to $39 million in 1977 (266). This
flowering of interest in slimming was accompanied by a growing rationali-
zation of the methods by which pounds were to be shed. Calorie counters,
fat farms, clinics, injections, surgery, jaw-wiring, stomach-stapling, regi-
mens of jogging, programs of fasting, hundreds of books offering the wis-

dom of doctors and psychologists (like Atkins, Tarnower, and Cott), now augmented the relatively simple appetite suppressants popular in the 1960s.

That this immense apparatus reorganized women's bodies for the paths of emancipation is made apparent by the change in the prevailing ideals identified with women's thinness. In the 1960s women's thinness was associated with little-girlishness. Waifs and adolescents, bodied forth by models like Twiggy and the young Jean Shrimpton, or the "daddy's girl" who could never quite manage anything on her own, played by Marlo Thomas in the TV series *That Girl*, were the hallmarks of feminine style. In the 1970s, by contrast, women's thinness began to be associated with women's ambition, strength, and self-control. The heroine of the decade was the slim, independent, emphatically single Mary Richards on *The Mary Tyler Moore Show*, who, unlike Marlo, didn't need daddy's help; she was going to "make it on her own."[14] Whereas 1960s fashions in women's dress sought to recapture infancy—baby-doll dresses, Mary Jane shoes—1970s fashions aimed at a rangy mannishness, with designers producing pinstriped suits, man-tailored shirts, hacking jackets, and stacked-heel loafers as part of the new working woman's "uniform" (see Milbank 240–42).[15]

Like the punitive reforms of the early nineteenth century, the rigors of dieting at once re-located women's bodies ideologically and addressed a consciousness they themselves helped to construct. It is concomitantly not without reason that Foucault shares with Rice, Chernin, and Krantz an emphasis on the term "soul." Discussing this same propensity in anorexics, who obsess about the expansion and purity of their spirits, Susan Bordo characterizes the "metaphysics" of dieting as an extension and "crystallization" of Western culture's privileging of spirit over flesh (92–96). But Rice, whose characters search for the "soul"'s grace, or Chernin (a former anorexic) who speaks of the "soul"'s nourishment, might agree with Foucault that the mind/body split encouraged by dieting is more than merely symptomatic of a long-entrenched preference for the ephemeral. Its generation of a psyche is real. As Foucault says of the prisoner, "A 'soul' inhabits him and brings him into existence"; "It would be wrong to say that the soul is an illusion, or an ideological effect. On the contrary, it exists, it has a reality" (30, 29). When modern women collectively converted to what Krantz calls the "religion of thinness" (*Scruples* 68), they perforce found at its altars the constituents of their own empowerment as politicized subjects.

But the "soul" doubtless gets ample space in the discourses of dieting not just because it blooms as the flesh disintegrates, but because it is an area of contending energies. Where the traces of dieting as a political technology—a strategy by which power is negotiated and exercised (Foucault 26)—reveal themselves is in the armature that originates and supports the "soul" of liberated womanhood—the soul's dependence, that is, on an ongoing, and therefore unwinnable, battle with the ghosts of mothering and domesticity. The insight of novels like *Lady Oracle* and *Scruples* lies in their sensitivity to the negotiations this battle requires. Although Atwood and Krantz pay tribute to slenderness as the key to personal development, they also realize that the heroine's selfhood hinges on her simultaneous acceptance of and resistance to traditional roles. Thus Billy's choice of marriage weirdly provokes a fresh bout of independence—"if she wanted to stay married to Vito . . . she had to establish an abiding interest in life that did not depend on him in any way" (568). The end of Atwood's novel finds Joan trapped in a maze and locked in permanent solidarity and contention with all her old "tenuous bodies" (342), the see-through women on whom her liberation depends: the Fat Lady, the Mother, the demure Good Girl, her enemies, her cohorts.

For Rice, of course, the conflicted terrain of the self is figured—indeed, allegorized—as the zone of war between good and evil, salvation and damnation, between compromised survival and all-out annihilation. It is a testimony to the extremity of her project in *Interview with the Vampire* that she dismisses the negotiations that characterize Billy's and Joan's development and forces a victory in the battle between emancipated selfhood and its vaporous domestic Other. The results may not be inspiring. Whether in Claudia's case, where, like a little balloon inflated with too much selfhood, she just explodes, or in Louis's, where the allure of plenitude wins over resistance, "nothingness" is equally the victor. With their subjectivity constituted by the conflict itself, Rice's vampires obliterate themselves at the instant they either win or lose. The delicacy of this equilibrium is illustrated by the aftermath of its upset. If Rice's later novels abandon the radical extremes of her first, they also suggest how closely the domestication of her vampires was tied to a larger defeat. Like the dieting iconoclasts of the 1970s who were reedified for 1980s consumerism and corporate culture, the vampire succumbed to the recuperative energies that were all along inherent in the strategies of abstinence.

And yet despite the pitfalls, the fits of hunger and longing that are too easily conscripted for mandates of self-indulgence, *Interview with the Vampire* insists on the wisdom of self-abnegation. In the end Louis gives up on "humanity" and starts eating his fill. His parting words to the journalist who is interviewing him speak eloquently of the choice he has made: "I drank of the beauty of the world as a vampire drinks. I was satisfied. I was filled to the brim. But I was dead" (324). Rice would go on in her other novels to rewrite this death as a necessary fact of vampire life, but her first novel acknowledges the bitter pressure exerted by plenitude on the self that will only find sustenance through resistance and loss.

Thanks to Nicola Nixon, Margot Young, and Michael Zeitlin for their invaluable comments on earlier versions of this essay.

10

When Hollywood Sucks,

or, Hungry Girls, Lost Boys, and Vampirism in the Age of Reagan

NICOLA NIXON

𝕬 few years behind his brother Ridley in the movie-making business, Tony Scott made his directorial debut in 1983 with *The Hunger*, a slick, glossy, upmarket vampire film based on the 1981 novel by Whitley Strieber.[1] Scott's emphasis on *The Hunger*'s trend-conscious currency—an emphasis that separated it quite decisively from the Hammer films of the late 1960s and early '70s,[2] and even from the novel itself—suggests that he had little difficulty parleying his experience in television advertising onto the big screen.[3] The initial scenes of New York nightclubs and fast cars zooming down the Long Island Expressway are intercut with shots of neo-goth Peter Murphy—complete with gaunt and powdered white face, lipsticked red lips, and monochromatic black clothing—singing the Bauhaus theme song, "Bela Lugosi's Dead." From Murphy, the virtual prototype of Anne Rice's Vampire Lestat, the camera shifts to two of the film's leads: the seemingly ageless Catherine Deneuve and David Bowie as the modern, very glamorous vampires Miriam and John Blaylock, who find their victims in New-York-style punk clubs and take them home to their chic Manhattan house—a house that is, of course, set up to facilitate the easy disposal of blood-deficient human husks.

From his casting and set design to his musical score, Scott stresses the essential up-to-the-minute contemporaneity of the film, representing vampirism in all its potential glamour, trendiness, eroticism, and appeal to '80s youth-cultism. Pop-star Bowie had, after all, just released two highly-acclaimed videos from his *Scary Monsters* album (1980), revitalizing his own claims to sleek and enduring fashionableness; and Bauhaus and neo-gothicism were finding a generic niche in the British not-so-underground music scene and London's "Bat Cave."[4]

Scott accentuates the contemporary appeal of his film, not only through its music and through the neat conflation of sex and vampirism, but also through its entire "medical" element, which focuses on Blaylock victim Dr. Sarah Roberts (Susan Sarandon) and her clinical research on sleep and human longevity. The film cuts back and forth between the time-lessly tasteful, artifact-filled interior of the Blaylock home and the stark, functional waiting rooms and research labs of Sarah's clinic, between the Blaylocks' white Steinway baby grand, and Sarah's microscopes. And in-deed one of the cleverest moments in *The Hunger* comprises the juxtapo-sition of scenes between Sarah, who is watching a video-tape playback of one of her rhesus monkeys—Methuselah—age at an astronomical speed, and John Blaylock, who is sitting in the waiting room outside the lab, ag-ing at the same extraordinary rate.

Blaylock's failure to retain his youth—his rapid slide from trendi-ness to antiquarianism, as it were—is highlighted in the subsequent scene where, as a new but now full-blown octogenarian, he fails miserably in his attempt to kill a young man who is roller-skate dancing to a beat-box play-ing Iggy Pop's "Fun Time." The remainder of the film involves Miriam's suitably regretful stowing of the terminally antique John in the attic with her other former lovers, her seduction and transformation of Sarah into a new vampire partner, and Sarah's initial rejection and then gradual ac-ceptance of the inevitability of being young and rich forever. In keeping with the film's emphasis on modernity, Ivan Davis and Michael Thomas's screenplay adroitly avoids Strieber's representation of John's fond memo-ries of his earlier centuries with Miriam and Miriam's memories of the per-secution of her vampire family in the Middle Ages; even the conclusion departs significantly from Strieber's novel. The novel envisions the ulti-mate endurability of the ancient race of vampires by offering a final glimpse of Miriam Blaylock's perpetuity in the face of John's reluctant and Sarah's deliberate demise; Miriam, the last of her kind, survives and sets off to find another partner. The film, however, presents the termination of both John and Miriam—the latter's in a highly unconvincing topple from one of the upper floors of the house—and Sarah's ascendance over the old-guard vampires (John and Miriam) to assume her position as the next-generation vampire, ensconced in a brand-new Manhattan highrise.

The Hunger never achieved much beyond B-movie status, despite its commercial aspirations to slickness and currency. Granted, it did not have much in common with the A-movies—the top grossing films of 1983 were, after all, *The Big Chill, Flashdance, Mr. Mom,* and *Return of the Jedi.* And the sensitive family-tragedy film *Terms of Endearment* won the Academy Award for best picture. Leonard Maltin, obviously disapproving of *The Hunger*'s yoking of vampirism and lesbian sexuality, dismisses it as "kinky trash masquerading as a horror film" (Maltin 571). But if we examine the film now, after more than a decade, it is not, in fact, its datedness—or trashy kinkiness—that stands out so starkly.

Let's reconsider *The Hunger* for a moment. It begins with two super-ficially-beautiful and sexually-charismatic but somehow invisibly-infected individuals, who get dressed up in leather, go to nightclubs, and seduce innocent, black-clad victims of either sex. They take their victims home, make love to them, then kill them. And if they do not kill their victims immediately, they simply infect them irrevocably. When Sarah Roberts is seduced by Miriam Blaylock, for example, she is first thrilled, then feels decidedly odd and unwell. Rushing back to her clinic, she has her lab assistant give her a blood test which reveals that her own blood is clinically tainted, that something foreign in her veins is waging war on and rapidly transforming her very cells. Then Scott offers us a quick cut from microscope and glass slide to the chimpanzee under scrutiny on the other side of the glass observation window, as if to clinch the connection between Sarah's undiagnosable ailment and an equally inexplicable disease afflicting the monkeys. Sarah's debilitating blood ailment, which gives her night sweats and renders her appetiteless, nauseous, sleepless, and disoriented, sends her back to Miriam, who promptly puts her to bed and cares for her, feeding and cleaning up after her when she pukes up dinner—her boy-friend, Tom—all over the lush oriental carpet.

There is something eerily familiar about the scenario of a seemingly-beautiful, charmingly-anonymous lover who, during an unusually passion-ate sexual encounter, transmits some virulent infection that cannot even be diagnosed, let alone cured. Indeed if we examine *The Hunger* now, it seems considerably less remarkable for its depiction of an early 1980s vampirism than it does for its stunning resemblance to an extended AIDS allegory. New York nightclubs and leather bars, anonymous sex with invisibly-infected strangers, transmitted and undiagnosable blood diseases that transform cells and have some sort of connection to lethal viruses af-flicting monkeys, and same-sex sexuality add up, now, to only one thing.

Even Scott's decision to stress the homoerotic component of vampir-ism is almost uncannily suggestive. Granted, the steamy lesbian seduc-tion of Sarah by Miriam is probably not quite as provocative as it might have been if the homoerotic element had been enacted as homosexual.

But then, again, Scott's casting of David Bowie as John Blaylock is oddly charged, since Bowie could hardly be separated from his androgynous self-promotion, his apparent bisexuality, and the implicit transvestitism that characterized him on the covers of, say, *Aladdin Sane, Pinups, Young Americans*, and *Diamond Dogs* in the 1970s. And Bowie's drag was revealed to be more than just play when Bianca Jagger, after her divorce from Mick in 1980, told the tabloids about Mick's sexual proclivities, confirming in the process that Bowie's alleged interest in men like her ex-husband was considerably more than mere music-industry gossip. While Bowie does not actually seduce and infect other men in *The Hunger*, then—his fruitless attempt to go after the virile young roller-skater notwithstanding—he nevertheless stands as a sort of icon to cross-gender sexuality.

But before we reach any firm conclusions that *The Hunger* is, in fact, an extended AIDS allegory, we would do well to remember when it was filmed and released. In 1983 there were only about 800 AIDS-type cases documented in the United States and fewer than 400 in England; the acronym itself was not even coined until around the end of 1982. The public heard little of the rapidly progressing epidemic until Hollywood released its astonishing statement to the wire services in July of 1985 that its "traditional, squarejawed, romantic leading man," Rock Hudson, was dying of AIDS (quoted in Shilts 575). *Time, Newsweek, People*, and most of the major American newspapers picked up the story instantly, initiating public speculation and misinformation about the so-called "gay plague" that "turn[ed] fruits into vegetables."[5] By then, however, more than 12,000 perhaps less-illustrious—and decidedly less iconographically heterosexual—Americans had been diagnosed as having AIDS, and half of them were already dead.[6] After Hudson's death three months later, his quarter-million dollar bequest founded AmFAR, whose national chair was to be Elizabeth Taylor. Hollywood thus had a fashionable new cause, even though its rather high-profile product—B-movie cowboy and President Ronald Reagan—had yet to acknowledge the existence of AIDS publicly. In terms of chronology at any rate, it is thus virtually impossible to make any case at all for *The Hunger*'s containing an oblique or embedded reference to AIDS.

If it is so tempting to read *The Hunger* as a curious and compelling but nevertheless impossible prefiguration of the iconography of an actual epidemic, I would argue that such is the case for several reasons. First of all, vampirism, with its connotative yoking of sexuality and contagion, has a long history of being linked to the horrors of venereal diseases—syphilis in particular.[7] And, as Sander Gilman has argued so convincingly, AIDS, with its initial categorization as an STD, has been represented consistently through an "appropriation of the iconography of syphilis" (90, 98). Consequently, vampirism has always already contained the constellation of signifiers currently clustering around AIDS. Witness, for example, the much-criticized vampire metaphors pervading media discourse on AIDS; this journalistic tendency to conflate the PWA and vampire is exemplified preeminently by Randy Shilts's much vaunted but highly problematic *And the Band Played On*, released in 1987. Shilts, a sort of modern-day Van Helsing with pretensions to journalistic objectivity and integrity, unearths and tirelessly tracks Canadian flight-attendant Gaetan Dugas—"patient zero"—the quintessential amoral, solitary, and infected predator, who, Shilts insists, had sex with men simply in order to kill them, using the cloak of darkness in nightclubs and bathhouses to conceal his telltale KS lesions, and gloating to his sexual conquests afterward that he had all but killed them. Even the vampire fanzines like *Fangoria* fielded readers' letters to the editors inquiring about whether vampires could get AIDS: the answer was, incidentally, a fairly consistent "no," because, of course, vampires are dead already.

Media representations of AIDS and PWAs as vampiric, and our filtered knowledge of the emergence and exponential growth in the 1980s of an epidemic that attacked and killed the young, the beautiful, the daringly promiscuous, the nightclub patrons—through their sexual practices—make it extremely difficult to read a vampire film like *The Hunger* without reference to AIDS, despite the prohibitive chronological details about when the novel was written and the film made and released. And part of that difficulty is exacerbated by the fact that Scott's film envisions a modern '80s vampire: a sexy, cool, leather-clad, dangerous vampire who, while apparently timeless, is very much a part of early '80s popular culture. If *The Hunger* can thus function almost paradigmatically as representative of modern vampirism and its inevitable slide toward AIDS iconography, what, then, are we to make of two later, equally modern vampire films emerging from Hollywood in 1987? Kathryn Bigelow's *Near Dark* and Joel Schumacher's *The Lost Boys* both surfaced in a climate of rampant AIDS paranoia, from a Hollywood loudly proclaiming a sense of mission.[8]

At first glance *Near Dark* and *The Lost Boys* are visually very different films: the former has all the dark, gritty appearance of an independent release, even though it came out of the De Laurentis studios, and the latter has all the slick, Hollywood feel of a Spielbergian techno-dazzler. But they have some rather remarkable similarities—similarities not limited to the

overdubbed, contemporary, pop-music sound tracks that serve to flag
the films as temporally immediate. Unlike *The Hunger*, with its undercur-
rents of homoeroticism and exploratory sexuality, both films are militantly
heterosexual and militantly pro-family, involving mildly bored teenaged
boys—Michael in *The Lost Boys* and Caleb in *Near Dark*—who are led
astray by cute, almost innocent, almost vampire girls—Star and Mae. And
both are, to all intents and purposes, boys-coming-of-age films, in which
Michael and Caleb rebel against their families and join a rough crowd
who just happen to be vampires. We could easily subtitle *Near Dark*,
"How Caleb Wins His Spurs" and *The Lost Boys*, "How Michael Becomes
a Rebel with a Cause"; they are twin celebrations of emergent heterosexual
manhood.

The American iconography of the cowboy/young gun informs *Near
Dark*, from Jessie's long, spaghetti-western coat, to Diamondback's chaps
and pistol, and Severin's spurs and stiletto-point cowboy boots. Equally
powerful American icons appear in *The Lost Boys*; Schumacher consciously
invokes the figures of boy-rebels James Dean and Jim Morrison, from the
motorcycle chicken games and black-leather, to Echo and the Bunnymen's
cover of "People Are Strange," the Morrison posters in the vampire lair,
and Jason Patric's brooding and Morrisonesque pout. But the rebel-boys
here achieve a manhood firmly situated in traditional familial structures,
even though Michael and Caleb are somewhat more susceptible to rebellion and bad influence because they come from single-parent families.

Although Michael is lacking a father and Caleb a mother, the families
they do have are nevertheless connotatively "good" and function, not surprisingly, as one pole of a symbolic opposition. In *Near Dark* the good
wholesome American family of Loy and Sarah is established as a counterpoint to the demonic vampire family of Jessie, Diamondback, Severin,
Homer, and Mae; and the same opposition holds true for *The Lost Boys*, in
which the good family of Lucy, Grandpa, and Sam is offset against the vampire family of Max, David, Marco, Laddie, and Star. Both films, in other
words, envision vampires not as sophisticated, sexy, charismatic, lone predators, but as dysfunctional families.

But why, we might ask, are the films structured so obviously around
families—both vampiric and all-American—complete with mom, dad, kids,
dog, and the family stationwagon? The American family was, after all—
and still is, if recent leadership conventions and presidential campaigns are
any indication—an ideological construct. In *Near Dark* the little boy vampire, Homer, refers to Daddy vampire Jessie (Lance Henrikson) as "dad"

and "gramps," and Jessie in turn urges him into the family wagon with "get into the car, bumster"; Severin (Bill Paxton) warns Caleb, "that's your mamma talkin' boy" when Mamma vampire Diamondback (Jenette Goldstein) gives Caleb a warning about not contributing to, or pulling his weight in, the family. Even Bigelow's casting of Henrikson, Goldstein, and Paxton, who were all in James Cameron's *Aliens* (1986), as Dad, Mom, and older-son vampire, accentuates their visual and representational appeal as a demonic family unit. At the end of *The Lost Boys*, Max says to Lucy: "It was all going to be so perfect, Lucy. Just like one big happy family. Your boys and my boys." And Edgar Frog comments wryly, "Great! A blood-sucking Brady Bunch." The individualistic, predatory, vampires of Bram Stoker, Sheridan Le Fanu, or even *The Hunger*, who deem people preeminently disposable, are displaced in these late '80s vampire films—and bad families collectively constitute the central threat.

But should we find it so strange that the powerful, amoral, single-minded individualism characteristic of the vampire, who profits by and capitalizes on the weakness or vulnerability of others, should not, in fact, represent the truly demonic or evil in Reaganite America? Let's remember that the maverick or renegade entrepreneur, tempered only by a strong dose of "family values," was nothing other than an American hero. When the American capitalist hero and the vampire thus have so very much in common—and the vampire has, after all, regularly functioned as a political metaphor for aristocrats, for the rich who suck the life blood and/or labor potential from the poor—does it not seem eminently appropriate, in the '80s, that true evil not be associated with the individualist vampire? Instead, the blood-sucking vampire has to be reconstructed as a demonized collective, as, connotatively, a sort of evil trade union that is bleeding the good entrepreneurs dry by cutting into their profit margin.

It is, of course, precisely this construction that Michael Moore deliberately attacks, inverting the demonization from the UAW to the American hero through representing him as entirely vampiric. In Moore's documentary *Roger and Me* (1989), for example, General Motors chairman Roger Smith is clearly the more traditional, conscienceless vampire who sucks the life-blood from Flint, Michigan, leaving behind only a dry husk of a ghost-town; Moore makes the case even more explicitly in his later *Pets or Meat: The Return to Flint* (1992). In the absence of such critique, or, better, in the presence of the strong complicity of *Near Dark* and *The Lost Boys* with '80s "family values"—aided representationally, no doubt, by Anne Rice's fictional community of vampires, who are, in fact, a far cry from the conventional family unit—evil vampires become a dangerous un-American "anti-family" that tempts the good American boy to stray, offering the promise of adult sexual license and the allure of rock music, all-night parties, and unchecked troublemaking in comic-book shops and dumpy roadhouses.

Not only is the vampire transformed—multiplied into a demonized family in *The Lost Boys* and *Near Dark*—but the entire dangerously enticing, erotic dark underside of vampirism we find in *The Hunger* or even Rice's Théâtre des Vampires is sapped of its seductive energy. First of all, Michael and Caleb are lured from their homes by sweet girls who are not yet committed to being vampires. *Near Dark*'s Mae, from Sweetwater, Texas, who first appears wearing a pink shirt and eating an ice cream cone, tries to protect Caleb from her corrupting influence, then later hides the fact that he cannot do his own killing by sacrificing her own well-being and sustaining him on her own blood. *The Lost Boys*' Star, sporting long flowing hair and diaphanous cotton skirts, tries to warn Michael away from the lair and has yet to make her first kill; apart from her appearance in one or two scenes where she actually functions as a sexual being, she is primarily maternal, preoccupied with little Laddie, a lost boy—and near-vampire— whose face appears on the back of milk cartons. The eroticism offered by Mae and Star is pretty tepid at best; it bears a far greater resemblance to teen romance with its vapid nice-girl heroines who have been led astray briefly and wait only to be saved, than it does to any steamy or transgressive sexuality that might potentially initiate the boys into some darkly-mysterious or dangerous sexual practices, the taste for which might prove irreversibly addictive and threatening to an ideal family order.

If vampirism is not in the least seductive, it is also not in the least binding. In both *Near Dark* and *The Lost Boys*, becoming a vampire involves a choice that is, oddly enough, not only personal but reversible. When Caleb's father, Loy, tracks his son all over the county and finally finds him at the Godspeed Motel, Loy kidnaps him away from Jessie and the vampire family; then, when Loy, Sarah, and Caleb are driving away, Caleb pleads, "Daddy, take me home." Loy does take Caleb home, sets up a portable transfusion unit in the barn, and proceeds to give his son a transfusion from his own arm. The good, wholesome blood of the Father is, of course, more than sufficient to wipe out all the bad blood/influence of the vampire family. Later on, Caleb redeems and saves the essentially good Mae when he gives her a transfusion and makes it possible for her to walk out into the morning sun once again.

Jessie and Diamondback's centuries of "good times" and road trips thus square off against Caleb and Loy's honest hard work on the farm. And to emphasize the difference, Bigelow offers us two, almost immediately counterpoised, scenes: in the first, the vampire family, who are out for an evening of fun, wreak havoc and carnage at a roadhouse, drinking blood out of beer glasses and dancing on tables while the Cramps play on the jukebox; and in the second, which occurs immediately after Caleb's trans-fusion, Caleb, Loy, and Sarah sit and eat dinner in the farmhouse kitchen. Dad offers to start the dishes, while Caleb goes upstairs to read Sarah her bedtime story. When Sarah is stolen from her room, Caleb sets out, just like his father, to track her down and rescue her from the machinations of little-vampire Homer.

While the homoerotic component may be absent from the demonic families in *The Lost Boys* and *Near Dark*, replaced in both by heterosexual relations, the relationships between the members of the demonic families smack of incest. In *Near Dark* in particular the "children" who are not related by blood, as it were, seek out additional brothers and sisters like Caleb and Sarah in order to have sexual, rather than filial, companions. While Caleb and Michael may be searching for appropriate sexual compan-ions, then, they are offered demonic siblings who desire them sexually; and it is this offer that consolidates their rejection of the vampire families in favor of their own, healthy families.

The same sort of temptation-regret-rescue trajectory holds true for both *Near Dark* and *The Lost Boys*. Michael is tempted by David, Marco, and the gang—playing chicken with David on his motorcycle, drinking strangely intoxicating beverages at the lair, and so on—but his inherent morality keeps him from making his first kill, just as it gives Star and Laddie pause. But brother Sam, with the help of the Frog brothers, Edgar and Allen, complete with combat fatigues and stakes, manages to keep Michael from falling completely under the control of David and the other gang members. When Michael is first feeling the effects of his transformation, he is ostensibly babysitting Sam. Wallowing in a bubble bath and washing his hair, Sam sings along to Clarence Henry's "Ain't Got No Home," a song that functions as a sort of musical commentary to Michael's increasing de-sire to forfeit real familial attachments, to sacrifice his home in order to feed off his brother. What, after all, could be more telling of Michael's moral jeopardy than his inability to drink milk, his dropping of the full carton—with Laddie's picture on the back—all over the kitchen floor? Later Sam articulates true filial bonds when he assures Michael: "Even though you're a vampire, you're still my brother."

Like *Near Dark*'s Caleb, who only needs a transfusion to save him,

Michael only needs the head vampire, Max, to be killed so that he can be freed of his transitory vampirism. In the end, it is Grandpa, the superannuated hippie, who saves the family by driving his antique car through the house and killing Max in the process. There are obvious parodic elements in *The Lost Boys*, Sam's comment to Michael, for example: "You're a creature of the night, Michael, just like out of a comic book. You're a vampire, Michael. My own brother, a goddamn shit-sucking vampire. Ooo, you wait till mom finds out buddy"; or Grandpa's final, anti-climactic observation: "One thing about living in Santa Carla I never could stomach—all the darn vampires." But those elements, while making for mild comedy, do not affect the film's essential substructure as a cautionary moral tale.

If *Near Dark* less self-consciously lampoons vampire stories, it nevertheless operates equally seriously as a monitory fable. And monitory fables were, after all, rather in vogue at the end of the '80s. *Fatal Attraction*, for example, appeared in the same year as *Near Dark* and *The Lost Boys* and was one of the top-grossing films of 1987, striking the fear of psychoretribution into wandering family-men. And Richard Wenk's truly awful film, *The Vamp* (1986), starring Grace Jones, offers a transparently cautionary tale of two frat boys who go out one night to the After Dark Club to hire a stripper for a Dipsa Phi party; Vic gets seduced by the vampire Katrina (Jones) and becomes a vampire, and Keith learns his lesson, heading home chastened at dawn after he and Vic have killed Katrina.[9]

In both *Near Dark* and *The Lost Boys* vampirism has been curiously purged: gone is the potentially transgressive homoeroticism, gone is the predatory individualism, gone is the permanent mortal danger, gone is the genuine allure of immortality and eternal youth, and gone even is the dangerous attractiveness of the vampire, all the components of vampire mythology that were realized so strongly in *The Hunger*. These two 1987 films in fact offer us up the vampire tale as a vehicle for moral interrogations and ideological reaffirmations, a vehicle that both draws from and essentially consolidates the legacy of Rice's late-'70s and '80s vampire novels, *Interview with the Vampire* (1976), *The Vampire Lestat* (1985), and *Queen of the Damned* (1988). Rice sets up the major tension in *Interview with the Vampire*, for example, as Louis's inability to accept that he is a cold-blooded killer. What makes poor Louis so fascinatingly attractive and so appealingly pathetic—to both the other vampires in the narrative and to the reader—is his moral dilemma, his contradictory need to kill to survive and his mortal unwillingness to relinquish his humanity and become truly evil. While Louis fights his hunger and tries to hold off from feeding regu-

larly in order to convince himself that he has not quite lost his human qualities, he must ultimately succumb.

But Caleb and Michael do resist feeding, precisely because both films
envision a curious middle zone of almost-but-not-quite vampirism. Either
the boys' strong beliefs in the sanctity of human life—derived, of course,
from their already ingested family values—or their redemptive families'
commitment to "saving" them, manage to pull them back as they teeter
on the brink of becoming real, permanent vampires. And, let's face it, a
comfy home looks just fine compared to crummy, flea-bag motels like the
Hideaway and Godspeed, cramped Winnebagos, tin-foiled and duct-taped
stationwagons and ratty vans, or minimalist boys' club-houses—the locus of a demonic, connotatively lower class, domesticity. Vampire families
can only offer migrant homelessness and a permanent and relentless "fun
time," which, because it loses its cachet as rebellion from sanctioned authority and domestic responsibility, seems almost boringly repetitive, an
empty enactment of rebellion from a non-existent authority.

Now, much as *Near Dark* and *The Lost Boys* presume to tell us about
how properly-raised teenaged boys can withstand bad influence, no matter
how weird or severe it might actually be, and much as they might caution
young rebels about the dire consequences of their getting involved with
attractive strangers, what do they reveal about late-'80s vampirism? And
what indeed are we to make of their delicate avoidance of any number of
its aspects? In fact, the only significant problem with being a vampire in
these two films is that one cannot have wild parties in the middle of the
day; one has to sleep in. Since such a restriction, operating as a sort of
inverted curfew, hardly constitutes a serious impediment to teen fun in
most cases, it would be unlikely to cramp the style of the average eighteen-
year-old boy-rebel. Then again, neither would an avoidance of churches—
or, for that matter, an avoidance of garlic, crucifixes, bibles, holy water, or
wholesome people brandishing pointed sticks.

But it is not simply the clichéd or common details of vampirism that
are neatly skirted. Actually, the two films' remarkable avoidance of precisely
those aspects of vampirism that make it sexy and attractive and compelling,
is, I would suggest, far more deliberate than delicate. Let's consider for a
moment how Caleb and Michael become infected: both are attracted to
girls, follow them home, and instead of having the desirable consummation of the evening, they are offered substitutes; both are given "nips"—
Michael gets his from a bottle of semi-fresh blood, and Caleb gets his as
a rather serious hickey on the neck. Once they have both become bona

fide addicts and substance abusers—blood-junkies—they must go back for
more: Michael returns to the lair for the bottle, and Caleb drinks from
Mae's wrist, since neither can bring himself to make his own "kills." Michael is saved when Grandpa kills head-vampire Max, who is the apparent
commanding source of contagion, and whose death will somehow guarantee that the infection not only ceases to spread but withers away and
disappears in those who have contracted it. Caleb is saved by a resurgence
of good, paternal blood, whose wholesome potency eradicates the bad
blood, the externally-contracted foreign infection, that is drawing him
away from his family.

These are provocative strategies of salvation—especially when we consider that California state senator, John Doolittle, had, only a year before
Near Dark and *The Lost Boys*, sponsored a Senate bill that "legalized the
creation of designated-donor pools to keep donated blood *within families*
so as to prevent transmission" of certain blood diseases passed from anonymous donors to "the general population."[10] It passed, in 1986, without a
murmur of opposition. Unfortunately, cobalt-bombing some sort of fictitious "patient zero"—the neatly-constructed and demonized daddy, if not
the absolute source, of an epidemic—would do little to arrest or limit the
spread of a certain blood-transmitted virus. But then, Michael and Caleb,
as nice, young, white, middle-class, and heterosexual boys from Texas and
Arizona were exactly what the American media and the Reagan administration conceived of as part of the ideologically-charged, unaffected "general
population," unlike, say, the anonymous truly "lost boys" ghettoized in
New York and San Francisco. Michael and Caleb do not even have much
sex, as far as we can tell, although there is a moment in *The Lost Boys* in
which the club-house curtain closes decorously on a scene between Michael and Star. But the boys do eventually become men through their
ordeals, and they are rewarded with sweetly appropriate girlfriends in the
end—which is more than they had at the beginning. More germanely,
however, Michael and Caleb finally come to appreciate the values of their
families.

Both films, in fact, conclude with a retrenchment of the good family
unit, after, of course, the vampire families have been destroyed—staked
and holy-watered to death in *The Lost Boys*, and quite spectacularly exploded and combusted in a conflagration at the end of *Near Dark*. The
penultimate scene in *Near Dark* offers us long shots of the demonic wood-
paneled family stationwagon—with Dad and Mom vampire (Jessie and
Diamondback) holding hands in the front seat—bursting into flames and

mushroom clouds, while Caleb, who is lying on the road, chants "Roast! Roast!" Oddly enough, at almost the same time that Schumacher and Bigelow's films were released, a strangely similar and even more sinister conflagration rocked Arcadia, Florida.[11] The Ray family, whose three hemophiliac and HIV-positive sons had been granted the right to return to the local school, had their home burned down by their Arcadian neighbors.

Of course, these representative conflagrations are mere coincidence, testifying only to the age-old mode that the self-righteous "general population" has preferred for the purging of the uncanny from its communities. And Paul Verhoeven's *Robocop*, also released in 1987, suggests that, in future, the general population will not need gasoline to expunge cancer-like inner-city undesirables from its clean, new communities: gun-slinging cyborgs with souls can perform such duties. What the Arcadia incident registered was the acuteness of AIDS paranoia in 1987. *People Magazine* did not, after all, lose a single beat, publishing a ten-page exposé of the Ray family and Arcadia's bigoted battle with them, in which *People* argued that the entire episode was symptomatic of the pervasive NIMBY—Not In My Back Yard—reaction of the "general population" to those testing positive to the HIV retrovirus. *People*'s sympathy was, of course, directed far more toward the suffering of innocent eight-year-olds than toward dying fags. But what makes the vampire films' and Arcadia, Florida's coincidental conflagrations especially provocative is that *Near Dark* and *The Lost Boys* are, in fact, supremely silent about fairly obvious parallels between vampirism and AIDS, parallels that make reading *The Hunger*, for example, as just another modern vampire tale, an effort of will.

If *The Hunger* invites a historically contextualized reading, no matter how fantastic, I would suggest that *Near Dark* and *The Lost Boys* do not—and they do not precisely because they retool the vampire tale so as to occlude any such recognizable contextual and metaphorical connections. The two 1987 films vaunt American ideals of normalized family values, offering placatory parables of the essential permanence and inviolability of such values in the face of the "bad" families who represent the potential decay of these ideals. Vampirism, like AIDS, consequently becomes a "lifestyle" choice, where the vampire, like the homosexual, is potentially curable, and if not curable, then surely deserving of death. The "general population" might have perceived itself as embattled, then, but its response, at least for Hollywood, was a righteously militant retrenchment against the demonic family that was threatening to pollute or infect American domestic purity and corrupt its sons.[12]

True, *The Lost Boys* and *Near Dark* hint that bad fun may *seem* dis-
tinctly tempting; but its appeal is transitory, and we should not succumb
to its addictive allure. Nancy Reagan's advice was, after all, "Just Say No."
And her husband seemed to take her anti-drug slogan as a panacea for
considerably larger American health problems. Reagan self-righteously said
"no" to unregenerate non-families too, without the slightest pang for their
demise: he never even mentioned AIDS publicly until November of 1987.
Three months after the Arcadia scandal, months after Shilts' popular *And
the Band Played On* was already on the bestseller list, months after Simon
Watney's more academic *Policing Desire: Pornography, AIDS and the Media* and *October*'s *AIDS: Cultural Analysis/Cultural Activism* were published, and after at least 26,000 Americans had already died of AIDS,
Reagan did, however, finally make a statement: "I have asked the Department of Health and Human Services to determine as soon as possible the
extent to which the AIDS virus has penetrated our society" (quoted in
Crimp 11).

It was rather obvious that the Hollywood cowboy-president just wasn't
going to clean up his town, especially when it was so populated—penetrated—with infected undesireables; clearly, there were far more important
targets for preemptive strikes in Cold War America. And Hollywood itself,
while prepared to endorse AmFAR fundraising and to sing dirges for lost
members of the Screen Actors' Guild, was not about to allow a whisper of
a reference to infect its box-office offerings. If its offerings since the late
1980s are any indication, Hollywood's red-ribbon campaign has had little
or no impact in cinematic terms, except, perhaps, as a joke in John Landis's
Innocent Blood (1992): when Tony (Anthony LePaglia) tries to resist making love to the lovely vampire Marie (Anne Parillaud), she asks him how
she can make him feel safer, then smiles knowingly and offers him a box of
condoms. While *Entertainment Tonight*'s Leeza Gibbons may well claim
that "blood-sucking [an old B-movie staple] is [now] big box office," [13]
then, we can only surmise that Hollywood's mandate is to make the vampire film an A-movie staple by avoiding the big A altogether.

11

Consuming Youth:
The Lost Boys Cruise Mallworld

ROB LATHAM

In his brilliant Marxist analysis of Bram Stoker's novel *Dracula*, Franco Moretti reminds us that the deployment of vampirism as a metaphor for capitalism derives from Marx himself, who described the process of capital accumulation as "dead labour which, vampire-like, lives only by sucking living labour, and lives the more, the more labour it sucks" (quoted in Moretti 91). Moretti stresses that, while the vampire is a perfect general image for the basic mechanism of capitalist development, individual vampire texts illuminate specifically the historical phases of capitalism in which they are produced. Thus Moretti analyzes Count Dracula as a crystallization of monopoly capital circa 1897.

In Marx's use of the metaphor, the vampiric relationship involves the forcible extraction of surplus value in production, an unremitting exploitation that is driven by a shadow of desire: "the capitalist devours the labour-power of the worker, or appropriates his living labour as the life-blood of capitalism. . . . By incorporating living labour-power into the material constituents of capital [i.e., fixed capital], the latter becomes an animated monster and it starts to act 'as if consumed by love'" (Marx 1007). Marx's allusion here is to Goethe's *Faust*, specifically to the refrain of a drinking song about a grossly corpulent rat who is poisoned by a cook and becomes wildly maddened, "as if"—in Walter Kaufmann's translation—"love gnawed his vitals" (215). The desire Marx speaks of here is, then, only a parody of amorousness; rather, it is gluttony transformed into tortured death-throes. In short, Marx is implying that capital's uncontrollable lust for endless accumulation will be its undoing, that the vampiric hunger of capital will culminate in a paroxysm of self-consuming destruction.

Much of twentieth-century Marxist thought has involved attempts to explain why this self-destruction was forestalled, why the vampire of capital has managed again and again to rise from the grave of economic crisis to batten upon the living. Marxists—often tutored by Freudians of one stripe or another—have been forced to admit that the desire animating capitalism is more complex than mindless gluttony, that the vampiric relationship between capital and labor involves a libidinal investment, an erotic complicity. As with Lucy in *Dracula*, the laborer-victim in some measure wills the capitalist-vampire's parasitical aggression, takes pleasure in the surrender of substance and identity to a remorseless force.

Stuart and Elizabeth Ewen's historical studies of the evolution of an American mass market allege that this self-surrendering desire was meticulously produced through the image-based apparatuses of product design, fashion, and advertising and directed toward an endless project of consumption, thus effecting what Richard Hoggart has called the "consumerization" of the working class.[1] In brief, the capitalist-vampire made willing accomplices of its laborer-victims by soliciting their desire with seductive promises—for example, perpetual youth—and profitably attaching it to an ever-expanding realm of commodities. Note the vampiric metaphors built into the Ewens' description of the results in their book *Channels of Desire: Mass Images and the Shaping of American Consciousness*: "Consumerism engendered passivity and conformity within this supposedly ever-expanding realm of the *new* [emphasis in original], which put leisure, beauty, and pleasure in the reach of all. . . . [T]he logic of consumption . . . is embroiled in our intimacies; tattooed upon our hopes; *demanding of our energies*. . . . The *insatiable urge* for new things" (75–76; emphases added).

Sut Jhally argues, in *The Codes of Advertising: Fetishism and the Political Economy of Meaning in the Consumer Society*, that the extraction of surplus-value in contemporary capitalism extends to the process of decoding advertising texts, that capital has now accomplished a "valorisation of consciousness" which expresses itself in television "watching-labour" (83–89). W. F. Haug's *Critique of Commodity Aesthetics: Appearance, Sexuality and Advertising in Capitalist Society* supports this thesis with a systematic metaphorics of vampirism, invoking capital as a cunning puppet-master whose mechanism of control is the apparatus of advertising, which proliferates a sensuous image-repertoire of commodities that, like Dracula himself, "becomes completely dis-embodied and drifts unencumbered . . . into every household. . . . No one is safe any longer from its amorous glances" (50) save perhaps for those rare few who do not invite it inside because they don't own television sets or buy magazines.

By these analyses, the individual laborer has been irreversibly penetrated by and infected with consumerist desire, an unquenchable, acquisitive lust on which, to return to the Ewens, "shopping centers and urban malls have been built. . . . [W]e have come to live in a visual space consumed by the imagery of commerce, a society organized around the purchase" (74). As Lauren Langman describes the situation: "Feelings are now mass produced and distributed in the shops, theatres and food centres of shopping malls." Subjectivity itself is constructed in the domain of mass consumption; this "is the secret of modern hegemony: the dominant classes, via media, control norms of affective gratification . . . in everyday life" (54). Again, a vampiric metaphor is invoked to describe the process: "everyday life in amusement society proceeds within a dialectic of enfeeblement and empowerment" (43)—enfeeblement because the vampiric regime has usurped the autonomy of individual experience, empowerment because consumption becomes the sole driving motivation. Thus Marx's gluttonous capitalist rat has been transformed into an army of consuming mall-rats, denizens of what Langman has called—updating Max Weber for the postmodern era—the "neon cages" of consumer society.

This specific transformation is cleverly enacted in Francis Ford Coppola's recent film of *Bram Stoker's Dracula*—that staple of mall multiplexes in the summer of 1992—wherein the master vampire converts himself into a multitude of rodents to elude capture. This visually arresting image culminates a scene in which Dracula (whose association with mass culture has already been established in earlier scenes set at his castle, a site dominated by filmic trickery, and at a cinematograph theater in London) promises Mina an eternal life of pathological consumption, an ambivalent empowerment/curse that she avidly seeks. Indeed, she even has to persuade Dracula of her committed desire, a major change from Stoker's original text, where she was his meek, passive victim. For the mall-rats watching Coppola's film, seeing teen idol Winona Ryder (as Mina) affirm her libidinal complicity with consumer capitalism could only, from the draconian Marxist perspective outlined above, serve to damn them to a similar fate.

This sort of judgment illustrates the extent to which the rigid Marxist view of the culture of consumption[2] partakes of what Fredric Jameson has identified as "left puritanism" ("Pleasure" 7); the problem becomes:

"Who is to break the news to them [consumers] that their conscious experience of leisure products—their conscious 'pleasure' in consumption—
is in reality nothing but false consciousness?" (3). In other words, who is
to drive the stake of critique through the vile undead heart of consumerist
desire? Perhaps in reaction to this rigorous negativism, a competing trend
in contemporary cultural studies has attempted critically to redeem the
pleasure taken in consumption. Annette Kuhn has succinctly formulated
the conviction animating this mode of analysis: "pleasure is an area of
analysis in its own right. 'Naive' pleasure, then, becomes admissible. And
the acts of analysis, of deconstruction and of reading 'against the grain'
offer an additional pleasure—the pleasure of resistance, of saying 'no':
not to 'unsophisticated' enjoyment, by ourselves and others, of culturally
dominant images, but to the structures of power which ask us to consume
them uncritically and in highly circumscribed ways" (8).

Indeed, much of the recent work in this area has alleged that the mo-
dalities of consumer culture—and the forms of subjectivity they enable—
do not necessarily integrate seamlessly into the capitalist society which has
mobilized them but may instead be potentially subversive of its purposes.
Recent feminist investigations of the evolution of the fashion system and
the culture of shopping—for example, the work of Rachel Bowlby, Elizabeth Wilson, Anne Friedberg, and Kathy Peiss—argue that consumerism
historically provided genuine empowerment, however limited, for women,
an agency that, according to Wilson, generated profound anxieties about
gender relations in bourgeois society: "The presence of women [in turn-
of-the-century department stores] created a special and ambiguous atmo-
sphere in these zones, which were public, yet aimed at the intimacy of the
private interior. . . . [B]ourgeois consumerism invaded the public sphere,
and the very spaces that were permitted to respectable women were in
many cases devoted to purchase and sale rather than to morally more ele-
vated activities. There, women looked, as well as being looked at" (*Sphinx*
59–60). Friedberg, too, argues for the construction, within the public sites
of consumption—culminating in the contemporary shopping mall, "a historical endpoint of increasing female empowerment"—of an active female
gaze, that of the mobilized flaneuse whose pleasure in the inspection of
commodities was active rather than passive, calculating rather than uncriti-
cal—although, as she stresses, women as a class were still economically
dependent on men and still, in their consumer choices, subject to "a constructed desire" (118–19).[3]

Kathy Peiss, while fully supporting Friedberg's crucial demurrals, also suggests a potentially subversive aspect to consumerism: "Leisure institutions played an intricate game of mediation in which the lines between cultural oppositions—female and male, domestic and public, respectability and disrepute, sexual purity and sensual playfulness—were shifting and indeed blurred" (114). However, as Peiss's work meticulously demonstrates, this shifting and blurring, for all the anxieties it produced in bourgeois culture, was not radically inimical to the ongoing capitalist project of commodification; after all, economic capital is not historically coterminous with the institutions of capitalist society and may in fact be profoundly unsettling of bourgeois norms and assumptions (as Marx himself well knew). Indeed, what the work of these critics suggests is that consumption may now be the terrain where contradictions between the economic forces and the ideological forms of capitalism are highlighted, negotiated, and contested, and that the public spaces of consumer culture stage these contradictions most forcefully. As Don Slater has concluded in his essay "Going Shopping: Markets, Crowds, and Consumption," "the market as a place of desire without obligation, of intimate fantasy in the midst of impersonal anonymity, of spectacle, entertainment and play, as a place where dreams can flow across a multitude of objects without yet being fixed permanently on any one probably still provides the single most potent space in Western societies in which one dreams alternative futures and is released (utopicly) from the unthinking reproduction of daily life" (207).[4]

Given such a viewpoint, it is hardly surprising that the mall-rat has been explicitly thematized—indeed, frankly celebrated—in recent cultural studies, and that this celebration has reversed the metaphorics of vampirism characteristic of "left puritan" discourse. In her discussion of the shifty pleasures of flanerie, Friedberg argues that "the fluid subjectivity of the spectator-shopper" potentially allows for the performative enactment of labile identities under the aegis of "the commodity's transformative power" (120)—a power that, like the shapeshifting vampire's, is protean but not necessarily demonic. In a related discussion, Susan Buck-Morss, building on the work of Walter Benjamin, has elaborated a "politics of loitering" in which "the fantasies which populate the reveries of the flaneur are also a form of resistance," a kind of "strike" against the instrumentalization of leisure ("Flaneur" 136). John Fiske goes farther, depicting malls as "key arenas of struggle" where shoppers "inflict a running series of wounds upon the strategic power" of capitalist calculation, "where the art and tricks of the weak" can overcome the "interests of the powerful" (14)—a reversal of the predatory relationship imagined by the more unyielding critics of mass culture.

Fiske's discussion builds on the work of Australian sociologist M. Presdee, who closely studied the shopping practices of working-class and unemployed youth in Elizabeth, South Australia. According to Presdee, these youth "cut off from normal consumer power" invade by night "the space of those with consumer power," an invasion that boldly lays claim to "the possession of consumer space where their very presence challenges, offends and resists. . . . They parade for several hours, not buying, but presenting, visually, all the contradictions of employment and unemployment" (quoted in Fiske 16). This passive-aggressive territorialism rattles the stolid bourgeois going about their business of consumption, invites the wary attention of mall security, and terrorizes and infuriates the shopkeepers. Presdee dubs their obstinate strategy "proletarian shopping," which Fiske glosses as the consumption of "images and space instead of commodities, a kind of sensuous consumption that [does] not create profits . . . an oppositional cultural practice" (17). If Presdee's marauding mallrats also toted around raucous boom-boxes, Dracula himself might be moved to remark: "Listen to them, the children of the night. What music they make."

Interestingly, this articulation of a subversive vision of consumer vampirism has been a project not only for contemporary cultural studies but for several recent vampire texts, in which Presdee's scene of cruising youthful terrorists has been explicitly staged. In Poppy Z. Brite's *Lost Souls* (1992), a master vampire passes a nightclub where a swarm of punkish kids "postured on the sidewalk, waving their spidery hands, tracking . . . [him] with their black-smudged eyes"; catching a snatch of their music—appropriately enough, New Wave band Bauhaus's song "Bela Lugosi's Dead"— the vampire makes an ironic allusion to "children of the night" (86). In the 1986 Joel Schumacher film *The Lost Boys*, the eponymous pack of adolescent vampires wander sullenly through a crowd of boardwalk shoppers, prompting the owner of a video parlor to throw them out of his store and a security guard to chase them away (much more on this film below).

The competing strands in left cultural analysis canvassed above may thus be said to mobilize contrasting vampire metaphors. Those who argue for an efficient, totalizing system, in which fixed desires are imposed, through the apparatuses of mass culture, on a passive audience of consumers for the dovetailing purposes of capital accumulation and social re-

Figure 1. *The Lost Boys*: Youthful consumers as "proletarian shoppers."

production, deploy a metaphorics of ruthless predation and dictatorial control. Those who believe rather in a less efficient, more contradictory regime, in which desire is relatively fluid, the audience active and even resistant, and economic capital less flawlessly articulated with social institutions, have recourse instead to a metaphorics of playful aggression and changeful identity. My purpose in this paper is not to decide finally between these options—an impossible decision, since I feel they mutually condition, reinforce, and sustain one another [5]—but rather to test the terrain of possibility they make available by analyzing a single vampire text, *The Lost Boys*, which I feel perfectly crystallizes—like *Dracula* for Moretti—the political/libidinal economy of vampirism characteristic of the specific phase of capitalism we inhabit.

*   *   *

Most significantly, *The Lost Boys* locates the vampire within adolescent (sub)culture and thus identifies youth as hegemonic in the contemporary sphere of consumption. This hegemony was empirically accomplished by the singular demographics of the baby boom: the postwar population saw a growth in the number of Americans under the age of 25 from roughly 62 million in 1950 to almost 80 million in 1960 to around 94 million in 1970 and 1980 (Russell 6). As Lawrence Grossberg has observed, the result has been an expansion of consumption, "not only by creating a huge demand for all sorts of products to service the needs of the children . . . , but also by creating an entirely new market. By 1957, the juvenile market was worth over $30 billion a year. This was the first generation of children isolated by business (and especially by advertising and marketing agencies) as an identifiable market" (172–73).[6]

Though Grossberg underestimates the extent to which previous generations of youth were targeted by advertisers,[7] he is certainly correct that the postwar period saw an exacerbation of this process to an unprecedented level of intensity and cultural obviousness. By 1970, a book by the president of an advertising agency was enthusiastically proclaiming *The Youth Market* to be a "$50-billion opportunity" for adventuresome marketers and their lucky clients (Helitzer and Heyel), and a decade later a market research firm was calling young adults "market pacesetters," a "Superclass . . . who have a concentration of buying power that is unique" (Fairchild 1). In 1987, the year after *The Lost Boys* was released, a book called *Youthtrends* estimated this superclass to be solvent to the tune of $200 billion (Graham and Hamdan).

Not surprisingly, the postwar consumerization of youth generated cautionary diatribes—frequently of conservative, as opposed to leftwing, provenance—that mobilized metaphors of vampirism, from Frederick Wertham's notorious 1954 polemic against comic books, *Seduction of the Innocent*, to Ron Goulart's synoptic 1969 indictment, *The Assault on Childhood*, to Neil Postman's 1982 lament over *The Disappearance of Childhood*, to the 1991 study sponsored by the Calvin Center for Christian Scholarship, *Dancing in the Dark: Youth, Popular Culture, and the Electronic Media*. According to Goulart, the "kid business" vampirizes youthful leisure, in the process spawning "an increasingly evident type—a person who is not a kid any more, but who is not really an adolescent or an adult either"—in short, an almost supernaturally transfigured being (Goulart calls it "Superkid") that devours everything in its path: "He graduates from kid consumer to affluent teenage consumer to young married consumer. He goes from having 2.6 billion dollars worth of toys bought for him each year to spending 20 billion dollars a year on lingerie, surfboards, motorcycles, deodorants, hamburgers, skis, mouthwash, eye makeup, phonograph records, used cars, movies, etc., to being 100 million dollars in debt through installment buying" (4).[8] These Superkids live eternally in a "cold antiseptic magic kingdom" of consumption, a "vast Disneyland" (95).

The vampiric implications of Disney's commercial appeal to youth are intriguingly glossed in Robert R. McCammon's novel, *They Thirst* (1991), which depicts the vampiric takeover of that capital of consumer fantasies, Los Angeles, and introduces its master vampire—wearing a Beach Boys T-shirt—at Disneyland. The theme park is closed for the night, but the vampire uses his powers to activate one of the rides: "He smiled, entranced, wishing that someday he could meet the one who had built this magnificent place; he thought that if he owned this place, he would never grow tired of playing here, not in the whole eternity of existence that lay before him" (110). Given Goulart's scathing portrait of Disney, the two would have had much in common: "Disney's greatest disservice to children was the persistent imposition of his lifeless dream on them" (66)—in fact, like the endless pall of vampire existence.[9]

Likewise, *The Disappearance of Childhood* and *Dancing in the Dark* depict contemporary youth as unmoored from traditional sources of community by the lures and snares of mass culture, united instead—according to the latter text—as "citizens in a new, commercially prescribed electronic culture" (47), entry into which is arranged by "ritual induction" into consumerism (141–42). This sort of vision is common on the left as well: Jacques Attali's critique of the commodification of popular music offers a similar view of the "confinement of youth" in "a separate . . . society with its own interests and its own culture"; in Attali's analysis, "socialization through identity of consumption"[10] produces a "channelization of childhood" that propels youth toward the "huge anonymous retail outlets where mass production is shamelessly displayed, where children come, fascinated by the Pied Piper of Hamelin" (109–11).[11]

These visions of swarming, feeding mall-rats were more than the paranoiac fantasies of mass culture critics; they were also observable realities. In 1956, the first enclosed mall opened; between 1964 and 1982, the number of shopping centers—including strip-malls as well as enclosed malls—increased 300 percent, from 7,600 to over 23,000 (Jacobs 45). By 1985, there were, as William Kowinski's *The Malling of America* details, "more enclosed malls than cities, four-year colleges, or television stations" (20) and Americans spent "more time in malls than anywhere except home, job, or school" (22). A Rutgers University study has found that a substantial number of suburban adolescents now locate their homes geographically as, for example, "Three miles from the Oxford Valley Mall" or "Near Quaker Bridge Mall" (quoted in Jones, *Great Expectations* 229), an unsurprising fact given the eagerness with which young people have taken to malljamming from the beginning. A study commissioned by the International Council of Shopping Centers concluded that "teenagers in suburban centers are bored and come to shopping centers mainly as a place to go"—a recourse the study advised management to encourage (quoted in Kowinski 350). Mall festivities, including the annexation of cinema culture into multiplexes,[12] combined with the widespread tendency of parents to use the mall as a babysitter, have led to the rise of a distinctive mall culture through which, in Kowinski's words, teenagers are "educated in consumption" (351).

According to the critics, the result is at once the premature sophistication of youth and the juvenilization of society generally—or, in the words of Joshua Meyerowitz, the simultaneous production of "the adult-like child and the childlike adult." Kowinski cites psychologist David Elkin's concept of " 'the hurried child': kids who are exposed to too much of the adult world too quickly" (351), while Jerry Jacobs, in his book on malls as "an attempted escape from everyday life," deploys sociologist Georg Simmel's notion of "the blasé attitude" to describe the cruising hordes (93).[13] Such critiques evinced deep anxiety that the collective confinement of youth in walled consumerist enclaves was producing a generation of precociously jaded hedonists and cynical delinquents, an anxiety that frequently crystallized around that rallying point of mall youth culture, the video arcade. Not only were these parlors sources of concern in the relative murkiness of their interiors—which made them potential sites for drug transactions—but teenagers' visceral absorption in the games was often attacked as itself a kind of addiction, a vampiric hunger.[14]

In 1982, Surgeon General C. Everett Koop declared that young people were in thrall "body and soul" to video game-playing, which caused "aberrations in childhood behavior" (quoted in Jacobs 84). Psychoanalytic critic Martin Klein agreed, arguing—in an article called "The Bite of Pac-Man"—that video games appealed to the oral-sadistic drive in adolescents, the very drive Ernest Jones, in his influential Freudian study *On the Nightmare*, identified with the vampire (120). Some accounts suggested that video games were producing new forms of consciousness in kids, hyperkinetic attunements of perception and reflex reminiscent of the preternatural sensory-motor apparatus of Anne Rice's vampires (e.g., Sudnow; Greenfield 97–126), while others depicted violence-addled teens as stupefied as the zombies shambling through George Romero's 1979 classic film of mall life, *Dawn of the Dead*. In the hysterical vision of novelist Martin Amis, the denizens of the arcades became subhuman fiends, a "blank-screen generation" moving through a hellish neon landscape: "Who are these that haunt the electronic grottoes . . . these proletarian triffids, these darkness-worshippers?" (20). Jacobs sums up the dystopic world constructed in gaming scenarios in terms of a stark, vampiric choice: "one is either the victim or victimizer. One eats or is eaten" (85).

This popular demonizing of video games figures as a major element in S. P. Somtow's novel *Vampire Junction* (1984), which centers on a vampire rock star, Timmy Valentine, whose consumer spin-offs include a video game called *Bloodsucker*, in which the player slays hordes of the undead. Ironically, however, the game itself is one of a series of commercial snares drawing teens into a vampiric world of cynical exploitation. Significantly, the story climaxes literally within the game scenario—"Terry hid in the shadow of the arcade machine, but it was a huge gravestone with a video screen instead of an inscription and the words strobing on-off on-off were ALL TIME HIGH SCORE TERRY GISH—VAMPIRE JUNCTION HALL OF FAME—WELCOME TO HELL" (345)—and the enticements of vampirism are truly warded off only with the explosion of this blood-sucking machine. For his part, Timmy Valentine, despite appearing perpetually pre-pubescent, is actually millennia old, and this lingering doom of a timeworn spirit inhabiting a juvenile body also becomes the fate of the teenage fans drawn in by his consumerist lures.[15]

The flip side of the premature adult-eration of children effected by the regime of mall culture is the pervasive juvenilization of adults.[16] As Tracy Davis has observed in her essay on " . . . the Mall That Ate Downtown," the video game functions as a microcosm of the mall as a whole, its spectacularization of perception and affect mirroring the shopper's experience of the entire glitzy, ersatz environment.[17] Marsha Kinder argues, in her book *Playing with Power*, that video games have become a major contemporary medium of socialization through consumption, one which need no longer be abandoned with adolescence but may become a lifelong project. The enveloping power of consumerist paradigms imbibed in youth was attacked by Goulart, whose vision of Superkids depicted them as victims of a Peter Pan complex, "growing up falsely, or never growing up at all" (3). According to Calvin Center's *Dancing in the Dark*, the result is a generalized "youthification," a "state of arrested development" that "encourages everyone, including adults and young children, to think and act like adolescents" (64–65).

The contemporary consumer is thus, like the vampire, trapped in a stasis of perpetual youth, an ongoing *Teenage Tyranny*, as Grace and Fred M. Hechinger put it in the title of their 1963 polemic, whose reign is as endless as the capacity of capitalism to generate ever-new, ever-youthful commodities. As *Dancing in the Dark* sourly observes, "Increasing years seem to breed not acceptance of mortality or the pursuit of wisdom" but rather "rapidly changing patterns of adult consumption, lifestyles, and leisure activities, all pursued in the hope of recovering adolescent bliss" (66). Stuart Ewen has shown how youth first emerged in the 1920s as a "desirable and salable commodity" in capitalist culture, as well as a fullblown consumerist ethos; for Ewen, "The symbolic ascendancy of youth represents the corporate infiltration of daily life and the creation of a family structure that might be ruled through the young, or through people's acceptance of a youthful ideal" (*Captains* 146). The hegemony of youth within consumer culture was consolidated in the postwar baby boom generation, for whom (according to Grossberg) "youth is something to be held on to by cultural and physical effort" (183), an immortality promised by the seductive apparatuses of fashion and advertising, where youth is displayed, modeled, and marketed.[18] Like Mephistopheles, consumer culture offers a Faustian bargain, a vampiric promise of undying youth which transforms its initiates into voracious consumers.

The title of this essay, "Consuming Youth," should thus be seen as a pun remarking three separate though intertwined dimensions of analysis; it refers to 1) an empirical youth culture of consumption, literal malljammers; 2) a libidinal impulse to (metaphorically) consume youth, through images and other commodities;[19] and 3) a general cultural obsession, a fanatical project (as in, capitalist society is "consumed by youth"). The modern vampire, then, can be a youthful consumer, a consumer of youth, or a figure consumed by a mythology of youth—or all three at once. Such a set of distinctions is necessary in order to tease out the complexity of contemporary capitalism's privileging of youth in its system of consumption. This complexity is strikingly enacted, for example, in the casting of David Bowie and Catherine Deneuve as seductive vampires in Tony Scott's 1983 film *The Hunger*, since both stars are famous for 1) marketing consumer objects—rock albums, skin lotions—to youth audiences; 2) maintaining a preternaturally youthful appearance into middle age; and 3) evoking a dream of eternal youth in their persons and in their product messages. Scott, erstwhile director of TV commercials and music videos, brought the visual register of these media in imagery and editing to the film, making *The Hunger* an exemplary work of consumer vampirism. However, it brings together my three modes of analysis largely extradiegetically, at the level of form rather than of story, while *The Lost Boys* does so more pervasively, especially in its foregrounding of contemporary youth culture as the site where the analysis must be performed.

*   *   *

The Lost Boys is set in the fictitious California town of Santa Carla (actually, the movie was filmed largely in Santa Cruz and makes prominent use of one of that beachside city's major attractions, an extensive carnivalesque boardwalk). The story centers on a family, Lucy and her two sons, Michael (roughly seventeen) and Sam (perhaps thirteen), who have moved from Phoenix following a difficult divorce to stay with the boys' maternal grandfather, a crusty old curmudgeon who lives a bucolic hermit's life in a rambling farmhouse on the outskirts of Santa Carla. While Lucy takes a job working at a video store on the boardwalk owned by the suave Max, whom she also begins to date, her sons fall in with the local teenagers—Michael with a pack of leather-clad motorcycle punks led by the charismatic David, Sam with a pair of survivalist weirdos, the Frog Brothers. David's gang lures Michael into a nocturnal life of drugs and dangerous thrill-seeking, while the Frog Brothers fill Sam's head with comic-book fantasies of exterminating the confederacy of vampires that, so they claim, secretly infests Santa Carla.

Of course, this undead coterie is David's gang, who are attempting to initiate Michael into their ranks. Michael is persuaded to drink from a decanter containing David's blood, which gives him the power to fly but also infects him with an incipient bloodlust. When David and his crew finally reveal their true natures to Michael by slaughtering a competing youth gang and urging him to join in the bloodshed, Michael tries to escape from their control and, in the process, to save the lives of two other initiate vampires—Star, a teenage girl with whom he has fallen in love, and Laddie, her pre-adolescent friend. Armed with such weapons as homemade crossbows and holy-water squirt-guns, as well as with knowledge provided by the Frog Brothers—for example, that initiate or "half" vampires will become human again if the "head" vampire is slain—Sam comes to Michael's aid,

Figure 2. *The Lost Boys*: The ingratiating master vampire of consumer capitalism.

and they mount a pitched battle with David's gang that destroys the latter
entirely. However, Michael, Star, and Laddie do not revert to normal but
continue to display vampiric qualities such as fangs, glowing eyes, and feral
appetites, indicating that the true head vampire has yet to be dispatched.
This villain turns out to be Max, who not only has been insinuating himself
into Lucy's good graces but has also been secretly stagemanaging David's
efforts to draw Michael into his own undead "family"—his ultimate goal
being to secure a mother for his footloose brood of bloodsuckers. Just as it
appears Lucy is about to break down and accept his proposal, her crusty
old dad appears and saves the day, staking Max and releasing the family
from his clutches.

   What Max represents, beyond the obvious threat of a usurper trying
to supplant the boys' absent father, is the incarnate power of consumer
culture itself, his video parlor vending mass fantasy to all of Santa Carla
("How may I help you this evening?" he asks Lucy when she first enters his
establishment. "We have it all"). Significantly, Lucy's father, who thwarts
Max's plot in the end, does not—indeed refuses to—own a television set;
this refusal is part of a hippie-style rejection of modern society, the lat-

ter focused in the figure of slick yuppie Max, the master vampire whose puppet-strings extend into every household with a TV and VCR.[20] His wooing of Lucy involves an infiltration of the domestic space of the home, a cozy privatization of consumption Lucy's children fully expect to enjoy. Not only is Michael the one who literally invites the vampire inside when he arrives at the house for a date with Lucy, but, more tellingly, Sam is anguished by his grandfather's banishment of television because he has no access to MTV, the national organon of mass youth culture (although he is not entirely happy about its personification in Max, whose designs on his mother disturb the boy).

That Max stands in for MTV and its consumer youth culture is proven by the appearance and lifestyle of his vampire brood. Max's minions, David and his blackclad gang of heavy-metal punks, are living their own ersatz vision of 1960s Dionysiac revels in a music-video-style cavern decked out with a giant poster of Jim Morrison. This lifestyle, for all its seductive appeal to Michael—and, by implication, to the teenage audience of the film itself—is ultimately depicted as a wantonly destructive fantasy manipulated by a cynical agency of power; it is Max's local version of MTV, a glitzy dream of illusory adolescent autonomy.[21] (As Anne Rice's *The Vampire Lestat*, another novel with a vampire rock star for protagonist, attests, there is "something vampiric about rock music," especially in its institutionalization on MTV [6].) Against this vampiric co-optation of a rock-and-roll ethos, the film counterpoints not simply the grandfather's literal autonomy, a rural idyll disconnected from the mass "channels of desire"— to borrow a phrase of the Ewens—but, more generally, an "innocent" version of the '60s, ultimately represented by Laddie, who runs around throughout the film wearing a Sgt. Pepper jacket and whose salvation from vampiric takeover becomes a central motivation of the plot. Basically, Michael, Star, and Laddie emerge at the end as a perfect neo-hippie family purified of the taint of teencult vampirism vended by the mercenary Max.

By contrast, the members of the original '60s generation are depicted as either naively complicit with power or blind to its effects, an easy-going generation of neglectful parents who have left their children ill-equipped to resist the blandishments of mass culture. Lucy, an erstwhile flower child who thinks the only real difference between her own youth and David's gang is that the latter "dress better," readily falls under the spell of Max, and her father prefers to ignore the spread of vampirism throughout the region, intervening only when it intrudes into his own home. The militant Frog Brothers (Edgar and Alan) have been fighting the vampires virtu-

ally alone, while their parents—a stereotypical pair of tie-dyed dopers—
snooze behind the counter of the family comic-book store. The film's title
can thus be taken to refer not only to David's crew but to the Frog Brothers, to Michael and Sam, indeed to the entire '80s generation, seduced and
abandoned in a garish teenage wasteland presided over by a vampiric
image-apparatus which has become a kind of surrogate father. That the
'60s generation is hopelessly muddled-headed in the face of this evolution
is suggested early on, as Lucy, driving her sons into Santa Carla—the
"murder capital of the world" according to a roadside graffito only Michael
notices—starts humming along to a lite-rock radio station playing the Ras-
cals' 1967 hit "Groovin'": "That's from my generation," she coos; "Mm,
mellow," Michael snorts contemptuously, while Sam moans, "Change it."

As this scene also demonstrates, "youth" taste in music has been
thoroughly segmented by generation, to the point where individual radio
stations appeal to specific demographics within the baby-boom population.
The same is true, of course, regarding cinematic taste. Whatever its view of
the pernicious effects of mass-marketed youth culture, *The Lost Boys* cannot
escape the fact that it also belongs in this category. Its awkward positioning
produces an ambivalence that can be perceived in the film's depiction of
David's gang, who, for all that they are intended as cautionary figures displaying the dangers of teencult posturing, nonetheless must be made to
seem genuinely attractive and fascinating, not only to Michael but to the
entire teenage audience. This sort of attraction-repulsion pattern is, according to Christopher Craft, a narrative strategy characteristic of vampire—and, more broadly, monster—stories: the text "first invites or admits
a monster, then entertains and is entertained by monstrosity for some extended duration, until in its closing pages it expels or repudiates the monster and all the disruptions that he/she/it brings" (167). In the case of *The
Lost Boys*, however, the monster is consumer youth culture generally, and
thus its expulsion is more a matter of bad faith than in other vampire texts,
since its genuine extirpation would require that the film destroy itself.

Beyond the obvious material constraints dictated by the conditions
of its reception, a more generous reading of the film's ambivalence about
youth consumption is possible: it can be viewed, simply, as a "realistic"
portrayal of the fundamental ambiguities of consumerism generally. Indeed, the film potently enacts the divided vision of consumer vampirism
adumbrated in the first section of this chapter: on the one hand, David and
his gang represent a delusory fantasy of youthful autonomy packaged and
broadcast by Max, a seductive vision of rebellious adolescent hipness that

is actually merely a cat's-paw of power; on the other hand, they are an unpredictable, even dangerous agency, mercurially resistant to Max's authority and perhaps finally uncontrollable.

The precise relationship between David's gang and Max is never fully made clear: while Max is identified as the "head" vampire who ostensibly uses David as his pawn to enslave other teens, the few scenes of them together suggest that Max is genuinely afraid of David and not entirely certain of his loyalty. When Lucy first meets Max at the video store, David's gang wander in, desultorily engaging in the sort of "proletarian shopping" outlined by Fiske above. "I told you not to come in here anymore," Max says to David, who smirks at him as he leaves; "wild kids," Max then comments to Lucy, with a note of tense irritation. Later, as Max is returning home alone from a date with Lucy, David's gang shadow him, frightening him by racing their motorcycle engines and sending crashing down onto his head a large kite with a comical bat-face painted on it—thus mocking Max's pretensions to vampiric domination and asserting a more playful vampire identity. This is not to suggest that Max is not a real threat or that he exercises no authentic power, but rather to indicate that the scope and limits of his control are in some measure undecidable.

Which is also to say that the seeming autonomy of Max's teenage prey—and, by extension, of all youthful consumers—may be in some measure genuine. The profound anxieties evinced by the critics of youth consumption canvassed above certainly indicate that the desires activated and the powers unleashed in youth by their interpolation into the market system disturb adult observers—who respond by denigrating teenagers' apparent independence as an ideological sham. Yet, as we have seen, some feminist critics have alleged that the solicitation of female consumers by mass-market capitalism is a real form of empowerment, however limited it might be by economic circumstance or by the range of self-fashioning available to women in a patriarchal culture. Likewise, the empowerment of teens as consumers, however stunted the horizon of their alternatives, can be viewed as progressive, in that it stakes out a domain of desire and decision for a population traditionally expected, like women, to be socially passive, to know their place.

In fact, just as, according to Wilson, turn-of-the-century department stores became an "ambiguous zone" where the conventional gender hierarchy seemed to dissolve, so too, it can be argued, contemporary mall culture has produced a space where teens, otherwise a subject population, move and act with the casual confidence of adults. And, just as nineteenth-century men were nonplussed by the lively presence of women shoppers, so too do today's adults fret about the insubordinate forwardness of adolescents flocking at the multiplexes and the gallerias—and, as we have seen, the video arcades—as if the mall belonged to them. But really, this insolent pervasion does no more than materialize the ethical privilege generally accorded youth consumption within postwar capitalism. As Martyn Lee describes the situation in his book *Consumer Culture Reborn: The Cultural Politics of Consumption*, "capitalism developed and defined the social category of youth which became the most prominent materialization of the new mass-consumption ethic," in the process "enfranchis[ing] youth with the material and symbolic resources which could be used as potential weapons of cultural subversion" (106–7). Grossberg offers a similar argument: "the privileged place of youth [in postwar society] enabled it to resist its own subordination by foregrounding the sense of its own difference, a difference which had already been constructed for it. If youth represented . . . [America's] most valued commodity, then why shouldn't it celebrate itself as an end in itself, as a distinct and independent formation standing apart from, if not in radical opposition to, the adult world which had created it and endowed it, unknowingly, with such powers?" (178).

In *The Lost Boys*, the central site of this militant assertion of empowered independence is the Santa Carla boardwalk, a sort of combination open-air mall, gaming arcade, and amusement park. Always aswarm with throngs of teens, this venue provides several carnivalesque montages throughout the film, snapshots of sundrenched festive abandon, with kids leisurely browsing (and shoplifting), playing video games, riding rollercoasters, cruising for dates or for trouble, and otherwise acting as if they owned the world. Within this bustling environment, Max's video parlor is merely one of a number of consumer choices available, however exalted Max's view of his youth-cultural power might be. Just across the way, in fact, is the Frog Brothers' comic book store, where horror titles like *Vampires Everywhere* and *Destroy All Vampires* provide information—not always reliable, as it turns out—on combating Max's infernal designs. As represented by the boardwalk, the youth culture landscape of the film is a confused and confusing domain of fun and danger, of surveillance and subversion, and the teens peopling it a volatile mix of hybridized subcultures, parading around to the discomfiture of the baffled adults. These look much more "lost" on the boardwalk than any of the boys or girls do, and most of them probably—like Lucy's father—prefer to avoid this raucous scene entirely.

All of which is not to say that teenagers really own the boardwalk—or the malls—or even that their empowerment amounts to a great deal more than the power to affront, to enact a mutinous posturing that is obviously susceptible to commodification and mass-mediation by teencult vampires like Max. As Dick Hebdige, that signal analyst of youth subculture, has observed, "The relationship between the spectacular subculture and the various industries which service and exploit it is notoriously ambiguous. After all, such a subculture is concerned first and foremost with consumption. . . . It communicates through commodities. . . . It is therefore . . . difficult to maintain any absolute distinction between commercial exploitation on the one hand and creativity/originality on the other" (94–95). Contemporary capitalism's fetishism of youth as a privileged category within the domain of consumption makes possible both a real cultural agency for adolescents and a cynical recuperation of youthful leisure as "lifestyle"; consumption thus becomes for teens both an avenue of self-expression and also of objectification in the form of fashion. The result is an ambivalent dialectic of empowerment and exploitation, in which teens are both consumers and consumed, vampires and victims. What Moretti says of *Dracula*—that it operates by means of "*dialectical* relations, in which the opposites, instead of separating out and entering into conflict, exist in function of one another, reinforce one another" (108; emphasis in original)—is equally true of *The Lost Boys*, which maintains throughout, in a state of dialectical tension, opposing visions of youth consumption—and, indeed, consumption generally.

Part Four

READING
THE
OTHER

12

The Gilda Stories:
Revealing the Monsters at the Margins

MIRIAM JONES

"You've searched admirably for your humanity. Indeed, this is the key to the joy found in our lives, maintaining our link in the chain of living things. But we are no longer the same as they. We are no longer the same as we once were ourselves."
—Jewelle Gomez, *The Gilda Stories* 210

[T]he deconstructivist can use herself (assuming one is at one's own disposal) as a shuttle between the center (inside) and the margin (outside) and thus narrate a displacement.
—Gayatri Chakravorty Spivak, *In Other Worlds* 107

These two quotations are emblematic of a tension in Jewelle Gomez's *The Gilda Stories* (1991): the tension between the rewriting of generic conventions from the margins of literary discourse, and the contradictory fixedness of the resulting narrative position. Michel de Certeau uses the term "Brownian motion" to refer to the ways the disempowered tactically consume elements of hegemonic culture to create more resonant meanings. Constance Penley uses this idea as a departure for her analysis of women who produce amateur 'zines within science-fiction fandom, although she points out that these women go beyond a transitory consumption to produce actual products that "(admiringly) mimic and mock" their mass cultural progenitors (139). Although Gomez's *Gilda Stories* was published commercially, albeit by a small feminist press, her approach to the vampire genre can best be understood in the context of de Certeau's term for the appropriation and rewriting of cultural artifacts: *poaching*. Of the response of indigenous peoples to the Spanish conquest, for example, de

Certeau writes: "They metaphorized the dominant order: they made it function in another register. They remained other within the system which they assimilated and which assimilated them externally. They diverted it without leaving it. Procedures of consumption maintained their difference in the very space that the occupier was organizing" (32).

Artists from groups that are culturally disenfranchised must by definition have a complicated relationship to the traditions within which they produce their work. The more culturally specific the historical location of the tradition, the more concrete the elements with which to interact. Given the structures and shared referents implicit in most genre fiction, it seems an ideal preserve for poaching. Both the vampire genre and book publishing, here specifically horror and science-fiction publishing, have excluded and continue to exclude African-Americans, lesbians, and writers from other marginalized groupings. By rewriting the vampire from an oppositional position and by publishing genre fiction with smaller feminist publishers, Gomez—like Pat Califia and Jody Scott, two other authors who play with the lesbian vampire—moves beyond the tactic of consumption, which de Certeau maintains is "a calculated action determined by the absence of a proper locus" (37), and reappropriates the cultural space of genre fiction from the subject rather than the object position.

The vampire, perhaps more than any other imaginative figure, has fulfilled, and has generally been *seen* to have fulfilled, a cluster of related metaphoric functions within literary discourse. Critical responses generally function to expand the existing shared generic referents, rather than to decode them in a separate stream of discourse. Historically, the vampire has figured as a danger from without. The vampire is the monster that threatens the white middle-class male protagonists in Bram Stoker's *Dracula* (1897): he is largely absent, an exotic metaphor for an unspecified contagion which they perceive to be preying on a vulnerable, homogeneous society. This is part of what Patrick Brantlinger identifies as the European fear of civilization reverting to a "primitive," atavistic state, or "going native" (230). This danger, the fictional narrative reassures, can ultimately be controlled and vanquished by scientific reason.[1]

In the earlier *Carmilla* (1872), J. Sheridan Le Fanu uses a similar model, although the impurity and contagion are more specifically—and titillatingly—figured as a voluptuous, unnameable lesbianism. In the 1993 "White Issue" of *The Village Voice*, Eric Lott offers a glossary of "whiteness" in which he alludes to Dracula as a "primitive nobleman from the East," a "sort of one-man miscegenation machine" who represents "hysterical fears of Anglo-American imperial decline" (39). This reading has for some time been held as a truism in cultural criticism, and now we see it reflected more accessibly.[2] However, Lott extends his meaning when he writes, "Dracula then and now portends the withering of empire by those on whom it formerly fed" (39). Here one could add that the vampire, by its very existence as an alternative set of meanings, simultaneously consolidates and threatens the idea of empire. With the use of the unambiguous term "fed," Lott's construction implies a shift in vision from the perspectives of the colonizers—Van Helsing and company—to those of the colonized. Instead of from "without," the threat is now from those who have done without. Further, his phrase "portends the withering" implies an even greater shift—a global historical shift to a post-colonial world where previous dominant subject positions are no longer tenable and new, perhaps unimagined ones, will replace them.

Gomez's *The Gilda Stories* self-consciously rewrites both the genre and the representation of the vampire figure. But most radical is her transformation of the metaphoric function of the vampire and vampirism. Her text evokes the traditional generic notions of social contagion at the same time as it unmasks the metaphors. It asks: who are really made monsters in contemporary hegemonic discourse? The broad answer is: the disenfranchised. Gomez inverts the historical metaphoric functions of the vampire and reinscribes them with meaning, both from within literary discourse itself and from a location outside, on the margins. To refer back to the quotation by Spivak that opens this discussion, *The Gilda Stories* narrates a series of displacements, some of which successfully challenge received subject positions and some of which, perversely, reinforce them. It undertakes a series of negotiations: 1) from inside the genre itself, 2) in relation to contemporary reworkings of generic paradigms, and 3) within the broader context of political discourse and scholarship.

As both *Carmilla* and *Dracula* colonize a mythical "East" as the site of all that threatens the British Empire—Le Fanu's text through its use of unnatural sexuality as a marker of degeneration and Stoker's through its frantic enforcement of heterosexual norms[3]—these canonical texts also colonize even the possibility of lesbian representation. Vampirism functions as a metaphor for lesbianism in Gomez's text as well, but this is neither the decadent, threatening lesbianism of the nineteenth-century popular imagination nor the pseudo-lesbianism of the B-movies of the 1970s that take *Carmilla* as their point of departure[4]; the vision in *Gilda* is explicitly politicized and finally has more in common with Pat Califia's de-

scription of lesbian sadomasochism from her introduction to *Macho Sluts*
(1988)—"this [painful] experience of radical difference, separate at the root
of perception" (9)—than it does with cleavage and fangs. Further, while
lesbianism is arguably foregrounded, it is indivisible from categories of race
and class: Gilda's outcast status is situated within a nexus of exploitation.

Gomez has herself spoken publicly against a false division of oppres-
sions when she critiques those who would separate her gender from her
race, class, and sexuality with their exclamation, "But you're a *woman!*"
(Gaylaxicon). The vampire, then, functions in Gomez's text as the vampire
often has in literature: as a floating category of all things "alien" to the
normative forces of official cultural discourses. However, instead of threatening from outside the frame of the narrative, Gomez's vampires construct
an inclusive vision of those traditionally absent from literary discourses in
general, and sf, horror, and especially vampire tales in particular.[5]

Gomez inverts textual conventions. Her text examines the real threat:
a black working-class lesbian, opposed by implication to the white, European, aristocratic, male vampire-norm of Count Dracula, Barnabas Collins,
and Lestat de Lioncourt.[6] If Stoker's Count is a "one man miscegenation
machine," as Eric Lott would have it, located where sexuality and politics
converge (Hatlen 133),[7] what then is Gilda, once enslaved, whose historical
counterparts were subject to enforced pregnancies because of rape and
other forms of sexual coercion? Gomez's generic reversal indicates who
paid the price when the colonizers felt threatened from without; it shows
us the face of the real monster.

It is here that the category of "vampire" ceases to be a fluid marker of
"otherness" and becomes a fixed subject position on a political and historical grid. As such, it both opposes the received Eurocentric assumptions
of the gothic and vampire genres, while it reifies the constant, shaping
consciousness of the classic realist text.[8] In this, *Gilda* is perversely more
conservative, for all its progressive politics, than the fractured perspectives
of the hallucinatory gothic that historically opposed the certainties of the
mainstream novel.[9]

Re/Writing History

Gomez's narrative is chronological, but episodic rather than continuous.
The character of Gilda produces a contemporary, engaged entry into historical events from the perspective of those marginalized by or made absent

from standard accounts. In brief, Gilda, as yet unnamed,[10] escapes slavery in 1850 and is helped by two vampires, Gilda and Bird. The original Gilda decides she has lived long enough and leaves her legacy to the Girl, who takes on her name. The new Gilda moves from place to place over the next two centuries. By the twenty-first century, the earth has become contaminated and all who can afford to do so live off-world. Vampires are hunted for their blood. Gilda and other vampires finally retreat to Machu Picchu to form a closed community.

Gomez's narrative is, in effect, a series of mini-narratives, set in different geographic locations in the United States and later in Latin America, usually at intervals of several decades. Gilda's movements through these locations play with the center/periphery metaphor discussed earlier in relation to the vampire genre. Gilda moves from the rural South to the boom town of San Francisco, then back east to a small town, then to the cultural center of Boston, and next to New York, the center of the universe. The latter part of the text reverses this movement from periphery to center: Gilda rejects the magnetic power of the metropolis and goes to rural New England, and then back to the southwest to hide, and then finally out of the United States altogether and into Peru. The roles of space, place, identity, and history intertwine and are played out in a concrete geographical journey that can be plotted on a map.

The term "stories" in the title implies both the separation of the narratives, and also their connectedness through the qualifier "Gilda." These are not stories in the sense of independent narratives; "stories" means episodes in an overarching whole. In a literal sense, of course, that "whole" is the extended life of the protagonist. But just as Gilda, as vampire, functions as a metaphor for marginality in general and the position of African-American women specifically, the episodes in her life function as markers of key historical junctures in African-American history. The fictional narrative cannot rewrite the historical one—Gomez says that she made a conscious decision not to have Gilda save Angela Davis and the Black Panthers, for instance, in the chapter set in the 1970s (Gaylaxicon)—but it can provide a cohesive vantage point from which to re-view it. While Gilda may "grow" as a character, her subject position is stable; her perspective orders the narrative without rupture.

The word "story" is resonant in the text; the characters discover commonalities by exchanging their life-stories. Bird teaches the recently-enslaved Girl, soon to be named Gilda, narratives from her own Native American culture: "Bird taught the Girl first from the Bible and the newspaper. Neither of them could see themselves reflected there," just as they are not present in the Eurocentric vampire genre. "Then Bird told the Girl stories from her own childhood, using them to teach her to write" (21). Bird encourages the Girl to recall her own memories of her Fulani mother: "Of the home their mother spoke about, the Girl was less certain. It was always a dream place—distant, unreal. Except the talk of dancing. The Girl could close her eyes and almost hear the rhythmic shuffling of feet, the bells and gourds. All kept beat inside her body, and the feel of heat from an open fire made the dream place real. Talking of it now, her body rocked slightly as if she had been rewoven into that old circle of dancers. She poured out the images and names, proud of her own ability to weave a story. Bird smiled at her pupil who claimed her past, reassuring her silently" (39).

Although the original Gilda says to the Girl, of vampires, "There are only inadequate words to speak for who we are. The language is crude, the history false" (43), it is not Vlad the Impaler and peasants with torches that the text foregrounds, but a Native American woman and an African escaped from slavery, searching for their own languages separate from the received narratives of the Bible and the newspapers. In this sense of "stories," then, the text itself can be read as a simultaneous sharing, and seeking, of personal and collective histories in the face of a monolithic, exclusionary discourse. This reading is reinforced by the production of the text as an artifact; the artwork on the paper cover simulates marbled endpapers and incorporates a turn-of-the-century photograph of the author's great-aunt: these design features are more consistent with the packaging of autobiography than with conventional vampire fiction. Gomez writes elsewhere that she has incorporated real people into the text, specifically her stepmother Henrietta Walker, who appears in the novel "as her own monument to the vibrant history of leadership that black women of little means have provided" ("Retta's House").

In this reading of the narrative, the immortality of the vampire functions as a metaphor for the continuities, as well as the evolutions, of the African-American community through time. At one point Gilda realizes that she has had no sense of the future throughout her life and that she has merely adapted to shifting events. She then determines to look forward and to think of herself as "part of another line of history" (216). She means, here, that she is different from mortals. But again, rather than tracing the histories of the more ancient vampires, Sorel and Effie, the text constructs a thread of African-American women's history, beginning with the struggle out from under slavery, and distinct from received white male narratives.

But if Gomez as author is functioning as a "shuttle," in Spivak's sense, between the margins and the center, she is doing so in a double way. She is representing black history from the perspective of the enslaved, and she is also writing genre fiction that inverts the traditional figure of the vampire as landowner and master of serfs as in *Dracula*, or more to the point, as Southern plantation owner as in Anne Rice's *Interview with the Vampire* (1976).[11]

In the second chapter, Gilda, newly made vampire, solidifies her persona and shifts from the position of prey to that of predator. Gomez has elsewhere spoken about the meaning of constructing a black protagonist, who because of her race has historically been hunted, as the hunter: she characterizes such an inversion as "terrifying" (Gaylaxicon). Terrifying but powerful: through Gilda the text refuses the imposition of a narrative of oppression. In her next incarnation, Gilda takes on the persona of a widow/farmer and helps another African-American woman become politically active within the context of community and church work, and obliquely, within the broader politics of the African-American cultural transformations of the 1920s.

In 1955 Gilda owns a hairdressing shop in Boston, the historical center of many significant political and social movements, among them abolitionism and the black women's club movement.[12] It is at this time that she first feels strong connection to an identifiable community: she says, "In the shop I've grown to understand the rhythm of their lives, their desires" (157). Gilda becomes a kind of voyeur of her own culture, trying to forge connections with the people she left behind by becoming a vampire. Vampirism functions here as a marker of the displacement from one's own history that oppression imposes.

The importance of the small neighborhood shops such as Gilda's, in their roles as cultural and informational clearing houses, should not be minimized. Gilda's notion of community is an inclusive one, as many of her clients, whom she befriends, respects, and protects, are prostitutes. Nor should the significance of hair—black hair—be underestimated as a marker of pride and cultural identity: "The shiny copper color of [her customer] Savannah's round face was topped by her crowning glory: a thick head of hair that she kept bleached white. She'd seen a picture of an aboriginal tribesman in *National Geographic* and was seduced by the dark skin in contrast to the stark plainness of sun-bleached hair. . . . Gilda closed her eyes and felt her mother's hands combing and braiding her hair. She remembered the sharp tugs and the pull of her scalp as the hair was caught

back in the thick braids running like rows of corn across her scalp" (129–
30, 131). Savannah takes control of the manipulated (mis)representation of
herself in the hegemonic mass culture of the American empire; she reappropriates the exoticized, commodified *National Geographic* construction
of peripheral "blackness" from the marketplace and brazenly recreates it
on her own body, "fronting-out oppression," as Kobena Mercer writes in
"Black Hair/Style Politics," "by the artful manipulation of appearances"
(49), just as Gomez stakes out occupied literary territory, recasts the marginalized "other," and allows Blacula to step into the center.

In 1971 Gilda lives and works within the wider white community in
New York. She critiques the Civil Rights movement for its failure to be
inclusive of women, Puerto Ricans, lesbians, and gay men: "Gilda was surprised at the depth of her own feelings, about the disappointment she had
seen on the faces of black women over the years" (170). In the next "story,"
the expansion of her life is paralleled to that of the progressive political
movements in the 1980s. She lives within a circle of lesbians and her upstairs
neighbor is a transvestite: sexuality is foregrounded and this segment can
be read as a marker of the rise of the women's movement and of lesbian
and gay liberation. At this point, the timeline of the text intersects with
"real" time. It is here that the two strains of history, mortal and vampire,
diverge. Gilda withdraws from society with her lover; the text abandons the
chronological historical narrative and turns to speculative rather than gothic
generic conventions. But until this point, the meta-chronology of political
and cultural struggle provides the narrative structure, and Gilda functions
as the site of insertion, constant although floating forward through time,
for contemporary historical interpretation.

Traditionally, the vampire exists in an adversarial relationship to a human "society" figured as seamless. S/he is other, alien. Her or his situation
necessitates hiding and "passing" in order both to remain anonymous and
to lull victims; this construction, of course, plays on fears of a secret corruption from within. In *Gilda*, passing as mortal is literally survival, a survival that resonates with the conflicted significance of "passing" to people
of color, lesbians, and gay men. Although a vampire—a superhuman, immortal creature who plays different roles over the years—Gilda is always
black. She is, for example, attacked by Klansmen in the rural South, although she effectively defends herself. But this is no facile turning of the
historical tables; unlike her blood-sucking counterparts in mass culture,
violence does not come easily to her. Nor is she only subject to the racism

of mortals; in one scene, white nineteenth-century vampires are reluctant to drink in the same bar with her.

As well as being black, Gilda is also visible as a lesbian: with rare exceptions she unrepentantly dresses, and acts, butch. She wears trousers; she is courtly to other women. Even in nineteenth-century San Francisco, she wears a suit made with floor-length culottes, and she reminisces about the times she has seen women tramping the countryside dressed as men, "just going around from place to place trying to live free. . . . Four times!" (66). She herself dresses for the hunt in clothes coded as "masculine," in a self-conscious adherence to recuperated narratives of lesbian history.[13] She is black; she cross-dresses; and, by deliberately not "passing"—by putting herself at risk by drawing attention to markers of race and sexual identity—Gilda perversely camouflages her real secret: her vampirism.[14] She flirts with the reader and the other characters alike in her flamboyant embrace of the visual codings of dangerous differences that obscure the central, undeniable difference of her nature. In this sense she too is passing, paradoxically by refusing to "pass."

Re / Writing Desire

As Sue-Ellen Case notes in "Tracking the Vampire," the "apparatus of representation" belongs to the unqueer (9). Le Fanu's *Carmilla* is narrated by the victim/heroine, Laura. She situates herself as heterosexual—or rather, as "normal," as there was, arguably, no such category as "heterosexual" in the mid-nineteenth century[15]—because there are no other nameable options. Despite this, she is tempted into unnatural same-sex desire by the vampire: "I experienced a strange tumultuous excitement that was pleasurable, ever and anon, mingled with a vague sense of fear and disgust" (90).

The figure of the lesbian as an aberration who threatens the sexual *status quo* has been translated virtually without modification into contemporary mass culture. Miriam Blaylock, Whitley Strieber's vampire in *The Hunger* (1981), provides just such a threat to Sarah Roberts. While Laura is theoretically protected by her position as a virtuous and innocent lady, Sarah, a medical doctor in contemporary Manhattan, has her knowledge and experience with which to defend herself. Neither shield is sufficient: "Miriam made another noise, one that was familiar to Sarah. It was her own little chortle, the one she always made when she was penetrated. To hear it under these circumstances [drawing blood for medical testing], in the throat of another woman, was faintly revolting. . . . She longed to be free of Mrs. Blaylock's touch. It was undeniably pleasurable and the very delight of it was what was so awful" (107).

Unlike the virginal Laura, Sarah is in a sexually fulfilling relationship with a man, and yet despite strenuous resistance she also falls prey to the contagion of homosexuality. Gomez exposes such conflicted constructions of same-sex desire as the hysterical rationalizations of oppressive practices. Vampirism, in the oppositional lesbian texts of Jewelle Gomez, Jody Scott, and Pat Califia—texts that are themselves as different from each other as they are from *Carmilla*—inverts the historical codings associated with the genre.[16] In these texts it functions as a metaphor for the alienation of the lesbian (or gay man) in a world that is compulsorily heterosexual.

It is useful in this context briefly to comment about the radical reappropriation, through amateur or fan writing, which has taken place in a related popular genre. I am referring here to a type of non-commercial writing known as *slash*, an examination of which can shed some light on the treatment of proscribed desire. *Slash* is a sub-genre of self-produced fan writing. In mainstream fan magazines, or "fanzines," the authors construct narratives within the parameters—or at least within their perceptions of the parameters—of a commercial media series. There are fanzines concerned with *Doctor Who*, *Beauty and the Beast*, and *Star Trek*, to name some of the most common. These 'zines are distributed through the mails, at conventions, and electronically.

Slash fanzines take the same general format, but with an important variation: they take their name from the phrase "Kirk/Spock" (Kirk-slash-Spock), and they involve same-sex relationships between the protagonists that concretize the homo-social relations implicit in the media originals. One frequent scenario is the coming-out, or first-time story.[17] In a similar fashion, vampire stories, particularly the soap opera *Dark Shadows*, have often been re-written by fans, and vampire-slash exists as a sub-genre of slash fanzines.[18]

Vampire slash is interesting in the context of this discussion because of the way it treats the revelation of the secret desire. In other, non-vampire slash, homosexuality is usually the issue: one character agonizes over his— and it is virtually always "his"—secret love for his police partner/fellow spy/starship captain, who is figured as straight, and who he assumes would be shocked, disgusted, and embarrassed to discover himself the object of forbidden lust. Much of the story-line is taken up with this dilemma, which is finally resolved when the star-crossed lovers come together in a glorious sexual encounter. In vampire-slash, however, there is no space to worry about coming out to the loved one as gay, because one is preoccupied with the even more problematic coming out as a vampire. The characters are still gay, but that gayness is perversely normalized by the "otherness" of vampirism. Vampirism serves the same narrative function as does homo-erotic desire in non-vampire slash. It is the literary trope of the guilty secret one fears, yet longs, to impart.[19]

Gilda is part of this dynamic; her characterization blends the trope of the dangerous secret, where the identity of vampire elides that of les-bian, with the affirmation of the coming-out story. She experiences some-thing like what Sue-Ellen Case calls the "plentitude and pain" of the word "queer" (1) when she first becomes vampire: "Gilda allowed the feeling of loss to drift through her as they sped into the darkness. Along with it came a sense of completion, too. There was certain knowledge of the world around her, excitement about the unknown that lay ahead, and comfort with her new life" (50). She sounds like nothing so much as a neophyte dyke contemplating her expanding horizons.

In this context, an interesting comparison can be made to Tanya Huff's vampire series, the fourth novel of which, *Blood Pact*, was published in 1993 by Daw, a mainstream commercial press.[20] Henry Fitzroy, who as the "bastard son of Henry VIII" can thumb his hooked nose even at Count Dracula, is a vampire, a bisexual vampire in a novel series where all the other sexual relationships are heterosexual. It is as if Henry were the only char-acter who could safely—in commercial sf and horror publishing—be in-vested with that euphemistic notion, an "alternate" sexuality, because he is a vampire and that position implies a certain decadence. As in the slash 'zines, blood has no gender.[21] Anne Rice takes this notion one step further; her vampires do not have genital sex at all. She depoliticizes Judith Hal-berstam's notion, in *On Our Backs*, of vampirism as the expression of same-sex desire in the imagining of a sexual practice that has no need for genital intercourse, or what Sue-Ellen Case characterizes as "a draining away" rather than "the impregnating kiss of the heterosexual" (15). Rather, her vampires are "hyper-Platonic"; they experience intense whole-body sexual feelings when they feed, as if they were involved in a mass-culture, bi-gendered enactment of Luce Irigaray's contention that women's entire bodies constitute an erogenous zone (28). Here the slippage between vam-pirism and pansexuality is complete.

Gomez, in a move that can be characterized as radical given the current parameters of the genre, has removed bloodsucking from sexual pleasure so that lesbian eroticism is foregrounded in its own right and not elided and normalized by vampirism. Her characters both feed and have sex, but usually not with the same people. When they exchange blood with other vampires, it is not exactly feeding, but functions as a symbolic sexual sharing. Conversely, taking blood to feed is about power and involves intense sensations, but it is not sex. This distinction desexualizes power and particularly the feminine helplessness that is usually so compellingly present in the vampire mythos. In *Carmilla*, for example, Laura is relentlessly pursued by the lesbian vampire even in her sleep. Of her dreams, Laura says: "Sometimes it was as if warm lips kissed me, and longer and more lovingly as they reached my throat, but there the caress fixed itself. My heart beat faster, my breathing rose and fell rapidly and full drawn; a sobbing, that rose into a sense of strangulation, supervened, and turned into a dreadful convulsion, in which my senses left me, and I became unconscious" (105–6).

Pat Califia brings the Victorian dream into waking reality when she uses the cultural codings of vampirism as a short-hand for lesbian s & m practices in her story "The Vampire": "it hurt so much for so long that she came, came even as the canines sank another notch into her cuts and drank fresh blood from the deepened wound. Which penetration made her come? She did not know" (259). The lesbianism in *Gilda* must be read in relation to this range of representation.

The blood-taking in Gomez's text is feeding, a compulsion, an urge or appetite. These terms are often used to evoke sexuality, but not by Gomez. The sex in *Gilda* is egalitarian, and minimal compared with current publishing practices. Gilda does not have sex with mortals. She carefully segregates feeding as a category separate from sexual practice; it is an enticing category, ultimately more compelling than the erotic passages. The scenes of feeding position the reader as voyeur, as an illicit viewer of the desire of another and as a consumer of erotically resonant images. The reader often follows Gilda after a victim down an alley, through a window, or into the small space of a parked car to view illicit private acts in public or semi-public spaces. The descriptions of sex, in contrast, explicitly deny voyeuristic pleasure:

[Bird] pressed Gilda's mouth to the red slash, letting the blood wash across Gilda's face. Soon Gilda drank eagerly, filling herself, and as she did her hand massaged

Bird's breast, first touching the nipple gently with curiosity, then roughly. She wanted to know this body that gave her life. Her heart swelled with their blood, a tide between two shores. To an outsider the sight may have been one of horror: their faces red and shining, their eyes unfocused and black, the sound of their bodies slick with wetness, tight with life. Yet it was a birth. The mother finally able to bring her child into the world, to look at her. It was not death that claimed Gilda. It was Bird. (140)

The reader is positioned as the outsider, her squeamish reactions anticipated, even specifically assigned. Yet the text goes on to reinterpret the image of the blinded, bloody women—simultaneously newborns and mothers both—as an affirmative evocation of female power in a graphic inversion of the usual treatment of monstrous birth in sf and horror, from *Frankenstein* to the *Alien* film series.

Re / Writing Power

At another level of metaphor, the text serves as a prescriptive model for a lesbian-feminist way of being. "Lesbian" is a political category, indivisible from the lived experience of women. In *Gilda* we see the creation of what more visceral fans of the genre might dismiss as the "politically-correct" vampire: she is interactive rather than a succubus; she eschews the conventional decadence and violence of the genre and replaces it with the purposeful violence of a metaphorical childbirth. Gilda gives back something when she feeds. She calls it "trading," or the "exchange":

She caught [her chosen donor] up in her gaze, then probed his mind for what he might be seeking. . . .
   Gilda had never encountered such a void of desire. . . . He seemed full of only himself. She sensed a greed for gold. . . . Little else appeared to be of consequence. . . . He was on his way to gamble and thought only of winning—even if it meant cheating. Gilda sliced the soft flesh of his neck and caught him up in her arm. She bent to him in the shadow. . . . She sucked insistently at his life blood, almost losing herself in the need for the blood and in her disappointment in the smallness of his vision. Gilda . . . slipped in among his thoughts with the idea that cheating was merely a way of shortening the possibilities for his own life.
   She urged this realization into his resisting mind as she took her share of the blood. (57)

There is a problem here, of course, around the issue of lack of consent: the passive partner to this "exchange" never agrees, either to the act of

feeding itself, or to the nature of the thoughts or impulses Gilda leaves
behind. This oversight presents an unresolved difficulty that indicates a potential rupture in Gomez's vision of respectful mutual dependency. An
ethic that would allow for such a construction must ultimately reject the
liberal notion of the sanctity of the individual will in favor of some greater
good, such as the community, however defined. This is certainly an un-
American idea; but then, one might ask what the American state ever did
for Gilda.

The appeal of the vampire has been recognized by many recent writers, and the vampire has consequently grown increasingly sympathetic,
even domesticated, since Stoker's influential description of a Lombrosian
sub-human criminal. Writers in the genre are then faced with the dilemma
of how to characterize the vampire's feeding: no matter how graphic, the
reader or viewer must not be completely alienated. The results are often
unsatisfactory. Anne Rice's vampires, if they become old and powerful
enough, cease to need to feed. In *The Tale of the Body Thief* (1992), for
example, Lestat admits that he still enjoys feeding, but he limits himself to
that most inhuman of criminals, the serial killer, "one of those splendid
human trophies whose gruesome modus operandi reads for pages in the
computer files of the mortal law enforcement agencies" (10). The text
does not deny the pleasure of the "big game hunt" (10)—rather, it sensa-
tionalizes it—but it reframes it in a moral universe far removed from the
nineteenth-century vampire's remorseless offstage visits to his or her slowly
languishing prey. Victorian moral categories have overtaken vampire morality, although a binary code is still in place.[22]

Other writers resolve the dilemma of feeding by eroding the conventional polarity between mortal and immortal, monster and human.
Chelsea Quinn Yarbro's Saint-Germain, as "a vampire living through the
centuries, would have to become a very compassionate person" (Riccardo
17); he does not kill when he feeds. Instead, he thoughtfully exchanges
extremely good sex for the blood he drinks: "Her back arched suddenly
and she shivered ecstatically. A cry escaped her before she could stop it, but
her joy was so profoundly private that the sound was not very loud. She
felt flushed, and her feet, which had grown colder, were pulsingly warm in
the sweeping delicious frenzy coursing through her. Her fingers were sunk
in his dark, loose curls that pressed her cheek as he bent his head against
her neck" (133).[23]

In *The Vampire Tapestry* (1980), Suzy McKee Charnas's vampire must periodically hibernate in order to forget the ties he inevitably forms during each of his forays among humans. His cyclical realization that the "sheep" are more like him than is comfortable threatens his continued existence and so nature compensates. In Steven Brust's *Agyar* (1993), Jonathan, whose initial patterns with his prey closely resemble the nineteenth-century model, falls in love with a mortal, Susan, and ends up sacrificing himself for her. Jody Scott's Sterling O'Blivion is a metatextual vampire who tactically positions herself along with her reader as a delighted consumer of the vampire mythos: "I adore being a vampire. I love the lore, history, rich tradition and sense of fabulous majesty it confers on an otherwise simple, sentimental, and perhaps boring older woman. The only part that wearies me is the convulsive outrage and vain lamentations, the barbed words of cruel slander, as a selfish world fights to hang onto that few lousy, crummy, measly drops of blood" (5).

These various possibilities—turning vigilante, refiguring feeding as consensual sex, becoming more "human," postmodern displacement, humor—are not possible within Gomez's framework. Since for her vampirism functions as a category apart—a site for African Americans and other people of color, women, lesbians and gays, and others written as monsters by dominant discourses—she cannot demonize criminals without accepting the punitive terms of the criminal justice system and creating division and hierarchy within the ranks of the marginalized. Gilda herself begins as a criminal, since by escaping from slavery, she steals herself.[24] Nor, as the "other," can she comfortably climb into bed for ecstatic sex with those who exclude and erase her. Instead, vampire and mortal must co-exist in uneasy symbiosis, and finally, the vampires must separate themselves from their former prey.

The text ultimately reformulates the hunter/prey relationship and emphasizes the importance of a vampire community quite different from Dracula's patriarchal family or Anne Rice's élite grouping. Gilda's extended community also includes mortal women, such as the young Boston hooker she rescues from her pimp, and her lesbian-feminist friends in New York. In the final segment, Gilda seeks sanctuary in Machu Picchu, a site resonant with the history of indigenous people, in the company of other vampires: two black lesbians, a straight black man, two gay white men, and a Native American lesbian. Barnabas Collins is pointedly not invited. Here the novel curiously evokes de Certeau's characterization of the indigenous peoples who faced the Spanish conquest: "they metaphorized the domi-

nant order: they made it function in another register" (32). The vampires
have literally returned to the site of original conquest and refigured it as
a haven.

It is possible to read in Gomez's text both a tendency to separatism
and a certain essentialism, particularly in its final chapter, but also throughout in her characterization of the respectful, sharing vampire. In this sense
Gomez does not locate herself in the postmodern tradition of Queer
Theory that deconstructs the fixed subject position and postulates a same-
sex desire that is not gender-specific.[25] Rather than constructing a binary
distinction, however, between "essentialism" (simple) and "postmodernism" (sophisticated), we might more usefully develop a more nuanced
reading of Gomez's apparent essentialism and what it might signify. Or
more importantly, what it might accomplish. Identity is not the same as
essence. Communities and alliances between different groupings based on
notions of shared identity can serve important tactical functions. Identity
in this wider, strategic sense is not the depoliticized, ontological position
described by critics, one based on notions of a fundamental essence. Ultimately, the otherness of the vampires is based on their relationship—their
lack of access—to power, rather than to any shared core identity; certainly
the final grouping is diverse in all respects but one, and that is their subordinate construction in hegemonic discourse. As Diana Fuss points out in
Essentially Speaking, African-American writers *begin* with a double—or in
Gomez's case, a triple or quadruple—consciousness: might not Gomez's
agenda have more to do with the integration rather than the deconstruction of the self?[26] By building the narrative completely around the stable
subject position of Gilda as a self-conscious alternative to the productions
of hegemonic literary discourse, Gomez's text displays its own fixed hierarchy of discourses, one of which is clearly privileged in much the same way
as in Catherine Belsey's prototypical classic realist text. She eschews the
playfulness and ambiguity of the gothic—a playfulness that Califia and
Scott have in their different ways embraced wholeheartedly, so that there
would seem to be more than one way to skin the same cat—as a conscious
political choice to reclaim the metaphoric representation of the exoticized,
threatening "other."

In the end, the vampires themselves are hunted. The categories
"hunter" and "prey" are reversed in a genocidal erasure of difference. The
vampires become commodities to humans eager to achieve immortality,
and the narrative echoes the first section, in which the Girl, by escaping
slavery, rejects her position as commodity. Who are the *real* monsters,

then? Racists, rapists, and pimps, and the power-hungry rich who hire the Hunters to track down the vampires and who, as governments and corporations, have poisoned the earth beyond repair. These are the people who literally feed off others.

Such *engagement* is hardly surprising from Gomez, a long-time activist with a clearly articulated perspective who has said that she does not regard political consciousness as a boundary to writing, but rather an opportunity to "open up." She has noted, for instance, that sf writers are not writing to the people of the future (Gaylaxicon); Gomez is here indicating her conscious use of gothic and sf tropes in isolation from the larger generic paradigms her text categorically rejects. Despite her radical appropriation of genre, the transparency of her agenda could perhaps be seen to have more in common with that of the second-wave feminist sf writers of the 1970s like Joanna Russ and Suzy McKee Charnas.[27] At the same time, Gomez is no doubt aware that this is a tradition that excludes African-American writers almost as completely as does that of hard sf. Gomez is rewriting history, and she is also rewriting the sf and horror genres, and Western print culture in general. She is locating herself as Gayatri Spivak's shuttle, which moves back and forth from the margins to the center and deconstructs literary and historical narratives simultaneously from without and within. In this sense she reappropriates the vampire genre itself as a metaphor—a metaphor of vilification, absence, and exclusion—and reinscribes it with other possibilities.

Preliminary work for this essay was presented at the Association of Canadian College and University Teachers of English Conference (ACCUTE), Carleton University, Ottawa, 1 June 1993. I would like to thank the Social Sciences and Humanities Research Council of Canada for their generous support, and Veronica Hollinger for her editorial suggestions. I also owe a debt of gratitude to Nancy Johnston and Joe Galbo for their insights here and elsewhere.

13

Coming Out of the Coffin:

Gay Males and Queer Goths in Contemporary Vampire Fiction

TREVOR HOLMES

The following preliminary look at gay male vampire fiction in the 1990s starts from two distinct but intersecting identity-places which I am calling queer and goth punk respectively. They do not exist independently of one another, although their overlappings are neither simply defined nor always obvious. The place I call *queer*—I'm going to let the term develop as I use it—has a terrain that has been variously mapped, and its borders are necessarily shifting, not so much to accommodate different populations but to produce difference itself. The place I call *goth punk* is characterized by local and international intersections of a style, a shifting scene of self-representations and productive reading practices. "Gothic punks," or "batcavers," or "goths" for short, are people who, since the late 1970s, have used the figure of the vampire to inflect their readings and productions of music, philosophy, literature, film, dance, fashion, and sexuality. To get from one place to the other is not so difficult: this essay functions, not unlike the Borgo Pass in *Dracula*, as one opening between these two geographies of subjectivity. I start from these places because they are zoned for construction—the construction of an object of study called gay male vampire fiction. I do not believe that such an object exists prior to the gaze of the surveyor's instrument, nor that it exists as a fixed datum point in that operation. I will argue that the iterability and conjoining of the terms gay, male, vampire, and fiction are very much conditioned by contemporary versions of the places from which I begin, though how and where and for whom is a question to which I do not assume any permanently fixed answer.

One of the assumptions I do make in the following pages is that a text is social: it does not exist in and of itself waiting to match certain pre-existent generic categories that guarantee its meaning. Although it would be easier to define gay male vampire fiction in terms of an identity between gay male authors, same-sex male vampire content, and a hypothetical gay male readership, the available fiction itself troubles this attempt at equivalence. Vampire narratives in which marks of male-male desire exist implicitly or explicitly have been written by men and women who self-identify as gay, straight, queer, lesbian, dyke, bisexual, transgendered, or transsexual, as well as by writers to whom these categories would not have been conceivable in their own day. For this reason alone, the meanings constituted over time and space by these taxonomies are completely unstable. The content of the works to be discussed varies considerably, and, as a category, "male" itself is thrown into disarray by the particular ability of vampires to transform themselves from moment to moment. The form of the works varies too: novels and short stories, bestsellers and niche-market erotica, editorial introductions, and original fiction downloaded from the internet all come into play. As well, new technologies of narrative production, like the internet discussion list to which I'll return later, entail new modes of subjective experience. So the being and becoming which occur in the narrativizations of writers, characters, and readers are fantastically over-determined.

When, therefore, I invoke and yoke together the terms "gay male vampire fiction," I do so most guardedly. While the 1990s have thus far seen the proliferation of stories about male vampires who desire men—whatever that may mean in terms of blood/lust, psychology, sex, predator and prey, or topographies of the vampire self—these stories are unifiable in only the most general sense. They are all about relationships, by which I mean those between (usually) men *in* the texts, and those which circulate *around* the texts, among authors and readers of multiple and varied gender and sexual identifications. It is in these relationships that the phenomenon of goth is rendered visible as a reciprocally determining strategy. What follows is, in part, an attempt to sort out how gay male vampires and queer goths get articulated together—and how they sometimes do not. In some cases queer goths are the writers and written-about in vampire fiction; in other cases, they are the style and the attitude that many gay writers and readers would rather forget, or, in fact, completely disavow.

Codes: Goth and Self I

The following narrative offers one way into the intersection of goth iconicity and sexual transgression. Though site-specific, it speaks to the elasticity of meaning-production on the part of at least two goth-identified and queer subjects in a manner that can be generalized: many marginalized communities find themselves in the rather unique position of offering "perverse" readings of otherwise fairly benign moments.

Some years ago, my partner and I went to see Peter Murphy, former lead singer of the goth punk band Bauhaus, perform in Toronto. The opening band was Nine Inch Nails, a neo-industrial band/artist destined to be featured on the soundtrack accompanying the 1994 film adaptation of the comic book *The Crow*.[1] The band was touring in support of its 1989 album, *Pretty Hate Machine*. We were struck by the NIN symbol on the opening band's concert shirts: we knew that Bauhaus had recorded a song called "Antonin Artaud" and my partner had recently been exploring the epistolary connection between Artaud and Anaïs Nin. The NIN/Nin connection seemed more than coincidental, so, correctly or not, we read this as an ironic display of a relationship between a literary/theatrical avant-garde in high modernity and a musical avant-garde in postmodern "low" culture. This is not the place to argue the point, but rather to demonstrate that, at any given staging of cultural phenomena, there are multiple entry points for readings based on embedded genealogical codes, whether or not these codes were intentionally put there by anyone. Our reading of this particular moment involves all sorts of boundary transgressions: in order to produce the meaning we attached to the scene, we both had to be familiar with a rich "underground" of alternative rock and a fairly unknown link between two figures in alternative "high culture"—as well as with the index that marks Anaïs Nin as bisexual.[2] To be thus familiar is often to script oneself as authentic in identity terms—the more arcane trivia available to me, the more I become an expert in subjectivity games. My point is that goth punk identities, by no means as stable as many would like them to be, exist by suturing the canonical and anti-canonical, the cynical and the romantic, the high and the low, the straight and the queer, most often via the index of the Gothic tradition in general and through one of its figures in particular: the vampire.

Not uncoincidentally, readers of gay and lesbian Camp also actively produce meanings out of embedded genealogical codes.[3] It matters little

what was intentionally placed "out there" for the purposes of canny recognition; what matters is the sense of community and difference circumscribed by the adeptness with which a group of people reads, shares, and
circulates meanings. Camp readers are equally camp writers, or, as Eve
Kosofsky Sedgwick puts it in her discussion about the difference between
"kitsch-attribution" and "Camp-recognition," the latter's operations acknowledge "that its perceptions are necessarily also creations" (156). Normally, certain linguistic and textual codes *mark* certain subject categories
while leaving a hegemonic set of subjectivities *unmarked*.[4] However, gay
and lesbian readers can and do produce alternate meanings even within the
most naturalized heteronormative scripts, marking those un- or otherwise-
marked categories with difference. Hollywood Romance, for instance, has
been the site for numerous constructions of gay and lesbian icons. As well,
beginning (as far as I know) in academic discourse with Sue-Ellen Case's
"Tracking the Vampire" (1991), the often archetypally-configured hetero
or homosexual predatory vampire has been the site for decidedly *queer*
re-writings. This process allows for identity to be something other than
sameness, for identity to be supplemented by difference. Identity is not
something that easily fits the taxonomies we construct for it. J. Gordon
Melton's *The Vampire Book: The Encyclopedia of the Undead* (1994) provides an example of exactly this desire to contain meaning by categorizing
phenomena.

Melton's form of taxonomizing defines both goth and homosexuality
in and through separate lists of attributes, while simultaneously drawing
dubiously wrought conclusions about how they relate to each other. The
main entry for "goth" in *The Vampire Book* is found under the heading
"Gothic" (262) and the subheading "The New Gothic Movement" (264).
This entry defines the "gothic counter-cultural movement that appeared
in most urban centers in the 1980s" (264) as a mixture of the gothic tradition in fiction and rock music subcultures of the '60s and '70s, and it offers
readers a list of the music, fanzines, and clubs that have defined what is
elsewhere in the book called a "special slice of rock and roll" (424). In
general, Melton's view of the goth movement in rock is characterized by a
listing of bands that focus on vampire motifs and gloomy music or physical embodiments thereof. He does, however, mention the connection between goth sexuality and gay politics:

As a secondary theme, based in part on the androgynous ideal, the gothic world has
continued a self-conscious critique of the dominant sexual mores of late twentieth

century society. This critique was also present in previous movements such as punk rock. . . . Some have noticed that the androgynous ideal (as articulated by [Anne] Rice and embodied most forcefully in her male characters) supported and was, in many ways, indistinguishable from the value system of the gay community. The homosexual aspect of the gothic world has been presented most clearly in Poppy Z. Brite's writing. (268)

It is interesting that "androgynous ideals" are generally thought to reside in both *male* characters and *male* goths.[5] In any case, Melton goes on to define the goth movement in terms of sexual subversions, creating as he does so a kind of hierarchy of degrees of subversion: "Beyond just a demand for sexual freedom or the acceptance of homosexuality, some gothic music and literature has also argued for the destruction of the taboos that surround sado-masochism (an essentially androgynous activity that explores the pleasure of pain), fetishism, bondage, and all sexual activities still considered perverted even by many who consider themselves otherwise sexually liberated" (269).

Though troubling to the extent that this definition of sado-masochism (S/M) insists on its essential androgyny, it is probably correct to suggest that these forms of subjective interaction are considered too extreme by several communities of sexually progressive individuals. The figure of the vampire, however, can mediate among goth, gay, and S/M in fiction, as we shall see in the novels and short stories to be taken up later.

What is missed by Melton's hierarchized taxonomies of identity is the possibility of crossover. Once we generate a listing of codes by which we know whether a vampire text is gay or not—creating a set of identity-guarantors such as the gender and sexuality of the author or the characters—we very much limit what counts as authentic or pure in terms of identity. Thus, for example, we are asked by Melton, in his discussion of "Homosexuality and the Vampire" (301–2), to accept Jeffrey McMahan's *Vampires Anonymous* (1991) as gay male vampire fiction while treating Jewelle Gomez's *Gilda Stories* (1991) as lesbian (under the heading "Lesbian Vampires" [362–65] and the subheading "Recent Additions" [365]). These categorical distinctions have a curious way of co-opting the gender and sexuality of the author as the marker of their authenticity. But there are times when texts like these ought not to be separated in this manner. For me, it is as important to interrogate the identity politics of Sorel and Anthony, the male characters marked as gay in *The Gilda Stories*, as it is to analyze McMahan's male vampires in relation to each other and to the female vampires around them, mainly because both texts embody a moral high ground not altogether satisfying to those readers with an appetite for the horrific. The answer is not simply to umbrella them with "queer"—for that in itself could conflate very different projects and effects. I would rather hold texts like these up against moments in the erotica I will be considering or against a novel like Poppy Z. Brite's *Lost Souls* (1992), because these moments tend to hybridize sexuality and goth punk impulses in a manner that no encyclopedic list of attributes can contain. The basic point I want to reiterate is that there is no necessary equivalence between gay authors, gay fictional characters, and gay readers. This is not a search for positive or negative representations, but rather a questioning of the ground on which we base our understandings of gender, sexuality, and identity.

Now and Then: Historical Notes

The title of my essay, "Coming Out of the Coffin," would seem to suggest that gay male vampires are currently enjoying an unprecedented relation to identity and public space—that is to say, they are "out of the closet" where they used to be "in" it waiting to be decoded or discovered, and this must therefore be something to celebrate. It is tempting to characterize such relatively recent novels as Jeffrey McMahan's *Vampires Anonymous* and Gary Bowen's *Diary of a Vampire* (1995) in terms of a progression. While previous incarnations of fictional vampires have manifested codes read as gay by—at the very least—those interested in decoding textual desires, contemporary versions of the vampire can unabashedly iterate their same-sex desires, orientations, preferences, or identities. It is certainly a welcome moment in the genre when communities largely informed by the decoding and recognition practices of Camp can openly own what has always been "ours," writing it into being and reading it in the context of an increasingly receptive audience. Unfortunately, to ascribe progressive *gay male* meanings in any simple way to texts which are often resistant to stable categories of gender and sexuality—and here I would include most vampire configurations ever penned—is to elide their power to actively elicit (and put into flux) subjective identity fictions.

There is a peculiar mix at work in end-of-the-millennium reanimations of the vampire figure, a mix that includes embodied decadence, cynical neo-Romanticism, HIV, savvy camp, and, I would add, a post-punk aesthetic. This mix happens not only in published novels and short story collections, but in film, in music, on e-mail discussion lists and World Wide Web pages, in comic books and fanzines, and in the performance of everyday life. I want to ask what difference this mix really does make in the rearrangement of taken-for-granted identity designations such as gay, lesbian, bi, and straight. How do exclusively gay male narratives fit or not fit the work of Poppy Z. Brite, for instance, the twenty-something crowd's answer to publishing-machine Anne Rice? There's also the issue of transgender vampire erotica, more and more of which seems to be "coming out of the coffin" in an interesting relationship to more novelistic interventions like McMahan's. Something else which has not received much attention from fans of narrative constructions of subjectivity happens electronically: what sorts of identity constructions are enabled or disabled by the phenomenon of the internet "persona"—a hybrid virtual subject who inhabits multiple spaces at once?[6] I will approach all these questions indirectly at first, by way of a particular reading of vampire heritage.

Genealogically speaking, when Pam Keesey organized the stories in her first anthology, *Daughters of Darkness: Lesbian Vampire Stories* (1993), the leading entry was obviously Joseph Sheridan Le Fanu's novella *Carmilla*, first published in 1872. What was it that made this filiative move so obvious? Beginning with Sue-Ellen Case's "Tracking the Vampire" and continuing now in films like *Dry Kisses Only* (dir. Kaucyila Brooke and Jane Cottis, 1990), and essays such as Tanya Krzywinska's "La Belle Dame Sans Merci?" (1995), lesbian theorizing about vampire identification in subjective self-construction has been far more sophisticated than that done by gay men about gay male vampires—the most notable exception being Ellis Hanson's "Undead" (1988), an essay on the connections between AIDS and *Dracula*. The recent publication of Michael Rowe and Thomas S. Roche's *Sons of Darkness: Tales of Men, Blood, and Immortality* (1996), arising, as it were, from the groundwork performed by Keesey's collections, seems to signal a catching up of sorts by those who want to think about vampires and gay males. Yet why is it that *Daughters of Darkness* can present a tradition of lesbianism which (by republishing it) posits *Carmilla* (the only male-written contribution to the anthology) as its originary moment, while *Sons of Darkness* seeks the beginning of its heritage in a Poppy Z. Brite story, "His Mouth Will Taste of Wormwood," first published in 1990?

Something like an answer lies in the different ways that gendered history operates: the rendering visible of male same-sex textual desire is performed in a different manner to that of female same-sex textual desire. Given patriarchy in articulation with capitalism, men could encode same-

sex desire at a safe remove from self through women.[7] I'm thinking here of
Aubrey and Lord Ruthven through Aubrey's sister in John Polidori's *The
Vampyre* (1819), as well as of Dracula and his hunters through Lucy and
Mina in Stoker's *Dracula* (1897). Again, given patriarchy in articulation
with capitalism, representations of women's same-sex desire—always already a threatening Other—have been, and still might be, less mediated
through the body or subjectivity of an other. It is worth reminding ourselves that the "original" women characters now readable as both vampiric
and lesbian—Coleridge's Geraldine and Christabel and Le Fanu's Carmilla
and Laura—are male-generated narrative constructions. This is certainly
not to suggest that there is some totalizing meaning in them that we can
therefore pin down, but simply to point out that it is through their appropriation from a differently situated perspective that one configures these
texts as lesbian narratives.

I don't think there can be much agreement at present about which
nineteenth-century vampire narrative signals the beginning of representational depth in gay male vampire fiction. Which codings "mean" gay or
lesbian and which demarcate at least non-heteronormative terrain among
vampire anthologists and readers are hardly agreed upon. Is *Dracula* the
first gay male vampire text, including as it does scenes such as the Count's
possession of the feminized Jonathan?[8] To take a different tack, let me suggest that it is perhaps by way of Count Eric Stenbock, creator of the lovely
(when sated) Count Vardalek, that certain of the generic codes become
settled, codes through which we might say with certainty in our glance
back that a text embodies gay male vampire subjectivity.

While it's impossible to take stock of all the means by which we might
uncover the presence of gay-themed content in literature, I do think we
can gesture towards some of them at work in Stenbock's "A True Story
of a Vampyre" (1894): the displacement of male-male desire through an
aged and desexualized "female" narrative gaze; reiterations of a Classics-
inflected cult of male youth; perhaps the absent mother and ineffectual
father; references to unfettered sexuality. In Stenbock's story, we find
ourselves addressed by an aged and eccentric woman named Carmela, who
narrates the story of her family's ruination at the hands of a vampire. The
path to the description of the vampire is not straight: along the way the
mother is absented, the foreign-marked governess is introduced, the benevolent father is described in the kindliest terms, and she spends a full
three paragraphs—quite full in relation to other paragraphs—describing
the "difficult to describe" (119) victim of the vampire's desire, her angelic

brother Gabriel. Gabriel will not eat meat and he is very much aligned with nature and the animal kingdom. His lips and mouth are feminized, and the sentence describing his form becomes breathless, a fragment punctuated by an exclamation mark: "Then that beautiful, lithe, living, elastic form!" (120). He is described as "praeterhuman, something between the animal and the divine" (120). The classical clue is brought in at the same point, though even this is not sufficient to the descriptive task: "Perhaps the Greek idea of the Faun might illustrate what I mean; but that will not do either" (120). Why will that not do? Because it is not enough in that historical juncture to leave description at the level of comparison. Gabriel's wildness must have meaning traced through ethnicity, his mother "having been of gipsy race" (120), which is the first suggestion of a sexuality coded as unconventional, unstable, and non-normative.

When Carmela finally begins to describe Vardalek himself, his heteroglossic perambulations[9] through linguistic terrains are as important as his effeminate features, foreshadowing as they do the dangerous worldly knowledge of Count Dracula.[10] The ensuing tale of romance, punctuated by suspicious boundary-traversings on Vardalek's part, is between the vampire and the nature-boy. Gabriel's becoming-languorous rivals Laura's, although Gabriel does not live to tell the tale. However, the resemblance between the two stories stops there, in that the narrative signals in the two texts produce same-sex orientations in very different ways. Le Fanu's triple-distanced narration—through the double framing device of the narrator who provides us with Laura's narration and the original addressee for Laura, the arcane Dr. Hesselius—may well be what enables a mid-Victorian text to co-operate in the production of a textual lesbian. On the other hand, Stenbock's mediation through a single older female voice produces precisely that almost-safe-enough narrative distance by which a late Victorian textual homosexual can show himself. And although it is a mistake to assume that it guarantees any meaning, it will become worthwhile later to mention now that Stenbock himself cultivated a very post-Byronic, decadent aesthetic. As Peter Haining notes in his introduction to the story, Stenbock was "one of the most talked-about and controversial figures in London" (117); he cultivated not only a taste for other young men, but also for cloaks, coffins, familiars, drugs, drink, death, and decay. His liver offered him an early retirement from life, although, were he to become a revenant, his candidacy for Lestat's rock band would be undisputed. Quite seriously, however, the meanings in his story are so bound up with a very much un-closeted authorial identity that it makes sense to begin asking what relationship vampire fiction has to the identificatory practices (among authors and/or readers) of everyday life.

Among other things, what is happening here is a micro-instance of proto-goth identity. In this case, what I mean by identity is a logical self-sameness constructed between narrative content and ontological style, between textuality and sexuality, between mediated representation and apparently unmediated existential reality. It is the same process for Stenbock as it is for many post-goth writers of gay male vampire fiction. He is, and they are, writing the self by writing the vampire, although with many different goals and traces and unforeseen effects.[11]

When I claim that there is a gay referentiality at work in Stenbock's text, and a proto-goth identification in Stenbock's life, I am digging for clues. Yet the clues themselves were what determined the direction I want my argument to take; the embedded codes therefore ought not to be taken as veins of gold waiting for the academic prospector to discover and mine their depths. What I want to get across in deploying this metaphor is that there is a difference between studying texts from the 1890s and texts from the 1990s—to state the obvious—particularly in terms of the relative embeddedness of codes. If we like to pretend that we are searching for that vein of gold in nineteenth-century vampire texts, then the gold in the 1990s comes to us already fashioned into rings and pendants of various shapes and sizes, all displayed on the shelves at discount prices—except for the rarest ones, of course. However, despite the occasional murmur of domesticity in novels such as McMahan's *Vampires Anonymous* and Bowen's *Diary of a Vampire*, the coffin/closet is far from being domesticated.

Camping Out: *Vampires Anonymous*

Partly an extended vampire hunt from the perspective of the Other, partly an allegorization of the search for a "cure" for male homosexuality among right-wing fundamentalists (some of whom are themselves disavowed gays), McMahan's vampire novel takes characters first introduced in his short story, "Somewhere in the Night" (1989), and weaves them into a decidedly campy tale of manners, ethics, parenting, and love.[12] The narrative is told by the protagonist, although not exactly in the first person, as Andrew Lyall often deploys the precious self-distancing tactic of referring to himself in the third person singular or with his proper name whenever he doesn't want to face his emotions. His adventures joining the fight to resist the fascistically-inflected Vampires Anonymous organization, which is responsible for his lover Pablo's dissolution, are also part of his journey to self-understanding.

The back cover of the novel provides a plethora of adjectives with which to describe McMahan's undead protagonist: Andrew is "wry"; "sassy and sexy"; "irreverent, campy, lascivious"; "stylish, sophisticated." All these are adequate to their descriptive task, but they suggest little more than a lighthearted romp through a fanged fairyland. It is, of course, a milestone in the genre when readers no longer need to play out the camp associated with vampires in queer circles, for all the snappy wit one could imagine is right in the text.

Where the story's humor becomes most useful in the material reality of queer politics is in its staging of an allegory. McMahan deploys two groups of vampires to figure the charged tensions between heterosexist culture at large and homosexuality as lived in that world; between right-wing Christian fundamentalist groups—comprising "former gays" them-selves—and more progressive gay subjects; and between pro-marriage and anti-marriage tendencies within the gay movement itself. In connecting vampirism to addiction and displaying the "cure" in the regular confessional meetings of Vampires Anonymous, McMahan is confronting the still-present discourse of "curing" homosexuality among "family values" adherents (who number doctors and psychiatrists among their ranks). The setting up of a nuclear family unit (Andrew Lyall, his adopted "bat-in-arms" Ryan, and his new partner, John Studnidka), can be interpreted in at least two ways. It might suggest an alliance with the rights discourse of gay marriage, or it might function as a subversion of the same simply by virtue of the open sort of contract Andrew and his partner seem to have established. Andrew's snappy phrase, "the anti-nuclear family" (252), colors this relationship with irony, yet the last sentence of the novel appears to cement it in more traditional terms: after his broken phrase "That's my—" in reference to Ryan's proficiency at transforming himself into a bat and taking flight, Lyall confirms "That's our boy" (253).

The subverted family structure developed in Anne Rice's *Interview with the Vampire*, in which Lestat and Louis attempt to infantilize the child vampire Claudia despite her always maturing intellect, is much differently wrought. Lestat is responsible for Claudia's becoming-vampire, yet the threat of his violence is ever-present—at least in Louis's version of the tale.[13] In contrast, McMahan is careful to erase any possibility of desire for little Ryan or his blood, preferring instead to demonize—in rather tra-

ditional terms—the woman who "turned" the child. While the usual
description of the men in the nefarious Vampires Anonymous group is
Nazi-inflected, the main female character, Anneliese, is coded as a destructive, aggressively sexual, unmaternal vamp. Ultimately, then, it seems as
though Andrew Lyall wants it both ways: he leaves open the possibility of
further romantic meetings with the human Eddie Cramer and perhaps
with Kane, the mysterious freedom-fighter vampire, yet he simultaneously
reflects—in his last sentence—the heteronormative pair bonding that has
structured his oppression.

S/M, Incest, and Disease: *Diary of a Vampire*

Unlike McMahan, Gary Bowen makes explicit and taboo sex one of the
main subjects of *Diary of a Vampire*.[14] His protagonist, Rafael, is immediately written as gay in a dream sequence in which Rafael recollects events
in 1957 Budapest at the grave of his "beloved Valentin" (9). The pursuit he
recalls is a nightmare's apprehension of external reality, for as he wakes to
the sound of his house alarm, he realizes there is indeed an intruder en-
croaching on the entombed safety within which he has been sleeping for
the past fifteen years.

The intruder turns out to be his now-adult nephew, Michael, with
whom he eventually enters into a relationship after ridding himself of his
untrustworthy S/M partner and estate-keeper James. The narrative is one
of redemption through transgression, in that the "queer uncle" is taught
by the love of his nephew that he needn't be an individual alone in the
world, acting only to survive and to protect his own self-interest. Michael's
love arouses Rafael's desire to donate his blood to end the fight against
AIDS, thus effecting a cure which he would not allow to be co-opted for
corporate gain earlier in the novel. *Diary of a Vampire* is interesting in its
contrast between what might be considered absolutely moral—Rafael's
ultimate altruism—and what might be considered absolutely transgressive—explicit rough sex, gay incest, and bestiality. This is anything *but* a
displacement of real relations: what is speculative about Bowen's fiction
are the extremes to which a vampire can go in already charged moments.
Bowen's vampire can cure AIDS; he can transform himself into a panther
and still be sexual; he can transform his anatomical features into those of a
woman; he can break all but the most carefully constructed bondage im-
plements—S/M has never before been so drastic as with a vampire.[15]

In terms of the problems encountered in attempting to define identity, the key scene in the novel is surely that in which Rafael confronts both Michael's bisexuality and his own conflicted identity by transforming himself into a woman (178–84). According to Bowen himself, this scene has elicited rancor among some gay male critics, who react with disdain at the inclusion of a woman in a sex scene, as if such an inclusion automatically disqualifies the novel from being a gay male vampire novel (electronic correspondence, 19 October 1996). Apparently some gay critics fail to note the manner in which Rafael so insistently returns to what he likes most, effectively reasserting "gay" as the ground of his identity. This reassertion suggests, I think, an interest in passing, transformation, and performance rather than a demand for essences.[16]

Generation V: Goth and Queer in Poppy Z. Brite's Fiction

While it could be argued that both McMahan and Bowen reiterate a philosophically normative sexual politics of coupling and family romance despite the potential for subversion embodied by the otherness of their vampires, Poppy Z. Brite's textual identities—both her own and her characters'—are more emphatically queer, even if not entirely or always "gay." Her first novel, *Lost Souls* (1992) stages a decidedly different set of problems from those played out in the more established New Orleans vampire scene created by Anne Rice.[17] Brite's road-and otherwise-tripping trio of pleasure-seeking vampires, Zillah, Twig, and Molochai, embody a neo-decadent Generation X sensibility. They have none of the ethical compulsions or moments of self-reflection of the older vampire Christian, who harbors young vampire-wannabe Jessy after her one-night stand with Zillah, until she dies giving birth to Nothing, Zillah's child. Christian brings Nothing to Missing Mile, North Carolina, depositing him on the doorstep of a nice, middle-class family. Part of the novel is a tale of teen angst as Nothing sets out fifteen years later to discover his birthright—though not before living in the context of a bisexual teeny-goth peer group; the other part of the novel involves a complicated model of teen male friendship in the ever-deepening relationship between Steve, a guitar-playing dropout, and his otherworldly best friend Ghost.

What catapulted Poppy Brite's initial novelistic endeavor to a certain level of subcultural notoriety in both goth and gay circles is partly the ease with which her vampires range over same-sex terrain. That women in the novel serve either as the inevitably destroyed vehicles for the propagation of male vampires or as titillating side-dishes for mostly male-male sex is a problem, although one not without precedent in the "real" world. The boundaries between what counts as masculine and feminine, what counts as kinship, and what counts as consent or desire are constantly transgressed in *Lost Souls*. Where Gary Bowen opens up the possibility of "incestuous" sexual activity with a young nephew (who is, in fact, in his twenties), Poppy Brite engages an amorality that seems boundless. At one point Nothing muses to himself about drinking his father's semen, imagines himself as his mother having sex with Christian, and then imagines himself as a fetus being bathed in Christian's sperm (227). Interestingly, there is the suggestion here that a vampire fetus might have a sort of agency in these matters. One can't get much younger than that—although even the unproblematic sexual subject/object status of Nothing as a fifteen-year-old would be enough to upset more than a few Canadian customs agents. To see Brite's work as an unapologetic display of the most politicized forms of queer sex-radicalism is to remind oneself of one of the purposes of vampires in general: the displacement of real social relations onto the fantastic in order to foreground the fault lines in what is taken as natural in any particular social sphere.

To make this claim is to accept the term queer as at once radical, productive, and multiple, whereas many now see it as a liberal whitewashing term that erases differences even as it attempts to form alliances. This suspicion of queer is not unlike suspicion of goth: queer means nothing if queer can include happy heterosexual couples with children in tow who can retreat to their nice middle-class homes in suburbia, just as goth's androgyny is momentary and always recuperable by the normative pressures of growing up in a binary logic of sexual identity.

The term queer will probably never be settled, nor do I wish it to be. A brief look at its use by two theorists of vampire fiction will demonstrate what I mean here. Both Nina Auerbach's *Our Vampires, Ourselves* (1995) and Ken Gelder's *Reading the Vampire* (1994) identify Sue-Ellen Case as one of the original queer vampire theorists, and both themselves deploy the term, although differently. Auerbach's title is the more plural and subversive, yet her notion of queer theory is too unitary, safely settled in a Reaganite politics, fixed in a certain era, and reified with its own canon and capital letters. For Auerbach, "Queer Theory" is a discrete body of temporally and geographically specific writing (and conferencing) that ultimately contains little worth adding to her own analytic frame (181–86).

Gelder wants to see queer theorizing as more open than this, yet he seems fearful of its potential for contagion, as his text almost always surrounds the term with single scare quotes. Queer Theory or 'queer' theory? I would suggest that queer theory is not an "it," but rather a varying set of texts and lived experiences that together work to produce turns of meaning in other texts and lived experiences. For example, the manner in which Brite narrates her past as a goth in her introduction to the collection *Love in Vein: Twenty Original Tales of Vampiric Erotica* (1994) demonstrates the construction of her authorial self as a text about identity, interiority, publicity, and queer desire.[18] However, even if Brite herself ends up in the "liberal" position of celebrating polymorphous perversity of all sorts equally, some of the stories in *Love in Vein*, as well as in Tan's *Blood Kiss* and in Rowe and Roche's *Sons of Darkness*, more effectively narrativize the radical identity issues involved in gay, queer, and goth politics at the end of the millennium.

Collecting Short Stories: Identity Politics and the Anthology

Love in Vein and *Blood Kiss* both embody a different sort of anthologizing project from that of either Pam Keesey's lesbian vampire anthologies or *Sons of Darkness*. The boundaries established by the introductions to Brite's and Tan's erotic anthologies and the actual fiction they collect encourage wide-ranging conjunctions of goth punk and queer sex, with the figure of the vampire functioning as the mediating transformational figure. As a result, readers will find in them a multiplicity of pleasures to consume: there are stories which will be of interest to some gay males, some which will be read as gay by non-gay non-males, and several on which the jury is still "out."[19]

The excitement with which *Sons of Darkness* falls into the picture is wholly deserving, given the quality of some of its offerings; however, the guiding principles of the book as set out in its introduction fall somewhat short of the mark set by Keesey's collections. Rather than attempting to summarize the stories collected here, I want to provide a reading of the introduction and its place in the identity politics that form the subject of my discussion.

Framed by an italicized narrative that cleverly maps the present state of gay male sexual politics through the figure of the vampire, the editors of *Sons of Darkness* provide an argument about why the vampire is an appropriate mode in which to write erotic relationships between men. Their historical account of why the vampire resurfaces in specific cultural arenas suffers from a unidirectional determinism, however. They open their claims with the all-too-familiar argument that *Dracula* appeared because of "repressive Victorian England," and follow this up with the contention that the "paranoid and depressed 1930s . . . were haunted by the vampire films of Universal Pictures"; the "conservative . . . and McCarthy-badgered late 1950s" (10) initiated the first of the Hammer vampire films; and so on. In a similar causal relationship, now "in the age of AIDS and the sex-phobia it has engendered, come a revival of gothic culture and a widespread interest in vampires" (10). What is troubling about this version of the wherefores of cultural production and consumption is its elision of pre-*Dracula* vampire popularity and its inability to explain the specifics of vampire metaphoricity—except by laying claim to safely installed received notions of historical periodicity. It may in fact be the case that vampire production itself determines what sorts of subjectivities are available to subsequent generations on both individual and historical levels.

It is equally interesting that the editors take a tone very much in keeping with the oedipal drama that structures altogether too much male subjective response. In order to assert their credibility, they lay claim to a radicality of experience and voice that both ignores and broaches the issue of paternity, perhaps inadvertently replaying, in the process, the hegemonic differences between sons and daughters. Unfortunately, their rhetoric follows the potentially misogynist pattern of violent erasure of the female that we also find in texts by McMahan and Brite. They assume a familiarity with their male readership when they suggest that "Many are the men who have watched Christopher Lee towering at the head of that stone stairwell, eyes burning, teeth bared, and thought: *Someone get rid of that whimpering bodice-ripped heroine and let me take her place*" (12; emphasis in original). While it is reasonable to assume that there ought to be a companion collection to *Daughters of Darkness* called *Sons of Darkness*, it is problematic to proceed with such a project without calling attention to the ways in which sons and daughters are differently situated in terms of gender norms, lineages, and inheritance codes in Western culture. Combining the discourse of an in-your-face queer movement with the anti-intellectual rhetoric of "vampires fuck shit up" (11) serves both to excite the pulse, which I like, and to call attention to the rebelliousness of the sons' refusals to behave in the "family dynamic." In the process, however, this unfortunately amounts to a mere reiteration of traditional oedipal roles. Given the quality and diversity of some of the stories, some of which are short and some long, some delicate and some rather harsh, some consensual and some downright not, it is unfortunate that the editors end up in this strange space somewhere between Tom Cruise and snurffling about in the woods with other "real" men. To the extent that the editors want to leave aside "gay" as a term in favor of the apparently less troublesome definitional term "men" (12), it seems to me that there is something about the 1990s that discourages, rather than encourages, gay male identifications of a queerer sort. My own suspicions about the efficacy of the term gay suggest that it needs complicating, not scrapping.

Cybergoth and Vampyre Fictions

The fiction I've discussed so far has occurred in book form, with its own particular modes of production and consumption. New modes of production and consumption, however, necessitate changes in the manner in which subjectivity is constituted, and one of the more interesting new modes pertinent to vampire fiction in its articulation with queer and goth is the virtual space of the internet.[20] For those with access to the required technology and end-user knowledge, the internet has become a field of contested meanings with considerable potential to both reiterate and resist normative constructions of being-in-the-world. While fanzines such as *Propaganda* and comix like *Hothead Paisan: Homicidal Lesbian Terrorist* have long been the staple of underground goth and queer reflexivity, the internet brings with it the chance for a collusion/collision of expression never before possible in quite the same way.

The "Vampyres-L" list, in operation since about 1990, is populated by an eclectic mix of teen goths and pagans, some of whom are otherwise isolated from those of like persuasions; twenty-something students; somewhat older denizens of the dark; and even a couple of bona fide academics. What is striking about this virtual community, however, is its ability to elicit and contain a multiplicity of narrative strategies in the self-identifications of its writing/reading subjects. The listowners encourage both discussion and the submission of original fiction—called "Fluff" in the linguistic peculiarities of the internet—which can be short or in serial installments, appearing regularly or infrequently. This mode of writing produces input, arguments, revisions, and cross-fertilization (intertextuality writ fast and large), as well as collaborative projects. It also potentially subverts conventional assumptions about authorial gender, sexuality, ethnicity, and race—a welcome subversion for anyone familiar with the actual multiplicity of both goth and queer scenes. Contributors of both Fluff and opinion discuss many of these issues. The remarkable thing about this type of discussion, however, is that each contributor writes either "in" persona or "out of" persona, the personae developing either prior to or alongside the writing of characters in Fluff contributions, or sometimes without any Fluff at all. The out-of-persona voices sometimes make more claims to the "real" than at other times, but it is just as likely that an out-of-persona voice will seriously discuss his or her vampirism or magickal ability as an in-persona voice—it is all narrative, all writing the self, whether in a fictional register or otherwise. Some long-time contributors have more than two names/personae with which to enter into narrative, and some sign persona-names even when they are out-of-persona in discussion.

Some of the most active members of this cybercommunity include Vyrdolak, Chaos, Nephilim, the Baron, Laybrother Bat, Bloofer Lady, Claudia, . . . Those acquainted with the history of vampire lore and fiction will recognize the gothic valence to many of these names. In terms of transgender possibilities and the potential for gay space, one of the most important instances of writing in the context of my discussion is that performed by the Baron, who is "actually" a Canadian woman, Anne Fraser. The Baron is an older gay male vampire, and when he finds his way into Fluff, it is of utmost relevance to issues I have already raised. While many of the stories generated by listmembers bring out the worst possible heterosexism available to the vampire ethos, Fraser's stories deal with ironic gay revisions of cultural phenomena ("Club Undead"—a holiday getaway for Children of the Night and their lovers), with AIDS, and with same-sex love in her primary and secondary characters' ongoing narratives. This fiction does not have a market as such: unlike Poppy Brite's novels, it cannot be found on trashy horror shelves by unsuspecting teens; unlike McMahan's or Bowen's work, it cannot be found in "special interest" bookstores; unlike the *Blood Kiss* collection, it cannot even be mail-ordered. Its market is the virtually immediate—though heavily mediated—community in which it is produced. This has resulted in both encouraging input and rampant homophobia on the part of readers; it has also meant that two affinity-minded contributors could meet and collaborate on a serial, "Gramps" by Chaos and the Baron, in which both writers' characters appear together. This differently organized mode of production initiates a rearrangement of identity politics, a rearrangement in which a writing and reading subject's gender and sexuality are not restricted to a demand for consistency or singularity. When such a demand does present itself, as one of the hegemonic conditions under which any of us can produce anything, it presents itself as a banality, a too-anxious reiteration of patriarchal heteronormativity whose signals are all crossed in the queer space of the virtual community.

Conclusion: Goth and Self II

In the context of the identity-work being done in the 1990s along so many different axes of inquiry, I hope to have situated in a narrativized present the emergence of a particular queer vampire subject as writer, as text, and as reader. In connecting goth to gay—or at the very least non-heteronormative—I have made a move that is not without its own problems. In conversations and e-mail correspondence, I have been struck by a reluctance among gay males to see goth as anything but a fad for privileged white boys and girls who play at bisexuality but who ultimately return to the comfortable fold of their suburban hetero-white middle-classness. However guardedly I might want to disagree with this, the fact remains that in the mainstream circulation of images, a relentlessly heterosexual family romance structures the thinkable around goth. Take, for example, the film versions of *The Crow,* or the focus in radio interviews on Peter Murphy's happily married life. Still, a residue of last night's eyeliner and lipstick invariably remains, functioning to generate a space in which it is perfectly acceptable for androgynous goth boys and hyperfemme goth girls to be out of the closet as teenagers—not an easy task in many youth cultures.

Having begun with a story, it seems only fitting to end with another elaboration of reading and identifying. In 1985 I cut out a letter to the editor of the *Toronto Star* which insisted that punk was far from dead; it cited alternative anarchist lifestyles clustered around bands such as Crass. The accompanying photograph was a representative pair of androgynous, male, multiply pierced, big-hair punks flanking an equally alternative-marked woman. I cut out this picture and for years kept the images on my bedroom wall, wishing that the trio would bite me or something and make me just like them. Years later, when I met the person who was to become my partner, I discovered that she had in fact known the two young men in the picture I had carted around with me all that time. Finding out that they were an "out" couple in the Toronto scene back in the mid-'80s was very much an epiphany in my own same-sex desire matrix.

I would never deny the power of certain aspects of punk, particularly goth, to undergird a space of safety for non-heteronormative identity politics. The last I heard about this pair, they were on the West Coast of Canada, one of them infected with the virus that has conditioned much of the vampire fiction and vampire analysis being written today. When Gary Bowen writes his vampire protagonist as becoming-humanist in the fight against AIDS, I might want to raise eyebrows at the heroic altruism displayed by a generally more conflicted denizen of the dark; however, I would not for a moment deny the power of the fantastic to shape our hopes and futures. Vampires function as more than just metaphors or archetypes in contemporary culture; in the case of at least some subjects in the boundary-crossing moment that is both queer and goth, vampires are sources of self-invention and the very much *out* staging of the problematics of gender identification and sexuality.

14

Techno-Gothic Japan:

From Seishi Yokomizo's *The Death's-Head Stranger* to Mariko Ohara's *Ephemera the Vampire*

MARI KOTANI

The Archetype of Japanese Vampire Literature: Seishi Yokomizo's *The Death's-Head Stranger*

In his book *Bloody Arabesque: A Vampire Reader* (1993), the distinguished critic of Japanese fantasy literature Asahiko Sunaga tells us that vampire literature was first imported to Japan around 1930, in the early Showa era. Vampire, in the first place, is a foreign cultural product that never existed in our country before 1930. But, secondly, it is noteworthy that vampire is also a cultural complex made up of the Others of gender, class, and race. Traditionally represented as the western Other, the figure of vampire, once inserted into our context, was transformed into the Other of the Japanese mentality. In our literature, vampire plays a double role, therefore, as the western Other as well as the Japanese Other. How, then, did Japanese vampire literature come to deal with, and to cognitively familiarize, the western vampire as the cultural Other?

The prototype of Japanese vampire literature, mystery writer Seishi Yokomizo's *Dokuro-Kengyo* (The Death's-Head Stranger, 1939), was the first successful Japanese adaptation of Bram Stoker's *Dracula* (1897). With the nineteenth-century Edo Castle as his central stage, Yokomizo narrates the way the stranger Shiranui (Dracula) and his female disciples Matsumushi and Suzumushi (female vampires) transform Lady Kagero ("Ephemera"), the daughter of the Shogun, into a vampire in the face of the maid-of-honor Kotoe (Mina Harker), who has made every effort to rescue her mistress. Eventually, the vampire Shiranui is counter-attacked, and reveals himself to be Shiro Amakusa, who had planned to assassinate the Shogun and overturn the Tokugawa government.

Yokomizo's characterization of the vampire is modeled on a Japanese historical figure, Shiro Amakusa, an incredibly beautiful boy of the seventeenth century who, despite his youth, became a leader of the Christian peasants of the Nagasaki prefecture who groaned under the heavy burden of taxation. He resisted the Tokugawa Government's anti-Christian politics and died in a battle with the imperialist army when he was only seventeen years old.

The stronger the Shogun got at this time, the more xenophobic the Japanese government became. Fearing the influence of foreign knowledge transmitted by Christian missionaries, the Tokugawa government made up its mind to control and limit the flow of information by closing the country, stopping the importation of weapons, and forbidding Christianity. The author Yokomizo, keenly aware of the popularity of the historical figure of Shiro Amakusa within Japanese popular fiction, radically recreated him as a potential vampire whose deep immersion in foreign culture could not help but transfigure him into a monster, a signifier of Japanese xenophobia. What is remarkable in *The Death's-Head Stranger*, then, is that, in the Japanese context both Christianity and the opponent of Christianity are denounced as wicked invaders. The year this novel was published—1939, the same year that marked the beginning of World War II—coincided with the dramatic emergence of the xenophobic spirit in Japan.

Ethnicity and Sexuality of the Japanese Vampire: Ryo Hammura and Moto Hagio

The appearance of Yokomizo's *The Death's-Head Stranger* at the peak of the first boom of Japanese vampire fiction in the 1930s[1] made it inevitable that later practitioners of this literary subgenre would, as they wove their texts, be deeply conscious of the binary opposition between their national culture and foreign culture. For example, let us take a glance at the second boom, the revival of Japanese vampire fiction in the 1970s represented by Ryo Hammura's cliffhanger novel *Ishi-no-Ketsumyaku* (The Blood Vessel of Stone, 1971) and Moto Hagio's marvelous *manga* (comic-strip) *Poe-no-Ichizoku* (The Clan of Poe, 1974–76). In this decade we find that how a vampire fictionist interprets foreign culture depends, at least in part, on gender.

For male Japanese writers, on the one hand, vampire/foreign culture has been closely related to the racial conflict between the Japanese people and the non-Japanese. Post-war Japan accepted the American occupation army as well as American high and pop culture. The rapid absorption of this culture helped revolutionize the Japanese industrial structure, which in turn initiated a stage of high economic growth based on petro-chemistry that took advantage of the national prosperity brought about by the Korean War (1950–53). In this period, Japanese intellectuals who could respond quickly to foreign culture came to constitute a new form of aristocracy. Ryo Hammura's *The Blood Vessel of Stone* clearly reflects this aspect of the 1970s. His vampire carries within its body an extraordinary virus that is capable of literally petrifying people and then reviving them as immortal beings after several thousand years. For the virus to petrify people, the carrier is required to drink vessels of human blood. Through sexual intercourse, this virus has been imported from abroad and pervades the Japanese aristocrats, who are literally dying for immortality. The novel contrasts two heroes, an elite "salariman" involved in the power structure of these aristocrats, and an ex-salariman who challenges their conspiracy. For the author, the vampire virus represents the ambivalence toward foreign culture embraced by most Japanese men who were witness to World War II. This is why Ryo Hammura, who was twelve years old in 1945, had to radically "Japanize" the western legend of vampire.

For female Japanese writers, on the other hand, vampire/foreign culture seems not so much a racial as a sexual issue. For Japanese women, the variety of foreign products imported into Japan—such as Hollywood movies, American novels, fashion styles, and electric appliances—seem more utopian than evil, encouraging as they do these women to transgress the Japanese tradition of patriarchy. In Moto Hagio's *The Clan of Poe*, for instance, there are no Japanese characters. In this narrative, vampires are all renamed *vampanella*, wandering travelers on the edge of time who ingest the idioplasm of the rose; thus, in this sense, they deflower the rose.[2] The protagonist is a fourteen-year-old boy named Edgar, who became a vampire too early to mature physically, in spite of his inner maturity. Hagio's comic-strip constructs an omnibus-style chronicle that covers the passage of time from the eighteenth century to the present; the action is set largely in England and Germany. Its episodes deal with incidents in the journey of Edgar and his sister Merrybell, as well as with that of Edgar and his friend Allan. What is at stake here is not only the binary opposition between physical childhood and internal adulthood, but also that between physical manhood and internal womanhood. We can see this in the descriptions of Edgar and Allan, who remind us less of natural boys than of boyish girls endowed with delicate and artistic sensibilities. What is more, the relationship between Edgar and Allan gave birth to more works of *Shonen-ai* (male adolescent-specific gay romances), which became tremendously appealing to adolescent female readers.

In this sense, *The Clan of Poe* can be designated as the precursor of science-fictional gay romances, even as Ursula K. Le Guin's *The Left Hand of Darkness* (1969) inaugurated the subgenre of gender-panic science fiction in the United States. And now in the 1990s, it is not very difficult to find the contemporary equivalents of *Shonen-ai* fiction in such works as American "K/S" or "slash" fiction,[3] Anne Rice's *Vampire Chronicles*, Storm Constantine's *Wraeththu* saga, and even Japanese *Yaoi* fiction (the updated version of *Shonen-ai* novels and comic-strips nicknamed after an abbreviation of *Yamanashi-Ochinashi-Iminashi* [no climax-no conclusion-no meaning, but only a never-ending description of homosexual intercourse]). We should not forget, however, that the ultimate brilliance of Moto Hagio lies in her representation of vampire as a physically immature but mentally hyper-mature adolescent boy who determines to become neither an adult nor a female in the orthodox sense, and who is not a symbol of monstrosity but a beautiful imaginary being much like Jorge Luis Borges's Unicorn. *The Clan of Poe*, therefore, is the story of social deviants who destroy existing categories of sexuality and embody their own visions of utopia.

Within the development of various theoretical constructions of gender in the 1970s, the figure of vampire has become familiar to the Japanese audience. As assimilated into Japanese culture, vampire is a creature superficially familiar but essentially alien. I call this mode of assimilation "cognitive familiarization," in contrast to Darko Suvin's theory of the "cognitive estrangement" of conventional science fiction.[4] Two vampire stories of the 1980s are exemplars of this subgenre: Kiyoshi Kasai's *Vampire Wars* series (1982–1992) reinvestigates how vampire/foreign culture is assimilated into the Japanese culture, while Hideyuki Kikuchi's ongoing *Vampire Hunter-D* series (1983–) illuminates the sense of alienation felt by a hybrid being in the neutral territory between the foreign (vampiric) and the Japanese (human), despite the privileged power he can enjoy.

In this context, Kasai's *Vampire Wars* series delineates the effects of cognitive familiarization of Japanese vampire literature per se. In the 1960s and '70s, Kasai was well known as one of the most aggressive theoreticians of the *Zenkyoto* (New Left) movement, and in the early '80s he started his literary career by writing superbly sophisticated mysteries and science fiction as well as post-Marxist literary criticism. Thus, it is natural for Kasai to characterize his vampire hero as an ESP-er sought by state authorities and enterprises. Through his deeper exploration, the hero discovers his roots in the huge power of both the sunken continent of Moo and an interstellar civilization. He learns that all Japanese people, not only himself, are hereditary vampires. Kasai's reinterpretation is incredibly radical, since he restructures vampire as no longer totally foreign, but as genetically indigenous to the Japanese.

Such a refiguration of vampire will make more sense if we are aware of the way in which the Japanese term for vampire was coined. "Vampire" was first translated as *Kyuketsu-ki*, which literally means "bloodsucking ogre." Although we have no equivalent to the western anti-Christian bloodsucker—most famously delineated in Bram Stoker's *Dracula* (1897)—it is possible to establish an analogy between the western vampire and the Japanese cannibalistic ogre called *Oni* (corresponding to *ki* of *Kyuketsu-ki*). Such a Japanese assimilation of foreign cultural products demonstrates how we have persistently translated unfamiliar things into familiar ones through rediscovering analogies between western and Japanese cultures in a process of cognitive familiarization.

In contrast, Hideyuki Kikuchi's *Vampire Hunter-D* can be called post-cyberpunk vampire fiction. The story is set in 12,090, when human civilization has totally collapsed and a vampiric high-tech society dominates the whole earth. In spite of the development of their space exploration and bio-technological experimentation, the vampires have to confront the limits of their species as well as the decline in their birth rate, developments that gradually transfer their hegemony to human beings. The hero, D, is a tall, skinny, and gorgeous vampire hunter, a vampire-human hybrid who, ironically, is hired by humans to fight against vampires. Feeling uncomfortable with both humans and vampires, the hero acts out a type of romantic agony as he hovers between human culture (= Japanese) and vampire culture (= foreign). Such an agonistic hero undoubtedly re-allegorizes the international conflicts of the high-tech hyper-capitalist post-'80s era that cognitive familiarization invites.

Furthermore, we should not overlook the topic of "originality" as the hidden agenda of such international conflicts, a topic that has been insistently pursued by both Hideyuki Kikuchi and Kiyoshi Kasai. With the rise of Japan as a hyper-economic power, Japanese people have often been ac-

cused of an essential lack of originality, of having skillfully stolen and recreated the original products of western culture. This is no doubt due to the
fact that, in its appropriation of western technologies, Japan has sometimes
outdone the West. It is, however, the western politico-metaphysical discourses that have traditionally claimed "originality" as a primary virtue.
Now that we have entered the post-simulationist age of Jean Baudrillard
and Donna Haraway, we can begin to question the ideological status of the
notion of "originality," exploring the significance of this "virtue" as one
of the most powerful and dominant fictions of western mental history.

From such a post-'80s perspective, Japanese vampire fiction can be
reread as a rhetorical reflection of the structure of a sensibility characteristic of a post-original and post-simulationist age. While western people
have conventionally hated the concept of the "imitation," it is time to re-
investigate the ethics of simulacra, not as kinds of imitation "originating"
from the Japanese, but as highly typical of the very age we all live in. Note
that Kikuchi's vampire hunter D becomes tormented because, without the
high technology the vampires have applied to his human mother, he himself would never have been born. It is in this paradoxical sense that Japanese
vampire fictions like those of Kikuchi and Kasai, in their process of cognitive familiarization, invite us to ask, not whether a culture is original, but
rather how we should speculate on the topic of "hybridity" in a post-
colonialist and post-creolian age,[5] a topic that puts into jeopardy the very
metaphysics of originality.

Mariko Ohara's Vampire Science Fiction:
From *Hybrid Child* to *Ephemera the Vampire*

The concept of hybridity is the keynote of Mariko Ohara's vampire fiction,
which makes use of the technique of cognitive familiarization in its exploration of gender issues. Mariko Ohara is a distinguished Japanese writer
who, in 1980, made her debut as the winner of the sixth annual *Hayakawa's
SF Magazine* New Talent prize. Since then she has published a wide variety of cyberpunkish and widescreen-baroque novels and short stories.[6]
Her longest novel, *Hybrid Child* (1990), a masterpiece that won both the
1991 Seiun Award (the Japanese Hugo) and the *Hayakawa's SF Magazine*
Readers' Poll, succeeds in metaphorically reflecting the Japanese postmodernist cultural matrix, in which the post-'80s high-tech principles of sam-

pling, remixing, and cutting-up disclose the socio-political intersections between western and Japanese "simulationist" culture.[7]

Here let us concentrate on one of Ohara's most recent novels, *Ephemera the Vampire* (1992), which reconstructs, in terms of the problematics of Japanese femininity, the figure of "vampire," a type of the Other skillfully and unwittingly imported into Japanese culture from the West. What is initially amazing is her portrait of the vampire as taking the form of the human heart. When they assault a human victim, Ohara's vampires enter the body through the back, removing and then taking the place of the human heart and parasitizing their living hosts. These vampires have a longer history than humankind, ensured by their parasitic lives. It is through their parasitic relationship with humans, finally, that they achieve a higher stage of intelligence.

The monologue of Ephemera the vampire makes it clear that Ohara picked up her idea for this novel from American movies like *The Thing* (1982) and *The Hidden* (1987):

I've not recovered from the impact of that movie, *The Thing*. On seeing it, I came to the presupposition that human beings, under the disguise of cattle, have long been aware of the secret of our species. Indeed, stories about our species helped them weave the legends of vampire. But they are no more than legends, which are more misleading than convincing, and totally unreliable right now. But *The Thing* is another story, for it seems about to reveal the truth. A member of our species might have directed that movie. If that movie tells us a truth, our species might have come from deep space. I kept giving myself wild fancies. (*Ephemera the Vampire* 22; my own translation)

While *The Thing* inspired Ohara to write her story, her vampire heroine inspires us to reconsider the film as truth, not fiction. I find her statement fascinating, for it testifies to the cognitive familiarization of foreign cultures, a process that has helped to construct the Japanese mentality.

What is also interesting is that Ohara's vampire is primarily characterized as a sign of the feminine. In this novel, vampires usually hide themselves within female bodies; once they enter a male body, they become pregnant and reproduce themselves, having to change their hosts in the process. Ohara's vampires identify with women and multiply with men. Nevertheless, the author's provocative representation of vampire allegorizes and questions the notion of femininity, another cultural concept imported from the West into Japan during its period of modernization.

Certainly, to us contemporary Japanese, the notion of femininity has long seemed self-evident, deeply influencing our gender politics. But in fact "femininity" is a western concept that has gradually been assimilated into Japanese culture only relatively recently. In retrospect, while the western discourses of femininity and vampiric monstrosity were constructed in the nineteenth century by the demands of modernization, they have become naturalized in the twentieth. I think a similar process of naturalization has occurred in the Japanese assimilation of foreign cultural products. Although the notion of femininity was a foreign product more or less alien to the Japanese, it is this very notion that has been politically naturalized in our national culture, without which neither modern nor postmodern Japanese sexuality would ever have been constructed. Contemporary Japanese women are all hybrid children, all cyborgs. Thus Ohara's narrative leads us to find that the cultural status of vampire is basically analogous to that of femininity. In Japan, both notions are at work as cultural blood-sucking ogres.

Ohara's vampires most conspicuously represent the cyborg gender structuring the mentality of contemporary Japanese women. Her plot itself is very simple, centering as it does around the entanglement of vampires (parasites) and ALiens (aliens from the planet AL) with Japanese hegemonic families, an entanglement that results in the birth of a new type of creature. The ALiens are intriguing because their horrible genocide of women on their own planet has made it difficult for them to reproduce themselves. Their present aim is to appropriate human women for sexual reproduction, but once they arrive on Earth, they are—ironically—"raped" by Ephemera and transformed into vampires themselves. In sharp contrast to the patriarchal, ultra-macho, even homosexual ALiens, here Ephemera the vampire is empowered as a kind of vamp, that is, another erotic figure of the femme fatale or *la belle dame sans merci*, whose fatal attraction cannot help but threaten and destroy men.

As for the relationship between humans and vampires, here we ought to consider the matriarchal role played by Mme. Mana, another vampire who attempts to enter and reappropriate a Japanese Zaibatsuary. It is difficult to determine whether Japanese motherhood is traditional or modern. But our history tells us that, patriarchal and anti-feminist as it seems on the surface, Japanese society enabled some women to have power through their sexual relationships with the hegemonic male figures of the Shogun family; if these women, either legal wives or mistresses, bore the Shogun-to-be, they could control the nation by controlling their own sons, with their relatives as fixers or counselors.

It is in this context that Mariko Ohara attempts to grapple with the structure of Japanese motherhood represented in the portrait of Mme. Mana. Unable herself to give birth to a human child, Mme. Mana is depicted here not as a literal mother but as a mother figure. She feels so anxious about the future of the vampire species that she becomes the second wife of Taro Daimon, the president of the Daimon Zaibatsuary. Daimon is as self-centered as a child, and Mme. Mana tries to indulge him very generously; but he cannot be satisfied with her devotion. Meanwhile, it is significant that the evil spirit of the postmortem Daimon haunts Lilium, a beautiful human girl, whose mother was raped by a vampire. This constitutes another conflict with Mme. Mana, in which Lilium/Daimon is gradually transformed into a feminist, fascistic, phallic daughter. Thus Daimon's metempsychosis clarifies the extent to which Japanese society is figured as a kind of great infant who cannot help but seek for motherhood in every woman. To put it another way, it is the discourse of motherhood that violently accelerates the hyper-infantilization of Japanese society, a process that works something like a weird caricature of the Pièta.

At its climax, Ohara's novel describes the way in which the conflict between Mme. Mana and Lilium induces them to commit double suicide, as the children of Ephemera fly from outer space to attack the Earth, a climax that brings about a magnificent revolution of consciousness. At this point, we witness the crash course between the Orientalist discourse of Japanese Woman heightened by the process of western cognitive estrangement and the Japanese discourse of National Femininity effected by our cognitive familiarization/assimilation of foreign cultures. Of course, we are deeply "familiar" with Darko Suvin's influential definition of western science fiction as a literature of "cognitive estrangement." But Japanese science fiction functions as a literature of cognitive familiarization, enabling us not to defamiliarize or estrange, but to import and familiarize such western cultural commodities as vampire and vampire fiction, as well as the modern western intellectual concept of femininity.

Let me conclude this essay by comparing *Hybrid Child*, Ohara's masterpiece of the 1980s, with *Ephemera the Vampire*, her masterpiece of the '90s. In the former novel, on the one hand, the author focuses on a hybrid child of the organic and the mechanic, that is, a hyper-tech sampling device with a perpetual engine that is capable of sampling, remixing, and transforming whomever and whatever it encounters. It allows us insight into the inner space of Japanese families by simulating the figure of a mother who murdered her own daughter and the figure of an old man who loves and indulges his granddaughter. Indeed, the device as such may sound familiar within the tradition of Anglo-American science fiction. But what attracts me most in Ohara's text is that the protean mechanics of the hybrid child correspond wonderfully to the Japanese aesthetics of the ephemeral. For example, we Japanese are always intrigued by the very moment of the cherry blossom's flowering and falling. This sort of mentality reflects not only the delicate Japanese response to the change of seasons, but also our mental elasticity in the face of whatever change we experience, which seduces us to consume whatever foreign information we import. In imagining a high-tech sampling device, Mariko Ohara seems unwittingly to have unveiled her own Japanese sensibility.

On the other hand, in *Ephemera the Vampire*, the way Ohara's vampires constantly put on and change human bodies can be considered a radical allegory of Japanese Femininity. Now it is the very foreign concept of gender that plays the role of bloodsucker, putting on, changing, and consuming Japanese bodies and cultures, and reconstructing a huge alternative universe of Japanese Femininity. While the nano-mechanics of the hybrid child illuminate the Japanese aesthetic sensibility, the hyper-consumerist and hyper-metamorphic gender politics of the vampire uncovers the Japanese feminist mentality, which will help us reinterpret the paradox of Japanese cultural strategies of cognitive assimilation, strategies whose originality lies in their reappropriation of the original.

15

Fantasies of Absence:
The Postmodern Vampire

VERONICA HOLLINGER

In her influential study, *Fantasy: The Literature of Subversion*, Rosemary Jackson argues that, in a secular world, the role of fantasy is no longer to explore aspects of various transcendent or supernatural realities. Increasingly, according to Jackson, fantasy has come to function as an expressive rather than escapist or compensatory mode of writing (17). Its role is to hold up the mirror to our own human desires and anxieties: "[Modern fantasy] does not invent supernatural regions, but presents a natural world inverted into something strange, something 'other.' It becomes 'domesticated,' humanized, turning from transcendental explorations to transcriptions of a human condition" (17).[1] In this discussion, I want to use Jackson's construction of modern fantasy to examine the ways in which some vampire texts "mirror" aspects of that peculiar human condition which has come to be termed "postmodern," since postmodernism is one of the more productive—and challenging—paradigms through which contemporary Western reality is currently being conceptualized.

One of the most succinct definitions of postmodernism, and certainly one of the most influential, is Jean-François Lyotard's summation of this "condition" as "incredulity toward metanarratives" (xxiv), that is, as the loss of faith in totalizing stories such as capital-H History, capital-S Science, or capital-R Religion. This loss of faith is, in part, responsible for what has come to be called "the legitimation crisis," a crisis that puts into question the grounds on which so many human behaviors and beliefs have previously been secured. And one of the more positive results of the legitimation crisis is the current widespread movement of decentering: for example, voices historically relegated to the margins of discourse, of representation, of authority have come to the foreground, and perspectives

rarely before privileged have begun to be considered as—at least potentially—valid. As a paradigm of "the human condition," therefore, postmodernism functions neither to explain nor to exclude those "abnormal"
features of contemporary existence that the projects of realism are inherently incapable of mirroring; rather, it aims to incorporate the abnormal *as
it is* within the field of analysis.

This process has had, not surprisingly, a significant impact in terms of
generic authority. The various genres of fantastic narrative, conventionally
relegated to the margins of cultural production within the context of the
authority of realism, have moved once again to the forefront of narrative
production. This is at least in part because, as Jackson argues, "The fantastic traces the unsaid and the unseen of culture: that which has been
silenced, made invisible, covered over and made 'absent.' . . . Its introduction of the 'unreal' is set against the category of the 'real'—a category
which the fantastic interrogates by its difference" (4).

This aspect of the shift to a postmodern perspective helps to explain
one important feature of the treatment afforded many kinds of monsters in
today's fiction, the fact that so many are, like Mary Shelley's Creature, delineated from the inside rather than the outside. Fred Saberhagen's *The
Dracula Tape* (1975), for example, a retelling of Stoker's narrative from the
point of view of his vampire, is an almost inevitable result of the postmodern exercise of decentering. And the widespread popularity of Anne Rice's
Vampire Chronicles is due in no small part to her readers' fascination with
the psychological make-up of her monsters. In fact, as has often been
noted, in Rice's novels it is the human characters, not the vampires, who
are relegated to marginal narrative roles.

Jody Scott's satiric *I, Vampire* (1984) is another text that emphasizes
the shift away from the perspectives of traditional fantasy: Scott mobilizes
one vampire, two different species of space aliens, and various human characters in a satirical parody of both vampire stories and science-fiction alien
invasion stories.[2] *I, Vampire* not only breaks down the generic boundaries
between fantasy and science fiction, but because Scott replaces a two-term
system—vampire/human—with a three-term system—vampire/human/
alien—her text also disrupts the tendency toward binary thinking that constructs the Other as unproblematically monstrous and outside the boundaries of the human.

Suzy McKee Charnas's classic novella, "The Unicorn Tapestry" (1980)
is one of the most successful of these attempts to explore the internal life
of the monster: it dramatizes a series of "therapeutic" encounters between

a psychiatrist and her vampire "client." It is no coincidence that Charnas's model for the interactions between her human and vampire characters is the model of the psychoanalytic dialogue. One of the most deconstructive aspects of this story is that it manages to keep both vampire *and* human at the forefront of the narrative: the point-of-view character is the psychiatrist, while the subject—not the object—of the analysis is the vampire.

In fact, contemporary psychoanalytic perspectives have had far-reaching implications for the rise in popularity of various kinds of fantastic literature, since they encourage us to question the distinctions we have taken for granted between "reality" and "fantasy." As Victor Burgin, James Donald, and Cora Kaplan observe in their introduction to *Formations of Fantasy*, "in popular understanding, 'fantasy' is always opposed to 'reality.' In this definition fantasy is the *negative* of reality" (1). They argue, however, that, at least in psychoanalytic terms, fantasy is as constitutive of "reality" as are the more fact-based and experiential events in our lives. Rather than functioning as a supplement to empirical reality, therefore, fantasy might be (re)conceptualized as a significant feature of its constitution.

The potential inherent in the archetype of the vampire, one of our most long-lived cultural icons, to function effectively as a metaphor for certain aspects of postmodernity is particularly striking. One result of the legitimation crisis has been the way in which certain previously sacrosanct boundaries—political, philosophical, conceptual, ethical, aesthetic—have tended to become problematized; postmodernism has undertaken to undermine and/or deconstruct innumerable kinds of inside/outside oppositional structures. This deconstruction of boundaries helps to explain why the vampire is a monster-of-choice these days, since it is itself an inherently deconstructive figure: it is the monster that used to be human; it is the undead that used to be alive; it is the monster that *looks like us*. For this reason, the figure of the vampire always has the potential to jeopardize conventional distinctions between human and monster, between life and death, between ourselves and the other.[3] We look into the mirror it provides and we see a version of ourselves. Or, more accurately, keeping in mind the orthodoxy that vampires cast no mirror reflections, we look into the mirror and see nothing *but* ourselves.

Clearly, the kinds of potential breakdowns threatened by the vampire, while quite familiar features of the postmodern landscape, pose a real threat in any cultural moment that invests heavily in assumptions about stable reality, essential humanity, and clear-cut ideologies of good and evil. This suggests not only why the vampire was such a popular monster in the late nineteenth century, when Bram Stoker's *Dracula* appeared, but also why its treatment was necessarily quite different than it frequently is today. It is not difficult to understand why Stoker, after inviting Count Dracula into the fictional world of his novel, must resolve the vampire's threat by ex- pelling it, the monstrous double, from the rational, virtuous, patriarchal world of Victorian England.[4] It is also worth noting that, however threat- ening Stoker's vampire is, it serves a crucial function in his novel: in its role as evil Other, it necessarily guarantees the *presence* of the Good.[5]

This observation, which is nothing if not obvious, is nevertheless an important one, since recent fantasy has tended to be more concerned with absence than presence. Fredric Jameson, for example, makes the claim that modern fantasy "circumscribes the place of the fantastic as a determinate, marked *absence* at the heart of the secular world" (*The Political Unconscious* 134). He goes on to describe what he perceives as the inherently suspensive nature of what I will call here the *fantasy of absence*: "its expectant hush reveal[s] an object world forever suspended on the brink of meaning, for- ever disposed to receive a revelation of evil or of grace that never comes" (135). This lack of revelation, of course, is not necessarily tragic. While modernist texts such as Franz Kafka's *The Trial* or Samuel Beckett's *Wait- ing for Godot* dramatize the sense of loss that may result from such a sus- pension of meaning, it is precisely this same loss that energizes some postmodernist narratives. In their expressions of the human condition as a postmodern condition, they tend to emphasize the more liberating impli- cations of this absence of the transcendent. Returning to Stoker's *Dracula*, we can see how, in effect, his vampire functions as the revelation of Evil in all its resplendent horror; as such, the vampire functions also to guarantee the presence of Good in the world of Stoker's human characters. Existing as he does beyond the margins of the Good, the human, and the natural, the vampire's very existence acts as a confirmation that these categories remain in place, demarcated against and defined by that which is not Good, not human, not natural.

Being postmodern, however, is about being complicit rather than vir- tuous; it is about approaching categories like Good and Evil with a certain ironic skepticism.[6] While some recent fantasies, such as John Skipp and Craig Spector's *The Light at the End* (1986), continue to relegate the vam- pire to roles in which it represents otherness, evil, and the corruption of life-in-death, there are many other works that construct the vampire figure in more interesting and complex—not to mention less horrific—ways. In such texts, Evil is not simple, not unproblematic, not outside the characters—whether human or vampire—not clearly marked off as something that can be expelled.

One of Anne Rice's most tellingly postmodern ploys is to characterize her vampires as themselves obsessed with questions about good and evil. In *The Vampire Lestat* (1985), in particular, the very idea of something like a principle of Evil is put into question. Such a principle, from the point of view of those so defined, serves an obviously exclusionary purpose. At the same time, however, it *is* at least a concrete definition, an identity, as well as an important foundational explanation for the way Reality really is. For a vampire like Armand, who has spent centuries lurking in graveyards and engaging in "unholy" rites—because this is how evil creatures behave—the loss of his belief in the principle of Evil is only belatedly liberating; initially, it also means the loss of his very sense of what he is—and, as I will return to below in my comments on the film *Vampire's Kiss*—the loss of a kind of *moral* justification for the killing which is necessary to sustain vampiric life. The fact that one is Evil is its own justification for the performance of evil acts.

In contrast, Rice's vampires are rather like revenant versions of Samuel Beckett's Vladimir and Estragon, whose world in *Waiting for Godot* is also defined in part as the vacuum created by the absence of any transcendent principle. The scene in which Lestat enters a church and proceeds to challenge God to destroy him for his temerity—a challenge that meets, in true absurdist fashion, with absolutely no response from the realm of the transcendent—is a powerful one, because it dramatizes a certain contemporary nostalgia for lost certainties. If Rice is "being postmodern" here, then this moment has the potential to be liberatory; in fact, this may be one of the ways in which we can read the difference between Armand and Lestat: Armand is the modernist, and, for him, absence is paralysis; in contrast, Lestat is the ironic postmodernist whose existentialism is also a celebration of the absolute freedom that arises from the suspension of revelation.

We can see here how some fantasies incorporate absence into their narratives as a thematic concern. Rosemary Jackson says of Stoker's vampire that "he occupies a paraxial realm, neither wholly dead nor wholly alive. He is a present absence, an unreal substance" (118). Contemporary vampires like Lestat are postmodern to the extent that they themselves are victims of the self-same absence they have come to represent; they are as trapped within the framework of meaninglessness as are their human counterparts. The frequently ironic tone of Lestat's narrative voice demonstrates his awareness of the truly ambiguous success of his efforts to construct an ethical system in the absence of traditional absolutes. It might even be argued that the less sincere Lestat is, the more postmodern he is.

Rice's novels, perhaps not too surprisingly given their best-seller status, do not manage to sustain their subversion of conventional moral categories. Before too long, these categories are back in place, simply displaced on to other configurations. In *The Queen of the Damned* (1988), both good and evil are roles played out by vampires: humans are merely the pawns in this particular version of the cosmic battle. And, in *The Tale of the Body Thief* (1992), a quite simple reversal takes place, in which evil is represented by the human Body Thief and Lestat, in spite of his by now rather tiresome occasional angst over his vampire nature, is obviously on the side of the angels. Finally, in *Memnoch the Devil* (1995), Rice raises her conflictual stakes to the maximum: both God and the Devil make their appearances in this novel and, although Lestat's ironic skepticism does not completely desert him, it is the struggle between cosmic binaries, writ larger than ever, which gives shape to the action of the novel.

One of the most interesting—and confusing—vampire stories to deal with questions of morality in the postmodern context is the blackly comic film *Vampire's Kiss* (dir. Robert Bierman, 1988), which tells of a despicable yuppie named Peter Low—played in completely over-the-top fashion by Nicholas Cage—and his encounter at a singles bar with the vampire Rachel. Singles bars, sites of sexual predation, are Peter's favorite milieu, so this is an ironically appropriate setting for his first encounter with Rachel. After Peter becomes Rachel's unwilling and powerless victim, it remains unclear whether or not he himself turns into a "real" vampire: he seems to develop a need for blood, and daylight seems to hurt him; however, although he is unable to see his own reflection in a mirror, the camera—and therefore the spectator—can see his reflection perfectly clearly; and he is forced to buy a set of Halloween vampire teeth since he does not grow any himself.

Vampire's Kiss cannot seem to make up its mind whether Peter is really a vampire or simply absolutely mad—or perhaps both. However, like Rice's Armand, Peter is convinced that he has become evil, and he uses this as the justification to behave accordingly. He rapes an already terrorized secretary whose brother, in revenge, kills him—by driving a wooden stake, which happens to be ready at hand, through his body. This, of course, leaves unanswered the question whether he really is a vampire. In any case, he welcomes his death.

What makes *Vampire's Kiss* interesting is its suggestion that, whether or not Peter becomes a vampire, he was already a morally corrupt human being and therefore already a kind of monster. Vampirism seems to function in this film as a kind of metaphor for behavior that cannot simply be explained away as the result of some kind of absolute Evil. The suggestion here is that human beings must take responsibility for their own actions, even as it becomes impossible to base these actions on any absolute and absolutely legitimizing moral foundation.

Charnas's "The Unicorn Tapestry" is unusual in this context because it is one of the few vampire narratives that refuse to be framed in the terms of a moral conflict. Categories like good and evil simply have no place in this story. Rather, Charnas defines the relationship between the vampire and its human victims as one of simple necessity, in which the hunter has no moral obligation to its prey. For her vampire, Weyland, this particular configuration is a necessary antidote to the dangers posed by empathy: the vampire who empathizes too strongly with its human victims risks starving to death. At one point in Weyland's ongoing discussions with the psychiatrist, he draws a telling analogy between himself and the unicorn, the magical beast betrayed by the human maiden and destroyed by human hunters (161).

If recent fantasy has absence at its heart, if it reveals only that there is no revelation forthcoming, perhaps one of the roles of the vampire now is to function as a metaphor for the unrepresentability of this absence that seems to characterize contemporary existence. The last story I will discuss here, Angela Carter's "The Lady of the House of Love" (1979), is directly concerned with the apparent destruction of the fantastic in its encounters with a clearly-defined human reality. And one of the nicely ironic twists Carter builds into her narrative is that the magical creature and the betraying maiden are one and the same.

Carter's story is a self-reflexive allegory about the disappearance of the fantastic in the face of an intensely smug human rationality whose definitions of the Real are clear-cut and confident, leaving no room for creatures like vampires. "The Lady of the House of Love" is perhaps the most postmodern of all vampire stories, a kind of meta-fantastic account of the crisis of authority that overtook the Victorian ideology of reason, an ironic parody of Stoker's *Dracula* which emphasizes that, in a world defined by the ideology of human rationality, it is, in fact, the vampire—here standing in for the realm of the fantastic as a whole—who is the real victim. "The Lady of the House of Love," from this perspective, is the fantasy par excellence about absence.

The climax of Stoker's Victorian horror story is the defeat of the evil other at the hands of human characters who are both associated with and strong supporters of the natural and the rational.[7] Carter's tale is a retelling of this same defeat, but in her contemporary reworking, the impulse behind the death of the vampire is a radical inversion of those values—social, sexual, moral—which Stoker affirms and defends in his earlier work.[8]

As Burton Hatlen describes them, Stoker's characters are "firmly committed to the values of technology, rationality, and progress" (125), and Stoker reinforces this commitment through endless details about timetables, for example, or the latest gadgetry with which his characters are obsessed. In these terms, the war in which Stoker's characters are enlisted is the defense of their ideological reality against the Evil that threatens its very foundations, an erotic and amoral Evil whose own very different reality comes into inevitable conflict with and nearly destroys the dominant one. It is not surprising that this struggle soon transcends the merely human, as even God is enlisted as a partisan in what is tantamount to a Crusade. As Van Helsing solemnly, if somewhat ungrammatically, intones: "Thus we are ministers of God's own wish: that the world, and men for whom His Son die, will not be given over to monsters whose very existence would defame Him. He have allowed us to redeem one soul already [Lucy Westenra's], and we go out as the old knights of the Cross to redeem more. Like them we shall travel towards the sunrise; and like them, if we fall, we fall in good cause" (354–55).

Stoker's evil Other is of such threatening proportions that his defeat only serves to demonstrate the fundamental rightness of the system against which he pits himself. In his diary, Jonathan Harker details the Count's "strong" face (25) and his "astonishing vitality" (26). During the struggle to save Lucy Westenra's life, John Seward expresses his fear that "there is some horrible doom hanging over" the human characters (160) as the vampire thwarts their every attempt to restore her.

Stoker gives to his monster the power of an almost inevitable and completely evil Fate, so that his final defeat takes on the stature of an apocalyptic battle that culminates in the reinstatement of the Victorian middle-class social and moral structure, more secure than ever after the ordeals and victories of its champions. If, as Jackson suggests, in works of fantasy "the very notion of realism which had emerged as dominant by the mid-nineteenth century is subjected to scrutiny and interrogation" (25), then Stoker's tale of terror ultimately repudiates the fantastic and aligns itself firmly on the side of that dominant realism. In the end, of course, Good emerges victorious, but it is a measure of both the threat and the allure of Evil that the Dracula archetype has enjoyed such a lengthy career in popular consciousness.

Carter's most obvious inversion of Stoker's narrative is in her construction of the vampiric other. Her vampire, the Lady Nosferatu, is described in suitably baroque terms as "the last bud of the poison tree that sprang from the loins of Vlad the Impaler" (94). Although she is thus connected to Stoker's vampire, she is only a decadent and attenuated shadow of the original Dracula, described by Hatlen as "more terrible and more magnificent than any other character in the novel" because of his "hunger for the infinite" (126). Dracula has chosen eternal life and an awful freedom, the results of a Faust-like bargain he seems never to regret. To his human opponents he has all the grandeur of an inevitable doom. In contrast, Carter's Lady is "a cave full of echoes, she is a system of repetitions, she is a closed circuit" (93). Her life is a helpless recreation of the lives of her ancestors, a mere "imitation of life" (95). Her fondest desire is for the finite and the human, a pathetic and ironic repudiation of the past grandeur of the original Dracula. Significantly, Carter's text tells us that, in the Lady's "derelict bedroom," "a cracked mirror suspended from a wall does not reflect a presence" (93). In her fastidious shrinking from her own nature, she is both Dracula and Mina Harker, or as Carter writes, she is "both death and the maiden" (93).

While in *Dracula* there is a genuine fear that the fantastic evil will invade and overwhelm the domain of the real, in Carter's parodic variation there is only an exhausted yearning to repudiate existence as the other and to become fully human. In her narrative world, the fantastic is faded and worn-out. To the young soldier who is lured to the Lady's crumbling château, this vampire/maiden seems "inadequately powered by some slow energy of which she was not in control; as if she had been wound up years ago, when she was born, and now the mechanism was inexorably running down and would leave her lifeless" (102). Far from being a personification of some evil destiny, she is herself the victim of her ancestors, whose portraits loom over her, always watching. She spends her time seeking a new future in her Tarot cards, "endlessly constructing hypotheses about a future which is irreversible" (95).

As it does for Stoker's Dracula, the Lady Nosferatu's downfall also appears in human form, in the person of a young English soldier who is traveling through the Carpathian mountains before taking his place in the drama of the Great War. If Stoker's characters sometimes feel trapped by an evil fate, this young soldier is indeed, all unsuspecting, foredoomed, but not because of any threat from the Lady Nosferatu. As the narrative informs us, he is a member "of that generation for whom history has already prepared a special, exemplary fate in the trenches of Europe" (97). His will be no transcendent battle against Evil, but a war of strictly human proportions, harrowingly real. Naturally—and ironically—he is sublimely unaware of the real fate in store for him as the vampire lures him to her as her next victim. Again, naturally—and ironically—she is overwhelmed by his beauty, his bravery, and his innocence, allowing herself to die for love of him rather than destroy him, thus preserving him, of course, for the greater horror of the trenches.

This doomed soldier represents the dominance of the real in Carter's narrative world. He is protected from the evil Other by his innocence—he is a virgin—and by his courage, but Carter slyly suggests that such innocence is really ignorance and such courage really lack of imagination (104). Stoker's Jonathan Harker is able to respond sexually to the three vampire brides at Castle Dracula, finding them, if "repulsive," also "thrilling" (48); while his desire must be repressed, it at least exists. In contrast, Carter's hero is asexual and cold. What little fear he feels is soon controlled and his desire becomes transmuted into a vague romanticism, an urge to embrace the Lady protectively (105). It is significant that when he looks at her he sees only himself reflected in her dark glasses (102). He is so grounded in his own reality that he is incapable of any other kind of awareness; he destroys the vampire because "in himself, he is an exorcism" (106). He thus becomes a parody of Stoker's protagonists. Noble, true, and good, but without any consciousness at all, he destroys the fantastic other, completely unaware of his interaction with something totally outside the framework of his own conception of what is real.

To the soldier, the Lady Nosferatu is just an undernourished and neurotic young girl whom he is eager to help: a clinic in Zurich can treat her for nervous hysteria; an eye specialist can treat her photophobia; a dentist will get her teeth into better shape, and "any competent manicurist will deal with her claws" (107). In this narrative world, the fantastic is neither evil nor alluring; it is simply irrelevant, and therefore nonexistent: "I will vanish in the morning light; I was only an invention of darkness" (107).[9] The young soldier sees nothing outside the framework of his own particular experience because he believes that there is nothing to see. He is protected ultimately by "a fundamental disbelief" (104), crushing an alternative reality of which he is never truly aware, then proceeding to the destiny prepared for him by a human horror far more truly evil, Carter's story implies, than any of the fantastic terrors that could still loom over Stoker's world.[10]

Carter seems to be suggesting that 1914 is a kind of demarcation between two views of reality. The solidity of the Victorian ideology reached its zenith just before the whole of human reality exploded in the first of the world wars, and commitment to such an ideology has been steadily weakening ever since. In fact, in his study of postmodern fantasy, Lance Olsen has suggested that, in light of the increasing complexities and ambiguities of our contemporary human experience, "The fantastic becomes the realism our culture understands" (14). Carter's account of the pre-1914 worldview is necessarily ironic and her main ironic device is the reversal of the conventions originated in Stoker's text.

Just as her vampire is an inversion of the ghastly magnificence of Dracula, so her narrative unfolds anti-climactically, in a kind of entropic dying fall of the fantastic, an inversion of the suspense and power of Stoker's narrative that climaxes in the final confrontation between fantastic and human realities. If *Dracula* is an admission that the borders of late-nineteenth century empiricism may be threatened by the other and must be defended at all costs, "The Lady of the House of Love" is a demonstration that this defense has been all too successful. Stoker's monster could still come near to toppling the structures of his narrative world, but Carter's creation is completely overshadowed, first by the solidity of empirical reality, and then by the events that will soon destroy that reality. Perhaps there is no room for an inhuman other, nor any need of one, in a human world that can provide its own apocalypse.

Carter does not suggest that this disappearance of the fantastic is in any way desirable. Her young hero, with his "golden head, of a lion, . . . of the sun, . . . of the lover" (105), recalls too clearly the kind of patriarchal worldview that has gradually overcome all opposition. Stoker, as an adherent of that reality, casts his female characters as prizes in the contest between the male vampire and his male human opponents—although strong characters like Mina Harker and Lucy Westenra constantly threaten to break through the textual boundaries of the roles assigned to them. It is no accident that Carter associates the female with the fantastic in her story, both of which must be either controlled or destroyed in Stoker's novel.

One of Carter's most significant narrative effects, then, is her identification of female and vampire, which makes clear the not-so-covert association of women with evil in the original *Dracula*. Even at the unconscious level of Stoker's text, his vampire—read "sexual"—women are both powerfully threatening and powerfully alluring, while Carter's Lady is "reduced" to the status of virgin. Virginity/ignorance may an asset to the hero, but for the Lady Nosferatu it spells helplessness and doom.[11]

While Stoker's characters are somehow aware that Evil is a part of our human nature and must be battled and expelled, Carter's narrative world no longer suffers from such guilt. Both the woman and the vampire have been expelled from the outset, neither enjoying any ontological status within the framework of the "real" world of reason and morality. As Jackson writes, "the dismissal of the fantastic to the margins of literary culture is in itself an ideologically significant gesture, one which is not dissimilar to culture's silencing of unreason" (173).

Carter's story provides some interesting contrasts to the narrative strategies, largely epistolary, of *Dracula*. While Stoker goes so far as to become tedious in his efforts at verisimilitude[12]—the novel is a compendium of diaries, journals, letters, newspaper articles, and other forms of eye-witness reports—Carter's narrative voice is clear and even intrusive, making no pretense that this fiction is anything but a tale being recounted by some outside and omniscient narrator. The effect of her self-reflexive strategies is to highlight the artificiality of the fiction, to name it clearly a fictive tale.

One of her most obtrusive techniques is to interrupt the narrative with rhetorical statements that clearly exist outside the world of the story itself, in the limbo of the text, as it were. Several times, for example, the narrative voice asks, "Can a bird sing only the song it knows or can it learn a new song?" (93, 103). Intrusions like this not only emphasize the fictive nature of the story, but also serve as a kind of commentary on the narrative events. The insertions of bits of nursery rhymes and references to *Sleeping Beauty* and to *Alice in Wonderland* keep the reader aware of the parallels to other obviously fictional narratives and effectively prevent any real emotional involvement in the story, as does the distanced coolness of the narrator's observations: "This lack of imagination gives his heroism to the hero" (104); "She herself is a haunted house" (103).

This commentary also provides the story with much of its ironic impact. While Jonathan Harker's journey to Castle Dracula is reminiscent of a descent—or, in this case, an ascent—into hell, Carter's hero arrives in the sunshine, on a bicycle which is the subject of the narrator's superbly ironic hymn to reason: "to ride a bicycle is in itself some protection against superstitious fears, since the bicycle is the product of pure reason applied to motion. Geometry at the service of man!" (97). It is not suprising that, throughout his adventures, the young man's chief concern is for this "product of pure reason."

Carter's concern is not to create an illusion of reality—the concern of the realist novel, and of Stoker's as well—but to maintain the reality of the illusion. This supports her narrative thematic that an unquestioning allegiance to empirical reality has threatened to destroy the fantastic; just as the Lady fades away in the glare of the young man's solidity, so there is no effort in Carter's text to give any reality to the fantastic elements of her story. The fantastic here is an absence, not a presence; stories of the fantastic should be read as the fictions they are.

Like Jameson, who writes of an "absent presence," of the "sense of the radical impoverishment and constriction of modern life" (*The Political Unconscious* 135), Jackson also recognizes the absence at the heart of contemporary fantasy: "As Victorian horror fiction evolves, it reveals a gradual apprehension of the demonic as mere absence, rather than as essentially diabolic" (112). From this perspective, Carter's story is both a demonstration of and a repudiation of the worldview that has resulted in this absence in the contemporary world. As Jackson goes on to suggest, "it is possible to discern [modern fantasy literature] as a desire for something excluded from cultural order—more specifically, for all that is in opposition to the capitalist and patriarchal order that has been dominant in Western society over the last two centuries" (176).

Significantly, the last image in Carter's story is that of a flower returning to life. Like a gothic Sleeping Beauty, the Lady lives trapped behind "a huge spiked wall" of red roses planted by her mother (95). It is these roses that arouse the young soldier's unease: "A great, intoxicated surge of the heavy scent of red roses blew into his face . . . , inducing a sensuous vertigo; a blast of rich, faintly corrupt sweetness strong enough almost, to fell him. Too many roses. Too many roses bloomed on enormous thickets that lined the path, thickets bristling with thorns, and the flowers themselves were . . . somehow obscene in their excess, their whorled, tightly budded cores outrageous in their implications" (98).

Here the threat of female sexuality parallels, is implicated in, the threat posed by the gothic fantastic. Carter emphasizes this homology even more strongly in the voice of the dead Lady: "And I leave you as a souvenir the dark, fanged rose I plucked from between my thighs, like a flower laid on a grave. On a grave" (107). Female sexuality, vampirism, death: aspects of what is most feared, aspects of that which the light of day destroys.

Plucked by the young soldier in memory of the dead maiden and tucked into the breast pocket of his jacket, this particular red rose seems quite withered and dead. He places it in water, however, and when he returns to it, "his spartan quarters brimmed with the reeling odour of a glowing, velvet, monstrous flower whose petals had regained all their former bloom and elasticity, their corrupt, brilliant, baleful splendour" (107–8).[13]

We might therefore read "The Lady of the House of Love" as a meta-fantastic text in which the vampire takes on all the metaphorical resonance of the suspensive absence at the heart of contemporary fantasy. And Carter's final image is a splendid one through which to announce the promise of a return of the fantastic repressed—in all its "corrupt, brilliant, baleful splendour"—to the stories we tell ourselves about ourselves. As "The Lady of the House of Love" suggests, the vampire, that figure that also signals a return, a re-birth into another mode of existence, is an especially significant metaphor through which to explore the mode of the fantastic within the context of postmodernity.

Notes

Epigraph

Our epigraph is from Allucquère Rosanne Stone's *The War of Desire and Technology at the Close of the Mechanical Age* (182–83). So pervasive has the vampire become that it (re)appears in the conclusion to Stone's study as a kind of metaphor for human subjectivity in contemporary technoculture, standing in, as it were, for the figure of the cyborg and functioning as a kind of (meta)metaphor.

1. Introduction: The Shape of Vampires

1. Like the vampire itself, this very popular novel is currently enjoying something of a resurrection, thanks to Neil Jordan's recent film version and to the vastly sophisticated—and quite entertaining—publicity campaign in which Rice herself participated with no small enthusiasm.

2. As has been frequently noted, Stoker's narrative voices are exclusively human. Dracula himself appears on only 62 pages of the original 390-page edition of the novel (Wolf, *The Annotated Dracula* 350).

3. This shift, in fact, is expressed quite literally as an integral element in the narrative structure of Robert Aickman's "Pages from a Young Girl's Journal" (1975). We are indebted to Joseph Andriano who called our attention to the particular relevance of this award-winning vampire story.

4. The vampire's ongoing "life" is not confined to popular culture alone; avant-garde writers like Angela Carter and Anne Hébert have also invoked this figure to create haunting allegories of contemporary life.

5. It is not surprising, perhaps, that, in the United States, most of these nonfiction popularizations of the vampire myth are shelved in the New Age section of Barnes and Noble bookstores.

6. Several fiction collections have also taken up the idea of the vampire-as-metaphor, most notably Ellen Datlow's two collections of short stories, *Blood Is Not Enough* (1989) and *A Whisper of Blood* (1991), Pam Keesey's collections, *Daughters of Darkness: Lesbian Vampire Stories* (1993) and *Dark Angels: Lesbian Vampire Stories* (1995), and Poppy Z. Brite's collection *Love in Vein: Twenty Original Tales of Vampiric Erotica* (1994). In particular, Datlow's two collections focus on what

Auerbach terms "psychic vampire fiction" (111); in many instances, energy replaces blood as the medium of exchange in these stories.

2. My Vampire, My Friend: The Intimacy Dracula Destroyed

1. S. S. Prawer's reading of *Vampyr* in *Caligari's Children: The Film as Tale of Terror* (138–63), is a particularly sophisticated tribute to Dreyer's consummate control over his dream tale.

3. Metaphor into Metonymy: The Vampire Next Door

1. For an interesting discussion of the traditional relationship between mirrors and aging, see J. A. Triggs's "A Mirror For Mankind: The Pose of Hamlet with the Skull of Yorick."

2. As W. S. Gilbert reminds us in *The Pirates of Penzance*:

When the enterprising burglar's not a-burgling—
When the cut-throat isn't occupied in crime—
He loves to hear the little brook a-gurgling—
And listen to the merry village chime—

5. Sharper Than a Serpent's Tooth: The Vampire in Search of Its Mother

1. Joseph Andriano's discussion of Carmilla's motherly role emphasizes its sinister nature, describing her as "the mother in her Terrible aspect, who withdraws the breast as punishment" (101).

2. I have written of this aspect of the vampire metaphor in my article, "Tiny Baby Bite: Vampirism and Breastfeeding."

3. See my article, "Rehabilitating Revenants, or Sympathetic Vampires in Recent Fiction."

4. Leonard Wolf describes a similar act, though more luridly, as a ritual among the Hell's Angels motorcycle gang in his popular treatment of vampire lore, *A Dream of Dracula* (9–11).

6. Meditations in Red: On Writing The Vampire Tapestry

1. "Advocates," co-authored with Chelsea Quinn Yarbro, brings Charnas's Weyland and Yarbro's Saint-Germain together in the same story. [ed.]

2. This is a reference to Rice's less than successful attempt to rewrite the figure of the mummy for contemporary readers in *The Mummy, or Ramses the Damned* (1989). [ed.]

7. Sang *for Supper: Some Notes on the Metaphorical Use of Vampires in* The Empire of Fear *and* Young Blood

1. Kenelm Digby (1603–1665) was the son of Sir Everard Digby, executed in 1606 for his part in the Gunpowder Plot. He was a courtier during the reign of Charles I, serving as a diplomat in various negotiations with Catholic nations, and a member of the council of the Royal Society who devoted his later years to scientific research. Simon Sturtevant applied to patent a process for hardening iron in the early seventeenth century, but died of the plague before explaining what the process entailed. Nobody knows, therefore, whether he had re-invented steel some time before Réaumur. I can't remember where I read this fascinating titbit of information, so I can't give further details.

8. Recasting the Mythology: Writing Vampire Fiction

1. *Worlds Apart*, ed. Camilla Decarnin, Eric Garber, and Lyn Paleo; *Embracing the Dark*, ed. Eric Garber; *Disorderly Conduct: The VLS Fiction Reader*, ed. Marsha Mark; *Children of the Night: Best Short Stories by Black Writers, 1967 to the Present*, ed. Gloria Naylor. [ed.]
2. See also the two anthologies of lesbian-vampire fiction edited by Pam Keesey, *Daughters of Darkness* (1993) and *Dark Angels* (1995). In addition, some excellent studies of the lesbian vampire have appeared in recent years, including Barbara Creed's *The Monstrous Feminine: Film, Feminism, Psychoanalysis*, 59–72; Andrea Weiss's *Vampires and Violets: Lesbians in the Cinema*, 84–108; Bonnie Zimmerman's "Daughters of Darkness: The Lesbian Vampire in Film," *Planks of Reason: Essays on the Horror Film*, ed. Barry Keith Grant, 153–63; and Sue-Ellen Case's important theoretical statement on queer theory, "Tracking the Vampire." [ed.]
3. As Suzie McKee Charnas mentions in her own essay in this collection, a section of her classic *The Vampire Tapestry* has also been transformed into a stage production. *Vampire Dreams*—scripted by Charnas and based on "The Unicorn Tapestry," the best known of the various segments which make up this novel—is a two-act play which debuted at the Magic Theatre in San Francisco in 1990. [ed.]

9. Dieting and Damnation: Anne Rice's Interview with the Vampire

1. In the 1995 video release of *Interview with the Vampire*, Rice appears in a kind of preface to the film and assures her audience that this film is "one that I love with all my heart."
2. According to Zillah R. Eisenstein, by 1979 women accounted for 41 percent of wage earners in the United States (89).
3. I should point out here that the vampire had always been distinguished by peculiar eating habits, but for writers and audiences before Rice these generally

represented, or were peripheral in interest to, the vampire's tantalizingly "abnormal" sexual practices. *Interview with the Vampire* is unique for focusing obsessively on the vampire's hunger for nourishment, often to the exclusion of its hunger for anything else.

4. As John Allen Stevenson's discussion of vampire sexuality in Stoker's *Dracula* indicates, Rice was inspired by a long tradition of vampire writing that formulated and stressed the vampire's sexual convertibility. According to Stevenson, Stoker's vampires are "beings in whom traditional distinctions between male and female have been lost and traditional roles confusingly mixed" (146). Where Rice differs from her predecessors is in presenting this gender confusion as potentially liberating.

5. While there is no direct causal relationship between ordinary dieting and anorexia nervosa, Susan Bordo has made the case that they are related in their "crystallization" of our culture's imperatives and ideals for women. Although first documented in the mid-nineteenth century, anorexia and bulimia became prevalent among young women in the 1960s and 1970s at about the same time that weight-watching became a widely popular trend. And just as dieting was touted in the popular press as a sign of liberation, anorexics frequently associate their emaciation with a freedom from traditional female roles, roles they identify with their mothers. Bordo says, "It is indeed essential to recognize in this illness a dimension of protest against the limitations of the ideal of female domesticity . . . that reigned in America throughout the 1950s and early 1960s—the era when most of [these girls'] mothers were starting homes and families" (104–5). Likewise, Kim Chernin suggests that in the postwar epidemic of eating disorders we see "a progressively growing crisis in the institution of motherhood" (*Hungry Self* 77).

6. This fantasy of "disownership" is articulated by anorexics as an ascetic ascendance of mind over body, an abandonment of matter for spirit. "The more weight I lost," says one anorexic, "the more I became convinced that I was on the right way. I wanted to learn to know what was beyond the ordinary living, what happens in the afterlife. Abstinence was just in preparation for special revelations; it was like the things the saints and mystics had done" (Bruch, *Conversations* 133). Equally relevant is Chernin's observation that the anorexic "disembodies herself, pretends the body isn't there" (*Hungry Self* 135). Bordo discusses the anorexic's revilement of the body in the context of traditions of dualism in Western thought (92–100), a point to which I will return.

7. In *The Obsession*, Chernin briefly discusses both of Atwood's "food" novels, *The Edible Woman* (1969) and *Lady Oracle*. Only the latter recounts what I have been calling the Virginia Slims narrative, the female success story based on loss of weight. For a reading of the diet story in *Scruples*, see Miner, 109–23.

8. Rice is not alone among writers of vampire fiction in her association of the vampiric diet and women's bodies. As Bram Dijkstra notes in his discussion of fin-de-siècle vampire tales, authors early on exploited the tantalizing associations among sucking blood, menstrual blood, and sucking milk to identify the vampire's sexual and gastronomic habits with a supposedly dangerous "primal" femininity. See Dijkstra, chapter 10. But much as Rice's metaphors may be indebted to her predecessors, the identification of the mother's body and food is also a central fea-

ture of anorexic fantasy. "[I feel] full of my mother," says one anorexic; "I feel she is in me—even if she isn't there" (*Golden Cage* 57). From such notions Chernin has evolved an extended model of female development, one that rejects Freud's Oedipal triangle in favor of a mother/daughter dyad derived from Melanie Klein's *The Psychoanalysis of Children*. The mechanics of this dyad are organized around "the horrifying image of the mother as literal food sacrifice" (*Hungry Self* 127). The mother's body is a "primal feast" which the daughter as an infant ruthlessly consumes and enjoys but which, as she grows older, becomes the repressed focus of illicit desire, rage, guilt, and the secret fear that, as an adult woman, she herself will be "sacrificed" next (*Hungry Self* 114–57). While different from my own analysis, Chernin's model offers a striking gloss on the unresolved mix of rage and longing aimed at women's bodies in Rice's novel.

9. It is interesting, in this regard, that the sisters begin by appearing in everyone's dreams and then gradually materialize for various characters as the story moves forward, concluding, of course, with Mekare's spectacular first appearance at the novel's finale.

10. Although not as relevant to my argument as *Queen of the Damned*, *The Tale of the Body Thief* (1992) and Neil Jordan's film version of *Interview with the Vampire* (1994) are worth mentioning here. *The Tale of the Body Thief*, in which the vampire Lestat trades bodies with a mortal and spends his entire mortal time disgusted with his new body's excretory, sexual, and digestive functions, confirms the extent to which Rice's vampires have all along been predicated on a freedom from fleshly needs. Those needs are here again associated with the female body: when Lestat is mortal he finds sexual pleasure with women; when he is a vampire again the objects of his desire return to being men. The film version of *Interview with the Vampire*, for which Rice wrote the screenplay, adds little to the novel, except that the film, in accord with the trajectory of Rice's writing generally, stresses consumption over appetite, an emphasis vividly manifested in the film's several gory scenes of blood-drinking.

11. Given the growth of political awareness in Claudia and Louis, we might speculate that a similar mechanism is at work in *Interview with the Vampire* itself. Its veritable "starving away" of traditional women's bodies, which hinges on its reinscription of those bodies as objects of hunger, seems to produce a more critical and unsettling analysis of gender relations than the fully gratified "good mother" in *Queen of the Damned*.

12. Foucault and his followers tend to emphasize the insidious dimensions of modern subjectivation. Judith Butler, for instance, describes Foucault's "soul" as a "normative and normalizing ideal according to which the body is trained, shaped, cultivated and invested" (33). She continues: the operation of power "produces the subjects that it subjects; that is, it subjects them in and through the compulsory power relations effective as their formative principle" (34). My emphasis here, however, is equally on the radical possibilities of modern subjectivation, its potential to produce politicized subjects through the liberalist processes upon which the formation of the modern "soul" is founded.

13. Stuart Ewen reads the ideal of female weightlessness as part of this century's dominant "aesthetic of abstract [market] value" (*All-Consuming Images* 176).

14. Mary's honed success as a career woman was set against the failures of her chubby neighbor, Rhoda, whose unredeemed flesh seemed to provide solid evidence of her longing to get married and have babies.

15. General information on the 1970s is from Edelstein and McDonough.

10. When Hollywood Sucks, or, Hungry Girls, Lost Boys, and Vampirism in the Age of Reagan

1. Strieber's *The Wolfen* (1978) had already been made into a film, directed by Michael Wadleigh in 1981; but his real success came later in the decade, when he became an authority on "how I encountered—and was raped by—aliens and lived to tell" in his alien-encounter bestsellers *Communion* (1987) and *Transformation* (1988). *Communion* was filmed in 1989, with Christopher Walken cast as Strieber.

2. The Hammer films include Terence Fisher's *Horror of Dracula* (1958) and *Dracula—Prince of Darkness* (1966), Freddie Francis's *Dracula Has Risen from the Grave* (1968), Peter Sasdy's *Taste the Blood of Dracula* (1970), Roy Ward Baker's *Scars of Dracula* (1970), *The Vampire Lovers* (1971), and *The Seven Brothers Meet Dracula* (1974), and Alan Gibson's more modern *Dracula A.D. 1972* (1972) and *Count Dracula and His Vampire Bride* (1973).

3. Ridley Scott's *Alien* appeared in 1979, and *Blade Runner* in 1981. Ridley and Tony had spent some years collaborating on British television commercials before they went into film making. Ridley was responsible for the highly polished Chanel advertisements of the '80s, which did not, incidentally, feature Catherine Deneuve.

4. Rice's borrowing from British neo-gothicism in her *The Vampire Lestat* (1985) has not gone unremarked. On Toronto's *The New Music* TV-special on vampires and rock stars, which aired in March 1987, Laurie Brown interviewed Murphy after his performance at RPM, asking him if he had read *Lestat*. He responded enthusiastically: "I'd like to play him." Interviewing Bowie after his gig at the Diamond Club, Brown asked the same question, and Bowie too expressed interest in Lestat, suggesting that his experience in *The Hunger* might qualify him for the role. According to Brown, Rice was "getting hundreds of letters saying that Sting should play Lestat in the movie," since Sting had apparently used the book as inspiration for his song, "Moon Over Bourbon Street." This obvious overlap between rock stars and vampires notwithstanding, the movie version of *Interview with the Vampire*, directed by Neil Jordan (*The Crying Game*), stars Tom Cruise as Lestat—in spite of Rice's vociferous public objections which, however, were later followed by her equally public endorsements of Cruise—and Brad Pitt as Louis.

5. See Paula A. Treichler's long list of the terms in which the media have characterized AIDS in "AIDS, Homophobia, and Biomedical Discourse: An Epidemic of Signification" (32–33).

6. Of course, given media confusion over the statistics, it is extremely difficult to establish any concrete numbers. Shilts, for example, provides the 12,000 victims figure (580). But Treichler points out that the number of Americans diagnosed with AIDS by the end of 1986 was almost 30,000, and half of them had died (63n92).

7. See Lorne Macdonald, *Poor Polidori: A Critical Biography of the Author of The Vampire*, 201.

8. *Near Dark* was Bigelow's first Hollywood film after she gave up painting; *The Lost Boys* was Schumacher's second film after *The Incredible Shrinking Woman* in 1981.

9. Robert Bierman's *Vampire's Kiss* (1989), starring Nicholas Cage, also operates as a monitory tale; but it combines the paranoia of Martin Scorcese's *After Hours* (1985) with the gothic, offering the possibility that Peter Low (Cage)—a Reaganite yuppy who picks up a woman in a singles bar—may or may not be inventing his vampirism. When Low determines that his date was a vampire and has infected him, he becomes obsessive about how he is gradually becoming a vampire—although he still has to buy a set of plastic teeth because his symptomatic long canines have not materialized.

10. See Jan Zita Grover's "AIDS: Keywords" (22–23).

11. The incident in Arcadia occurred in August 1987. *The Lost Boys* was released in July 1987 and *Near Dark* in October 1987.

12. Hollywood's resistance to representations of AIDS and vampirism seems ongoing. Given Neil Jordan's subsequent comments about *Interview with the Vampire*, we might consider why he may have been hired: "I think all these efforts [to make *Interview*] went wrong because they [presumably other directors and screenwriters] wanted to treat the vampirism or exchange of blood as a metaphor—for drug taking, for sexuality, for AIDS. . . . In fact it's not a metaphor for anything" (Abramowitz 72). Critics have indeed commented on the decided lack of eroticism in the film, and the separation of vampirism and the erotics of blood exchange, despite the unusual production involvement of David Geffen, one of the few "out" producers in Hollywood.

13. She made this comment on the *Entertainment Tonight* episode, aired 3 August 1992, about Hollywood's vampire offerings for that same year: Fran Rubel Kuzui's *Buffy the Vampire Slayer*, Francis Ford Coppola's *Bram Stoker's Dracula*, Fred Gallo's *Dracula Rising*, Adam Friedman's *To Sleep with a Vampire*, and Landis's *Innocent Blood*.

11. Consuming Youth: The Lost Boys Cruise Mallworld

1. For more on the evolution of an American mass market, see Strasser, and the various essays in the anthologies edited by Bronner and by Fox and Lears; for more specific studies of American advertising history, see Fox and Pope.

2. Other examples of this rigid viewpoint may be found in Williamson, Raymond Williams, and Ewen, *All-Consuming Images*.

3. For a contrasting, more monolithically negative view of the historical construction of the female consumer, see Ascher. See also Wolff, who argues that the flaneur is always and necessarily a male subject position and thus unavailable to feminists seeking critical "purchase" on modern culture, not to mention to women shoppers generally.

4. This analysis builds upon a left tradition, which extends back at least to Walter Benjamin, of viewing the marketplace as the "dream world" of capitalism, where mass fantasy is activated as a potentially critical utopian force; on this, see Rosalind Williams and Buck-Morss, *Dialectics*. Also, see Jameson, "Reification," which argues for a critical practice devoted to locating and unleashing the utopian impulse buried within the texts of mass culture.

5. In support of this thesis, I offer in evidence the careers of Jean Baudrillard and Roland Barthes, both of whose thinking on the subject of consumption traced a parabolic arc between these poles. Their early work—Baudrillard's *Société de consommation* (1970), Barthes's *Mythologies* (1957)—limned an invidious system of meaning-production which operated with faultless efficiency, while their later work—Baudrillard's *In the Shadow of the Silent Majorities* (1978), Barthes's *Pleasure of the Text* (1973)—celebrated an audience whose strategies of reception were willfully aberrant and uncontrollable. Interestingly enough, for Baudrillard, the reversal in his thinking came with an investigation of an implicitly vampiric image: capitalist society's baffled and tormented attempts to see itself in *The Mirror of Production* (1973).

6. Grossberg's book culminates a tradition in British and American cultural studies of identifying youth (sub)culture as the privileged site of analysis, the performative locus of contemporary capitalism's most pointed contradictions; see also Hebdige, McRobbie, the essays in Hall and Jefferson, and in Cole and Skelton.

7. Hollander and Germain show that such an advertising strategy extends back into the late nineteenth century, and Nasaw draws a compelling portrait of children as consumers in early twentieth-century American cities (115–37).

8. This final phase suggests a symbiotic vampirism, as credit-spending both spurs mindless consumption and feeds on the consumer as well. Milton Bradley's recent (1990) game, *Mall Madness*, is of interest in this context, since it both empowers players as shoppers armed with ATM and credit cards and also subjects them to the electronic "Voice of the Mall" that dictates a feverish strategy of consumption (see Friedberg 256).

9. Interestingly, in the early '90s the comic strip *Doonesbury* projected the emergence of a "virtual mall"—coordinated between the Disney and Fuji corporations—that combines elements of theme park, consumer wonderland, and cyberspatial dystopia, a conflation Friedberg's work supports: "The shopping mall developed as a site for combining the speculative activity of shopping with the mobilities of tourism; . . . as a mobilized gaze becomes more and more virtual, the physical body becomes a more and more fluid site, [resulting in] the privatized public space of the shopping mall . . . [being] replaced by the 'electronic mall' and the 'home shopping network'" (109–10). For more on the confluence of shopping mall, theme park, and electronic arcade, see Crawford; Davis; and Bukatman (227–40).

10. Consumer socialization is a concept explicitly deployed in the work of marketing analysts who focus on youth: see Moschis; Ward, Wackman, and Wartella; and McNeal.

11. Helitzer and Heyel advise marketers to "avoid the pied piper image" by remaining "above suspicion" in their solicitation of youthful buyers; yet, as befits

good capitalists, they resolutely defend the advertiser's right to go "hammer and tongs after the youth market, in whatever segment he thinks he can make a contribution and earn a profit—infants, moppets, preteeners, teeners, young adults. . . . Ours is a competitive system" (31–32).

12. Friedberg pursues connections and analogies between cinematic spectatorship and shopping flanerie (120–25).

13. This sort of criticism is ubiquitous: see also Langman (58–61) and Lasch.

14. The video scare reached epidemic proportions in Britain; see Amis. More judicious sociological surveys are John Graham (for Britain) and Kubey and Larson (for the United States).

15. Somtow, under his real name Somtow Sucharitkul, has also authored a science-fiction novel called *Mallworld*—set in a planet-spanning shopping mall—in which teens are impenned—for fun this time—in a lifesize pinball/video game (58–60).

16. For an historical study of the juvenilization of American culture through the patterns of movie-making and movie-going since the 1950s, see Doherty.

17. Gibian depicts the mall's environment as "*visionary freedom in enclosure*" (44; emphasis in original), an apt description of a video game as well, although Gibian's analogy, like Friedberg's, is with the cinema.

18. For a discussion of the contemporary craze for "body maintenance" as an effort to cling to an ideological vision of youth, see Woodward and Featherstone.

19. For a fascinating discussion of the construction of the child as an object of erotic desire/contemplation in modern culture, see Kincaid, who also mobilizes vampiric imagery; interestingly, in his analysis, the vampire figure too is an object of consumption: "by attributing to the child the central features of desirability in our culture . . . we have made absolutely essential figures who would enact this desire. Such figures . . . come to define us: they are the *substance we feed on*. . . . The pedophile is thus our most important citizen. . . . We must have the *deformed monster* in order to assure us that our own profiles are proportionate" (5; emphases added). Many contemporary youth vampire texts touch base with a Victorian classic that provides the starting point for much of Kincaid's analysis—J. M. Barrie's *Peter Pan*; see especially S. P. Somtow's *Vampire Junction* and its 1992 sequel *Valentine*, in which the desire solicited by androgynous teen stars involves an urge to consume the substance of youth which converges with pedophilia.

20. Butsch offers a detailed overview of the economic conditions and social effects of VCR market penetration, arguing that the spread of the new technology was guided less by a systematic capitalist plan than by the decisions of individual consumers and retailers in a historical context where "divisions within capital limited its ability to control people's leisure" (229). From Butsch's perspective, then, master vampire Max would actually be allied not with the settled interests of capitalist entertainment industries but with the burgeoning ranks of video retailers, whose threat was less to consumers than to the film studios, theater chains, and television networks whose profits and market-share they were steadily bleeding off. Thus, to pursue a more strictly historical allegory than I argue for in this essay, one can read the demonization of Max in *The Lost Boys* as the response of a beleaguered movie industry to the rise in the 1980s of a new service class catering to the privati-

zed consumption of film product. See also Lardner and the essays in Levy for more on the so-called "VCR revolution."

21. On the role of MTV as orchestrator of youth consumption, see Goodwin (especially 37–48), and Kaplan.

12. The Gilda Stories: *Revealing the Monsters at the Margins*

1. See Ernest Fontana's "Lombroso's Criminal Man and Stoker's *Dracula*" for an examination of the ways in which Dracula is characterized in the language of the Victorian social sciences.

2. See Burton Hatlen's "The Return of the Repressed/Oppressed in Bram Stoker's *Dracula*" for a persuasive materialist reading of Dracula as a floating category of "otherness." He is alternately exotically Eastern, earthy in the manner of workers and peasants, and a European aristocrat. These categories may appear to be mutually exclusive unless they are read in relation to their shared opposition to the Victorian bourgeoisie. See also Patrick Brantlinger's *Rule of Darkness: British Literature and Imperialism, 1830–1914*, for a broader exploration of Imperialism in British literature, particularly his chapter, "Imperial Gothic: Atavism and the Occult in the British Adventure Novel, 1880–1914" (227–53).

3. In *Dracula* both bloodsucking and vampire-staking are coded as heterosexual practices. Jonathan Harker is at risk from the "red lips" of the three vampire brides, while the Count can only approach the men by feeding on "your girls that you all love," as he tells them. Once she is undead, Lucy Westenra is "released" by her fiancé with a stake: "The thing in the coffin writhed; and a hideous, blood-curdling screech came from the opened red lips. The body shook and quivered and twisted in wild contortions" (241). As Christopher Bentley writes, "The phallic symbolism in this process is evident, and Lucy's reactions are described in terms reminiscent of sexual intercourse and orgasm, and especially the painful deflowering of a virgin" (30). Instead of being staked in his turn, Dracula is cut down by a sword, man to man.

Contemporary fiction writers have not missed the point: in zana's "dracula retold," van helsing advises jonathan to confront his new neighbor, a radical feminist woman named dracula, and "kill the evil in her by driving your, uh, stake into her" (20). With her use of small case letters, zana is making a parodic point about feminist deconstruction of hierarchy.

4. Films such as Jimmy Sangster's *To Love a Vampire* (a.k.a. *Lust for a Vampire*, UK, 1970), Jean Rollin's *Les Frissons des Vampires* (trans. *Sex and the Vampire*, France, 1970), Harry Kumel's *Daughters of Darkness* (Belgium/France/West Germany/Italy, 1971) and Hammer productions like *The Vampire Lovers* (Roy Ward Baker, UK, 1970) and *Twins of Evil* (John Hough, UK, 1971) are all representative. Of these films, Sue-Ellen Case writes that "Only the proscription of the lesbian is literally portrayed—the occult becomes cult in the repression" (15). See Pam Keesey's *Daughters of Darkness* (237–43) for a more complete filmography/bibliography.

5. Such films as *Blacula* (William Crain, US, 1972) and *Scream, Blacula, Scream!* (Robert Kelljan, US, 1973), both heavily mediated "blaxploitation" features from mainstream studios, hardly count as attempts at inclusivity.

6. Lestat is, of course, the main protagonist of Anne Rice's *The Vampire Chronicles*; Barnabas Collins is a central character from the television series *Dark Shadows*, which first ran on ABC in 1968–1971. Set in New England, this weekday daytime show began as a gothic romance-style soap opera; after it introduced the vampire Collins, its ratings soared. Martin Riccardo comments that, "as the series progressed, [Collins's] character gradually took on a more sympathetic nature" (59).

7. I am not implying here that sexuality can exist outside politics, for I do not believe it can. Hatlen makes the persuasive argument, however, that the appeal of *Dracula* is not due simply to the fact that it indicates a sublimated sexuality, but also because it locates that sexuality in the context of Victorian imperialist politics.

8. Catherine Belsey offers a concise and useful definition of the classic realist novel in her *Critical Practice*. In her discussion of "the seamless narrative," she observes that "a high degree of intelligibility is sustained throughout the narrative as a result of the *hierarchy of discourses* in the text. The hierarchy works above all by means of a privileged discourse which places as subordinate all the discourses that are literally or figuratively between inverted commas" (70).

9. I am speaking here not of the intensely conservative texts of Stoker and/or other "Imperial Gothic" writers, to use Patrick Brantlinger's phrase, but of the development of the gothic as a largely feminine genre a century before. In *Consuming Fiction*, Terry Lovell outlines what she terms the "fantastic as subversion thesis" about the function of the gothic in which "Two different kinds of subversion have been elided . . . : subversion of a socially constructed class society in which women are systematically subordinated to men; and subversion of a precarious psychic order which secures a viable personal identity for the individual within the social order" (67).

10. We can presume that the Girl was given a name by the people who enslaved her. The text rejects this hypothetical false name, and she remains nameless until she goes through a legitimate naming process. However, the text does not completely disenfranchise her: it grants her the dignity of writing "Girl" with a capital.

11. Science-fiction writer Octavia Butler's novel *Kindred* (1979)—not a vampire tale but an sf-fantasy hybrid—also engages with slavery, from the perspective of a contemporary black woman inexplicably sent back in time to the pre-Civil War South. Both *Kindred* and *Gilda* imply, in markedly similar ways, the simultaneous impossibility as well as the compelling necessity of engaging with the history of slavery across more than a century. Butler's text is further conflicted by the fact that the protagonist Dana has a white husband to whom she returns between her periodic trips to the plantation owned by a brutal white ancestor whom she must protect in order to ensure her family line.

12. For a full discussion of political activity in the late nineteenth and early twentieth centuries, see Paula Giddings's *When and Where I Enter: The Impact of Black Women on Race and Sex in America*, particularly her chapter 6, which deals with the phenomenon of the club movement, whereby tens of thousands of African-American women organized over one thousand different clubs; most of them

worked on reform issues such as education, poverty, childcare, and suffrage. In 1896 an umbrella organization, the National Association of Colored Women, was formed, the motto of which was "lifting as we climb." Giddings notes that the clubs became vehicles for "the recognition of women as a distinct social and political force" (96). They continued strong into the first few decades of the twentieth century.

13. Both historians and writers of fiction have paid attention to the phenomenon of women who lived as men. See, for example, Julie Wheelwright's *Amazons and Military Maids: Women Who Dressed as Men in Pursuit of Life, Liberty and Happiness*; Lynn Weiner's "Sisters of the Road: Women Transients and Tramps," and Ingrid MacDonald's "The Catherine Trilogy."

14. Jody Scott's Sterling O'Blivion is also a lesbian vampire concerned about her vulnerability: "And I'm sick, too, of getting the crap beat out of me, which happens oftener than one would like to believe" (5).

15. See Jonathan Katz's *The Invention of Heterosexuality*.

16. Neither the parodic postmodern detachment of Scott nor the liberative s & m rituals of Califia seem at first glance to have much in common with *The Gilda Stories*. This would be rich material for another study.

17. Nancy Johnston, "Kirk Loves Spock: 'Homosexual' Confession, Repression, and Orgasm," presented at the 22nd Annual Popular Culture Association Meeting, Louisville KY, 18 March 1992. For a fuller discussion of slash writing, see Henry Jenkins's "*Star Trek* Rerun, Reread, Rewritten: Fan Writing as Textual Poaching" and *Textual Poachers: Television Fans and Participatory Culture*; see also Constance Penley's "Brownian Motion: Women, Tactics, and Technology."

18. *Dark Shadows* has generated an abundance of spin-offs, both professional and fannish. Thirty-four commercial novels were released between 1968 and 1981, 27 of them published by Paperback Library (New York, 1968–1972). There was also a comic-book series (Gold Key, 1969–1976), and a movie. More interestingly, however, are the several fan organizations and the various fanzines, many of which, like *World of Dark Shadows*, ran for some years and provided a unique forum for fledgling writers (see Riccardo). Vampire *slash*, as a sub-genre, sexualizes the vampire mythos. One representative example is Dovya Blacque's *Dyad: The Vampire Stories*, which contains stories slashing media favorites like *Miami Vice*, *The Man from Uncle*, and *Lethal Weapon*.

19. I am grateful to Glenn Mielke, member of the Tleilaxu Gay and Lesbian SF/F Club (Toronto) and 'zine artist and producer, for introducing me to vampire slash by lending me his copy of *Dyad: The Vampire Stories* and sharing his thoughts on the elision of vampirism and "gayness"—I here place "gayness" in quotation marks because of what Mielke calls its tenuous link to gay experience and culture—in vampire slash. Several critics, notably Penley and Jenkins, have speculated about the appeal writing and reading slash holds for the straight women who produce and consume the bulk of it. Penley suggests that the answers to this question "range from the pleasures of writing explicit same-sex erotica to the fact that writing a story about two men avoids the built-in inequality of the romance formula, in which dominance and submission are invariably the respective roles of male and female" (153–54). Penley also speculates about the expanded possibilities of the sf genre.

20. The first three novels in the series are *Blood Price* (1991), *Blood Trail* (1992), and *Blood Lines* (1993); the fifth is *Blood Debt* (1997).

21. Blood has no gender, and it is also no longer uncritically characterized as a life-force, stolen by the creatures of the night. The AIDS crisis has destroyed that binary; blood can now be more dangerous than the ones who seek it. In her fourth Henry Fitzroy novel, Huff alludes to—in fact, she cures—AIDS. Gomez does not refer to AIDS specifically, but in the final segment of *The Gilda Stories*, she does indicate that the general health of humanity has becomes compromised by contaminants. Other recent vampire narratives have engaged with the AIDS crisis, notably Dan Simmons's *Children of the Night*. Simmons effectively integrates horror with science fiction by explaining vampirism genetically, linking the "condition" of vampirism to the human immune system. Vampires have come full circle from contagion to cure.

22. The vampire in John Landis's film *Innocent Blood* (US, 1992) prefers to "eat Italian": she preys on mafiosi. In a segment that has more in common with the slasher subgenre of horror than it does with vampire tales, the vampires in Nancy Baker's novel *The Night Inside* (Toronto: Viking, 1993) decimate a houseful of people gathered to make snuff films. The reader is co-opted; s/he must surely approve of such targets. Other cinematic vampires are not such good citizens. The characters in *The Lost Boys* (Joel Schumacher, US, 1987) and *Near Dark* (Kathryn Bigelow, US, 1987) are figured as contemporary criminals, murderous juvenile delinquents and transients respectively. These anti-social vampires do not survive. Taking the dynamic one step further, in the parodic *Sundown: A Vampire in Retreat* (Anthony Hickox, US, 1991), there are both good and bad vampires, and the former helpfully rid humanity of the latter.

23. Yarbro's vampire may be gentle, but her texts can be hyper-violent; the bloodshed, however, is displaced from Saint-Germain. Tanya Huff's Henry Fitzroy is also in this tradition, as the following exchange between Henry and the mortal Vicky indicates:

"I know you feed from others. It's just . . ."
"No. I didn't feed from him." Her involuntary smile was all he could have asked . . . .
"You're probably hungry, then."
"Yes." He took her hand and gently caressed the inner skin of her wrist with his thumb. Her pulse leapt under his touch. (*Blood Pact* 11)

Drake, the lesbian vampire of Katherine V. Forrest's "O Captain, My Captain," goes one step further: "I learned that another kind of fluid can also nourish me. It too is a vital fluid—from that place in a woman that creates life. You give it generously" (222).

24. This phrase was suggested by the title of Billy G. Smith's paper, "Black Women Who Stole Themselves in 18th-Century America," presented at the Berkshire Conference on the History of Women, Vassar College, 11 June 1993.

25. See Sue-Ellen Case's persuasive "Tracking the Vampire" for an exploration of the differences between queer and lesbian theory. Case maintains that the more

gender-specific lesbian and gay theories "reinscribe sexual difference, to some extent, in their gender-specific construction" (2). She traces representations of the
lesbian vampire, a figure who is "Outside the mirror, collapsing subject/object relations into the proximate, double occupancy of the sign, abandoning the category
of woman as heterosexist, and entering representation only in a guise that pro-
scribes her" (17). Case acknowledges her awareness, as a feminist, of the potential
problems with her position on queer theory; it is at exactly this point, I suspect, that
Gomez might distinguish her own politics.

26. See Fuss for a refreshing unpacking of political terms that have too frequently been used uncritically. She points out that each position has its own internal
contradictions, and warns against a reliance on binaries (119).

27. See Joanna Russ's *The Female Man* (1975); see also Suzy McKee Charnas's
Walk to the End of the World (1974) and *Motherlines* (1978), as well as her latest
addition to the sequence, *The Furies* (1994).

13. Coming Out of the Coffin: Gay Males and Queer Goths in Contemporary Vampire Fiction

1. Although not precisely a vampire film, *The Crow* and its sequel, *The Crow:
City of Angels*, both draw heavily on the gothic punk musical "canon," as does the
comic book itself, though always in the service of a resolutely heterosexual romance
narrative. See, for example, the liner notes accompanying *The Crow: City of Angels*
soundtrack (Miramax Records/Hollywood Records, 1996). The presence of "industrial" and other "alternative" bands on both soundtracks marks these bands as
having an affinity with goth, and it is this sort of intertextuality which I would like
to see function as an analogy for the interdependence which subtends relations between writers and readers of goth and gay vampire fiction.

2. While I am referring here to ambiguous sexuality, I am not in any way assuming that Nin's (or goth's, for that matter) reputation as bisexual is necessarily
liberating or even simply defined. For an excellent reading of Anaïs Nin's positioning in the textual and historical development of the naming of female same-sex
desire, see Judith Roof's *A Lure of Knowledge: Lesbian Sexuality and Theory*.

3. For a useful overview of the ways in which camp can be thus configured, see
Moe Meyer's "Introduction: Reclaiming the Discourses of Camp" in his edited
collection, *The Politics and Poetics of Camp*.

4. Examples of how meaning thus circulates in our culture include "ethnic press" versus "the Press," "gay marriage" versus "marriage," and "Franco-
Ontarian" versus "Ontarian." The answer to this problem of marking is not simply
to ignore difference, but to mark the categories heretofore left unmarked as the
definitionally privileged set of codes.

5. This raises a question, for instance, about the "invisibility" of the femme
lesbian *as* lesbian, which, while not the subject of this present essay, is surely related
to popular assumptions that all hyperfemme goth women are straight. This is most
emphatically *not* the case.

6. The personae on the Vampyres-L discussion list can inhabit speculative fiction (as characters), "real" discussions (as the objects of those discussions), and a kind of in-between space as alternative identities on discussion lists and in internet live-chat parties. (Readers wishing to become part of an interactive list on which original fiction and discussion both occur should search the World Wide Web for "vampire" or "vampyre" pages which have up-to-date subscription information. The address for Vampyres-L will have changed by the time this essay appears in print.)

7. This is my reductive way of signaling an affinity with Eve Kosofsky Sedgwick's vastly more complex argument in her first study of the patterns of male homosocial textuality (which includes some discussion of gothic textuality), *Between Men: English Literature and Male Homosocial Desire*.

8. Why not the homosocial parts, then, in which blood is shared between Dracula and the Good Guys through Lucy's veins? Surely one must go further back, to Polidori's Lord Ruthven and Aubrey—but how much of this are we reading indexically through Polidori's own relationship to Byron? Indeed, Stoker's own possible secret/not-secret (Henry Irving), as well as various textual clues in *Dracula*, might lead one in similar directions, as might Stoker's connection to Oscar Wilde through Florence Stoker (see, for instance, David Skal's discussion in *Hollywood Gothic*, 34–39).

9. I've used the term "perambulation" here in an effort to connect Walter Benjamin's sense of Baudelaire (himself not unrelated to vampire figurations) as a *flâneur* to the scripting of Vardalek in the late nineteenth-century condition of decadence. While this is not the place to undertake such a comparison, it would be interesting to pursue it in the context of Benjamin's essay "On Some Motifs in Baudelaire."

10. I use the adjective "dangerous" to signal the all-consuming threat posed by the one who knows too much about the colonizer's culture (see Stephen D. Arata's "The Occidental Tourist: Dracula and the Anxiety of Reverse Colonization").

11. I want to be clear, however, about what I'm *not* claiming here: it is not by way of Stenbock's own gender that I'm exploring male self-representation in the writing of male-male desire. I'm not suggesting that only a man could have written this piece, nor that only men are writing gay and queer selves now. I *am* suggesting however, that authors are real people who read certain codes and write them, inadvertently or not, into texts. It is the relative embeddedness of these codes which marks the difference between "now" versions of this process and "then" versions of it.

12. McMahan's original story appeared in his Lambda Literary Award-winning collection, *Somewhere in the Night*.

13. I'm thinking here of Lestat's threatening "Perhaps you should sleep with Louis. After all, when I'm tired . . . I'm not so kind" (95). Readers might also recall the displaced pedophilia described in the scene in which Claudia attempts to poison Lestat by drugging two young boys whom—er, whose blood, I mean—she knew he would find irresistible (135–36).

14. Bowen is a prolific, multiple-genre writer of erotic fiction. He has contrib-

uted stories to Cecilia Tan's *Blood Kiss: Vampire Erotica* and to Pam Keesey's second vampire collection, *Dark Angels: Lesbian Vampire Stories* (1995), as well has having published his own collection of vampire stories titled *Winter of the Soul* (1995).

15. This intriguing excess is also ably demonstrated in Pat Califia's contribution to *Sons of Darkness*, "Parting Is Such Sweet Sorrow" (146–69).

16. One moment which tends to reiterate rather than resist gender and sexuality norms did not make it into the novel, but was published as part of a short story called "Brass Ring" in Tan's *Blood Kiss* collection. In this excised scene, Rafael and Michael—the former in female drag rather than being physically transformed—kiss by a carousel ride at a local fair. They are taken for a heterosexual couple by a child, who exclaims "Look Grandma, that man is kissing that woman!" to which Grandma replies "Yes, dear. They're in love. Don't bother them" (109). Rafael, now liberated by convincingly performing the usual display of heteronormative ownership conveyed in the public kiss, states "I can't go back in the closet" (109). One wonders, however, how "out" one is if a child and a grandma, two of our culture's most potentially threatened observers in the discourse of gay display, mistake the couple for a man and a woman. The inclusion of this scene might have undercut the novel's radical claims a little too obviously.

17. *Drawing Blood* (1993), Brite's second novel, also contains goths and gay sex, but isn't specifically a vampire novel. The controversy that is bound to ensue over her third novel, *Exquisite Corpse* (1996), will surely be about a perceived equivalence between "gay," "pedophile," and "serial killer."

18. Poppy Brite here seems to be arguing for a liberal tolerance of difference—what I might be tempted to call "vanilla queer." Students of Poppy's persona will want to find such interviews as Bruce C. Steele's "Poppy Art: Horror Novelist Poppy Z. Brite Turns Stomachs and Opens Eyes." On the other hand, it is possible to conceive of queer as an anarchic politics of alterity, a postmodern logic of difference rather than of identity. This is hardcore queer, or "queercore," a term coined by Canadian underground filmmaker Bruce LaBruce, according to Paul Burston and Colin Richardson in their introduction to *A Queer Romance: Lesbians, Gay Men and Popular Culture* (7). It owes as much to a postpunk aesthetic as it does to deconstruction. Perhaps queercore is one of the means by which goth vampire fags might narrativize identity.

19. Interested readers will allow me temporarily to deploy provisional categories in order to point them toward Pat Salah's transsex, transgender "The Perfect Form" (*Blood Kiss*, 1–18) in which a young gay goth boy is turned by an older male vampire into a younger female nymphomaniac, and Gary Bowen's previously mentioned "Brass Ring" (*Blood Kiss*, 85–110). In *Love in Vein*, Ian McDowell's "Geraldine" (27–56) is a fascinating queer vampire updating of Coleridge's poem, with goth undertones and a moral code which seems to share some elements of, while in fact being quite inimical to, Jewelle Gomez's lesbian vampire stories; Christa Faust's "Cherry" (125–38) involves a goth-coded male transvestite sex worker who goes home with an apparently male vampire and—I won't spoil it; Brian Hodge's "Alchemy of the Throat" (263–92), which narrates the tale of an older male vampire who buys a castrato, might usefully be discussed in relation to Wayne Koestenbaum's "The Queen's Throat: (Homo)sexuality and the Art of Singing"; and fi-

nally, Mike Baker's "Love Me Forever" (295–312) stages a scene of unrequited college roommate lust which is tragically mediated by a shapeshifting vampire with purple eyes.

20. New, of course, is a word I use with hesitation: there are instances even in the history of vampire fiction in which the discourse of the author is not freighted with the same singularity of identity formation as is the case with more canonical literary modes. The penny-weekly format, for example, in which *Varney the Vampyre* (1847) was written, was part of a mode of production of texts in which the actual author's identity was hardly a selling point compared to the publishing house's reputation for thrills and chills.

14. Techno-Gothic Japan: From Seishi Yokomizo's The Death's-Head Stranger to Mariko Ohara's Ephemera the Vampire

1. According to Asahiko Sunaga, it is after 1930 that vampire-related novels and essays began being published. Rampo Edogawa's novel, *The Vampire*, Konosuke Hinatsu's essay, "Vampire," and Masayuki Jo's short story, "Vampire," were all published in 1930; Yoichi Nagakawa's tale, "Vampire," as well as Hinatsu's translation of Montague Summers's *The Vampire: His Kith and Kin*, were published in 1931; and Haruo Sato's translation of Polidori's *The Vampyre* appeared in 1932. As Sunaga says, there was no folklore of vampire or bloodsucking ogres before 1930.

2. Here I would like to clarify how Hagio's creation of *vampanella* diverges from the conventional western figure of vampire. Hagio attempts to reinterpret and refigure—almost disfigure—the traditional biology of vampire by inventing an imaginary homogeneity between human blood and the ether-like "idioplasm of the rose." In order to satisfy his or her immediate hunger, vampanella has only to substitute the idioplasm of the rose for human blood, dropping the extract of the idioplasm into a cup of tea and drinking it. At this point, then, it is worth noting some of the effects of Hagio's brilliant re-creation of western vampire: she visually conflates the image of vampanella as a beautiful western boy with the image of the red rose; and she promotes the Japanese adoration of western aesthetic and fashion culture by means of the fusion of vampirism with British tea culture and horticulture. It is this combination of red rose (signifying imported culture) with vampire legends which introduces a kind of utopianism into Hagio's vampirism.

3. Miriam Jones discusses "K/S" (slash) fiction in more detail, elsewhere in this volume. [ed.]

4. Darko Suvin's very influential study of the poetics of science fiction defines the genre as one "whose necessary and sufficient conditions are the presence and interaction of estrangement and cognition" (7–8).

5. By "post-creolian," I mean the age of "heteroglossia" in the cyborgian and post-colonialist sense suggested by Donna Haraway in her "Cyborg Manifesto." As Haraway concludes, "This is a dream not of a common language, but of a powerful infidel heteroglossia" (181). Here I want to emphasize the linguistic aspect of post-colonialism.

6. At the time of writing, Ohara's story, "Girl" (1984) is the only one of her works available in English. Another story, "Mental Female" (1985) is forthcoming in Takayuki Tatsumi and Larry McCaffery's guest-edited issue of *Review of Contemporary Fiction, Avant-Pop Japan*. In the latter, Tokyo's mother computer and North Siberia's father computer appear on TV as a girl and a boy, Ms. Kipple and Mr. Techie. They fall in love and begin to play catch, a form of foreplay that launches missiles from both sides. As is clear from this outline, "Mental Female" is an example of Japanese proto-cyberpunk fiction, its appearance coinciding with the cyberpunk movement in North America.

7. When William Gibson paid his second visit to Japan in the fall of 1991 and talked with myself and Takayuki Tatsumi, he referred to the writings of Storm Constantine as "techno-gothic." Because of this, two years later I was inspired to guest edit the *Techno-Gothic* special issue of *Hayakawa's SF Magazine*, which included stories in translation by Constantine ("Immaculate"), Elizabeth Hand ("The Investiture"), Greg Egan ("Reification Highway"), and Angela Carter ("The Loves of Lady Purple"). At that time, I defined "techno-gothic" as a literary tradition obsessed both literally and figuratively with the nemesis of "blood," an obsession that has become more visible and readable in the wake of cyberpunk (see my "Techno-Gothic: An Introduction"). This concept enables us to radically reread writers like Tanith Lee, Michael Moorcock, Stephen Milhauser, Umberto Eco, Richard Calder, and David Blair, to say nothing of hardcore cyberpunks like Gibson and Bruce Sterling. From this perspective, I designate Mariko Ohara, as well as Baku Yememakura and Yasutaka Tsutsui, as Japanese Techno-Gothic writers.

15. Fantasies of Absence: The Postmodern Vampire

1. For this section of her discussion, Jackson draws on Jean-Paul Sartre's 1947 essay, "'Aminadab' or the Fantastic Considered as a Language." As described by Jackson, this is Sartre's "defense of fantasy as a perennial form coming into its own in the secularized, materialistic world of modern capitalism" (17).

2. For a more detailed discussion of the appearance of vampires in science-fiction scenarios, see my "The Vampire and the Alien: Variations on the Outsider."

3. This also suggests the potential usefulness of Julia Kristeva's meditation on abjection, *Powers of Horror*, as a theoretical framework within which to consider the vampire, a figure which exists precisely in that in-between state which Kristeva identifies as the source of true horror. Her commentary is extremely suggestive. For example, she writes of the corpse: "It is death infecting life. Abject. It is something rejected from which one does not part, from which one does not protect oneself as from an object. Imaginary uncanniness and real threat, it beckons to us and ends up engulfing us" (4). And she observes that "many victims of the abject are its fascinated victims—if not its submissive and willing ones" (9).

4. See R. E. Foust's "Monstrous Image: Theory of Fantasy Antagonists" for a useful discussion of the binary assumptions through which the category of the monstrous is constructed.

5. Like Good, of course, Evil is a socially-constructed category. As Fredric

Jameson notes: "The concept of good and evil is a positional one that coincides with categories of Otherness. . . . The essential point to be made here [about the Other] is not so much that he is feared because he is evil; rather he is evil *because* he is Other, alien, different, unclean, and unfamiliar" (*The Political Unconscious* 115).

6. In his wide-ranging discussion of modern and postmodern irony, Alan Wilde makes the following useful distinction: "Modernist irony . . . expresses a resolute consciousness of different and equal possibilities so ranged as to defy solution. Postmodern irony, by contrast, is suspensive: an indecision about the meanings or relations of things is matched by a willingness to live with uncertainty, to tolerate and, in some cases, to welcome a world seen as random and multiple, even, at times, absurd" (44). Wilde's use of the term "suspensive," it should be noted, differs from Jameson's in that it implies a more positive approach to "liv[ing] with uncertainty."

7. It is no accident that the frontispiece of Leonard Wolf's *The Annotated Dracula* is a reproduction of Goya's *The Sleep of Reason*—"which breeds monsters" (n.p.).

8. While Carter's story is extremely brief relative to Stoker's lengthy novel, it has all of the original behind it, so that it resonates with much that need not be written, but only suggested in passing. In this sense, her story is virtually a parody of *Dracula*, in that the conventions initiated by Stoker and solidified since in numerous stories and films are always present in Carter's text, to be echoed, inverted, or subverted as required by her own particular narrative objectives. Note Linda Hutcheon's definition of parody as "imitation with critical ironic distance, whose irony can cut both ways" (*A Theory of Parody* 37).

9. In Eric Rabkin's words, "the truly irrelevant tends to be excluded not only from art but in some sense from all experience . . . , As McLuhan says, 'I wouldn't have seen it if I hadn't believed it' " (14).

10. Carter's is not the only story which suggests the relative insignificance of vampiric predation when it is considered within the context of what human beings are capable of achieving all on our own. Jack Dann and Gardner Dozois' "Down Among the Dead Men" (1982) situates its vampire in a Nazi concentration camp and the action in Connie Willis's vampire story, "Jack" (1991), takes place during the London blitz. British playwright Caryl Churchill's *Mad Forest* (1990), set in Romania, contains a vampire who "came here for the revolution, I could smell it a long way off. . . . There's been a lot of good times over the years" (44–45).

11. Various literary critics and theorists have examined the conflation of women with vampires in Stoker's novel; see, for example, Phyllis A. Roth's "Suddenly Sexual Women in Bram Stoker's *Dracula*" and Gail B. Griffin's " 'Your Girls That You All Love are Mine': *Dracula* and the Victorian Male Sexual Imagination." For an excellent analysis of the novel from the perspective of gender and homoeroticism, see Christopher Craft's " 'Kiss Me with Those Red Lips': Gender and Inversion in Bram Stoker's *Dracula*"; and see also Andrea Weiss's discussion of the lesbian vampire film in *Vampires and Violets: Lesbians in the Cinema* (84–108).

12. Stoker works hard to give his readers the impression of objective, factual reality; his prefatory note, included in Wolf's *The Annotated Dracula*, makes his intentions clear: "How these papers have been placed in sequence will be made manifest in the reading of them. All needless matters have been eliminated so that a

history almost at variance with the possibilities of latter-day belief may stand forth as simple fact. There is throughout no statement of things past wherein memory may err, for all the records chosen are exactly contemporary, given from the standpoint and within the range of knowledge of those who made them" (n.p.).

13. Nina Auerbach's comments on the "unquenchable life" and "corporeality" of nineteenth-century female vampires such as Coleridge's Geraldine and Le Fanu's Carmilla suggest a direct link between these earlier figures and Carter's Lady Nosferatu, in spite of the faded quality of her twentieth-century presence. Auerbach argues that, "In nineteenth-century iconography, male vampires are allies of death who end their narratives by killing or dying, but females are so implicated in life's sources that their stories overwhelm closure" (49–50). The Lady Nosferatu's story also "overwhelm[s] closure."

Works Cited

Unless otherwise specified, all Japanese titles have been translated into English for the reader's convenience.

Abramowitz, Rachel. "Young Blood." *Premiere* 8 (November 1994): 62–72, 116.

Aickman, Robert. "Pages from a Young Girl's Journal." 1975. *Vampires: Two Centuries of Great Vampire Stories*, ed. Alan Ryan. Garden City, NY: Doubleday, 1987. 382–414.

Aldiss, Brian. *Dracula Unbound*. New York: HarperCollins, 1991.

Amis, Martin. *Invasion of the Space Invaders*. London: Hutchinson, 1982.

Andriano, Joseph. *Our Ladies of Darkness: Feminine Daemonology in Male Gothic Fiction*. University Park: Pennsylvania State University Press, 1993.

Arata, Stephen D. "The Occidental Tourist: *Dracula* and the Anxiety of Reverse Colonization." *Victorian Studies* 33 (Summer 1990): 621–45.

Ascher, Carol. "Selling to Ms. Consumer." 1977. *American Media and Mass Culture: Left Perspectives*, ed. Donald Lazere. Berkeley: University of California Press, 1987. 43–52.

Attali, Jacques. *Noise: The Political Economy of Music*. 1977. Trans. Brian Massumi. Minneapolis: University of Minnesota Press, 1985.

Atwood, Margaret. *The Edible Woman*. 1969. New York: Popular Press, 1976.

———. *Lady Oracle*. 1976. Toronto: McClelland-Bantam, 1977.

Auerbach, Nina. *Our Vampires, Ourselves*. Chicago: University of Chicago Press, 1995.

Baker, Mike. "Love Me Forever." *Love in Vein: Twenty Original Tales of Vampiric Erotica*, ed. Poppy Z. Brite. New York: HarperCollins, 1994. 293–312.

Baker, Nancy. *The Night Inside*. Toronto: Viking, 1993.

Barber, Paul. *Vampires, Burial, and Death: Folklore and Reality*. New Haven, CT: Yale University Press, 1988.

Barthes, Roland. *Mythologies*. 1957. Trans. Annette Lavers. New York: Hill and Wang, 1972.

———. *The Pleasure of the Text*. 1973. Trans. Richard Miller. New York: Hill and Wang, 1975.

Baudrillard, Jean. *In the Shadow of the Silent Majorities*. 1978. Trans. Paul Foss, Paul Patton, and John Johnston. New York: Semiotexte, 1983.

———. *The Mirror of Production*. 1973. Trans. Mark Poster. St. Louis: Telos, 1975.

———. *Société de consommation*. Paris: Gallimard, 1970.

Beckett, Samuel. *Waiting for Godot*. 1954. New York: Grove Press, 1994.

Belsey, Catherine. *Critical Practice*. London: Methuen, 1980.

Benjamin, Walter. "On Some Motifs in Baudelaire." *Illuminations*. 1969. Trans. Harry Zohn. New York: Schocken Books, 1985. 155–200.

Bentley, Christopher. "The Monster in the Bedroom: Sexual Symbolism in Bram Stoker's *Dracula*." *Literature and Psychology* 22 (1972). *Dracula: The Vampire and the Critics*, ed. Margaret L. Carter. Ann Arbor, MI: UMI Research Press, 1988. 25–34.

Bergstrom, Elaine. *Shattered Glass*. New York: Berkley, 1989.

Blacque, Dovya, ed. *Dyad: The Vampire Stories*. Poway, CA: Mkashef Enterprises, 1991.

Bordo, Susan. "Anorexia Nervosa: Psychopathology as the Crystallization of Culture." *Feminism and Foucault: Reflections on Resistance*, ed. Irene Diamond and Lee Quinby. Boston: Northeastern University Press, 1988. 87–117.

Bowen, Gary. "Brass Ring." *Blood Kiss: Vampire Erotica*, ed. Cecilia Tan. Boston: Circlet Press, 1994. 85–110.

———. *Diary of a Vampire*. New York: Masquerade Books, 1995.

———. *Winter of the Soul*. Elkton, MD: Obelisk Books, 1995.

Bowlby, Rachel. *Just Looking: Consumer Culture in Dreiser, Gissing, and Zola*. New York: Methuen, 1985.

———. *Shopping with Freud*. New York: Routledge, 1993.

Brantlinger, Patrick. *Rule of Darkness: British Literature and Imperialism, 1830–1914*. Ithaca, NY: Cornell University Press, 1988.

Brite, Poppy Z. *Drawing Blood*. New York: Dell, 1993.

———. *Exquisite Corpse*. New York: Simon and Schuster, 1996.

———. "His Mouth Will Taste of Wormwood." 1990. *Sons of Darkness: Tales of Men, Blood, and Immortality*, ed. Michael Rowe and Thomas S. Roche. Pittsburgh: Cleis Press, 1996. 135–45.

———. *Lost Souls*. New York: Dell, 1992.

———, ed. *Love in Vein: Twenty Original Tales of Vampiric Erotica*. New York: HarperCollins, 1994.

Bronner, Simon J., ed. *Consuming Visions: Accumulation and Display of Goods in America, 1880–1920*. New York: Norton, 1989.

Brownworth, Victoria A., ed. *Night Bites: Vampire Stories by Women*. Seattle: Seal Press, 1996.

Bruch, Hilda. *Conversations with Anorexics*, ed. Danita Czyzewski and Melanie A. Suhr. New York: Basic/Harper Collins, 1988.

———. *The Golden Cage: The Enigma of Anorexia Nervosa*. 1978. New York: Vintage/Random House, 1979.

Brust, Steven. *Agyar*. New York: Tor Books, 1993.

Buck-Morss, Susan. *The Dialectics of Seeing: Walter Benjamin and the Arcades Project*. Cambridge, MA: MIT Press, 1989.

———. "The Flaneur, the Sandwichwoman, and the Whore." *New German Critique* 39 (1986): 99–140.

Bukatman, Scott. *Terminal Identity: The Virtual Subject in Postmodern Science Fiction*. Durham, NC: Duke University Press, 1993.

Burgin, Victor, James Donald and Cora Kaplan. "Preface." *Formations of Fantasy*, ed. Burgin, Donald, and Kaplan. New York: Methuen, 1986. 1–4.

Burston, Paul and Colin Richardson, eds. *A Queer Romance: Lesbians, Gay Men and Popular Culture*. New York: Routledge, 1995.

Butler, Judith. *Bodies That Matter: On the Discursive Limits of "Sex."* New York: Routledge, 1993.

Butler, Octavia. *Kindred*. Boston: Beacon Press, 1979.

Butsch, Richard. "Home Video and Corporate Plans: Capital's Limited Power to Manipulate Leisure." *For Fun and Profit: The Transformation of Leisure into Consumption*, ed. Richard Butsch. Philadelphia: Temple University Press, 1990. 215–35.

Califia, Pat. "Parting Is Such Sweet Sorrow." *Sons of Darkness: Tales of Men, Blood and Immortality*, ed. Michael Rowe and Thomas S. Roche. Pittsburgh: Cleis Press, 1996. 146–69.

———. "The Vampire." *Macho Sluts*. Boston: Alyson, 1988. 243–62.

Calvin Center for Christian Scholarship. *Dancing in the Dark: Youth, Popular Culture, and the Electronic Media*, ed. Roy M. Anker. Grand Rapids, MI: Eerdmans, 1991.

Carrington, Dorothy. *The Dream-Hunters of Corsica*. London: Weidenfeld and Nicolson, 1995.

Carter, Angela. *The Bloody Chamber and Other Stories*. 1979. New York: Penguin, 1981.

———. "The Lady of the House of Love." 1979. *The Bloody Chamber and Other Stories*. New York: Penguin, 1981. 93–108.

———. "The Loves of Lady Purple." *Fireworks: Nine Stories in Various Disguises*. 1974. New York: Harper and Row, 1981. 24–40. *Techno-Gothic*, special issue of *Hayakawa's SF Magazine* 443, 34/10 (September 1993).

———. *The Sadeian Woman*. London: Virago, 1979.

Carter, Margaret L., ed. *Dracula: The Vampire and the Critics*. Ann Arbor, MI: UMI Research Press, 1988.

———. "Interview with Suzy McKee Charnas." *Vampire's Crypt* 2 (Summer 1990): 3–10.

Case, Sue-Ellen. "Tracking the Vampire." *Differences: A Journal of Feminist Cultural Studies* 3, 2 (1991): 1–20.

Charnas, Suzy McKee. *The Furies*. New York: Tor Books, 1994.

———. "The Unicorn Tapestry." *The Vampire Tapestry*. 1980. New York: Tor Books, 1986. 107–82.

———. *The Vampire Tapestry*. 1980. New York: Tor Books, 1986.

———. *Walk to the End of the World*; and *Motherlines*. 1974, 1978. London: Women's Press, 1989.

Charnas, Suzy McKee and Chelsea Quinn Yarbro. "Advocates." *Under the Fang*, ed. Robert McCammon. New York: Borderlands Press; New York: Pocket Books, 1991. 123–56.

Chernin, Kim. *The Hungry Self: Women, Eating and Identity*. 1985. New York: Perennial/Harper and Row, 1986.

————. *The Obsession: Reflections on the Tyranny of Slenderness.* 1981. New York: Perennial/Harper and Row, 1982.

Churchill, Caryl. *Mad Forest.* New York: Theatre Communications Group, 1990.

Cole, Mike and Bob Skelton. *Blind Alley: Youth in a Crisis of Capital.* Lancashire: G. W. and A. Hesketh, 1980.

Coleridge, Samuel Taylor. "Christabel." 1797. *Selected Poetry and Prose of Coleridge,* ed. Donald A. Stauffer. New York: Modern Library, 1951. 24–43.

Constantine, Storm. *The Bewitchments of Love and Hate: The Second Book of Wraeththu.* London: Macdonald, 1988.

————. *The Enchantments of Flesh and Spirit: The First Book of Wraeththu.* London: Macdonald, 1987.

————. *The Fulfillments of Fate and Desire: The Third Book of Wraeththu.* London: Macdonald, 1989.

————. "Immaculate." *New Worlds 1,* ed. David Garnett. London: VGSF, 1991. 15–31. *Techno-Gothic,* special issue of *Hayakawa's SF Magazine* 443, 34/10 (September 1993).

Copjec, Joan. *Read My Desire: Lacan Against the Historicists.* Cambridge, MA: MIT Press, 1994.

Craft, Christopher. "'Kiss Me with Those Red Lips': Gender and Inversion in Bram Stoker's *Dracula.*" *Representations* 8 (1984). *Dracula: The Vampire and the Critics,* ed. Margaret L. Carter. Ann Arbor, MI: UMI Research Press, 1988. 167–94.

Crawford, Margaret. "The World in a Shopping Mall." *Variations on a Theme Park: The New American City and the End of Public Space,* ed. Michael Sorkin. New York: Hill and Wang, 1992. 3–30.

Creed, Barbara. *The Monstrous Feminine: Film, Feminism, Psychoanalysis.* New York: Routledge, 1993.

Crimp, Douglas. "AIDS: Cultural Analysis/Cultural Activism." *AIDS: Cultural Analysis/Cultural Activism,* ed. Crimp. Cambridge, MA: MIT Press, 1988. 3–16.

Dann, Jack and Gardner Dozois. "Down Among the Dead Men." 1982. *Blood Is Not Enough: Seventeen Stories of Vampirism,* ed. Ellen Datlow. New York: Morrow, 1989. 228–55.

Datlow, Ellen, ed. *Blood Is Not Enough: Seventeen Stories of Vampirism.* New York: Morrow, 1989.

————, ed. *A Whisper of Blood: Eighteen Stories of Vampirism.* New York: Morrow, 1991.

Davis, Tracy C. "The Theatrical Antecedents of the Mall That Ate Downtown." *Journal of Popular Culture* 24, 4 (1991): 1–15.

Decarnin, Camilla, Eric Garber, and Lyn Paleo, eds. *Worlds Apart.* Boston: Alyson, 1987.

de Certeau, Michel. *The Practice of Everyday Life.* 1974. Trans. Steven Rendall. Berkeley: University of California Press, 1988.

de Gourmont, Remy. "The Magnolia." 1894. *Angels of Perversity.* Trans. Francis Amery [Brian Stableford]. Sawtry, Cambridgeshire: Dedalus, 1992. 90–94.

Dickstein, Morris. "The Aesthetics of Fright." *Planks of Reason: Essays on the Horror Film*, ed. Barry Keith Grant. Metuchen, NJ: Scarecrow Press, 1984. 65–78.

Dijkstra, Bram. *Idols of Perversity: Fantasies of Feminine Evil in Fin-de-Siècle Culture*. New York: Oxford University Press, 1986.

Doane, Janice and Devon Hodges. "Undoing Feminism: From the Preoedipal to Postfeminism in Anne Rice's *Vampire Chronicles*." *American Literary History* 2 (Fall 1990): 422–42.

Doherty, Thomas. *Teenagers and Teenpics: The Juvenilization of American Movies in the 1950s*. Boston: Unwin Hyman, 1988.

du Dubovay, Diane. "If lady is a four letter word, what does 'femininity' mean now?" *Vogue* (Sept. 1976): 100–101.

Edelstein, Andrew J. and Kevin McDonough. *The Seventies: From Hot Pants to Hot Tubs*. New York: Dutton-Penguin, 1990.

Edogawa, Rampo. *The Vampire* [Kyu-ketsu-Ki]. 1930. Tokyo: Shunyoudou, 1987.

Egan, Greg. "Reification Highway." *Interzone* 64 (October 1992): 6–13. *Techno-Gothic*, special issue of *Hayakawa's SF Magazine* 443, 34/10 (September 1993).

Eisenstein, Zillah R. "The Sexual Politics of the New Right: Understanding the 'Crisis of Liberalism' for the 1980s." *Feminist Theory: A Critique of Ideology*, ed. Nannerl O. Keohane, Michelle Z. Rosaldo, and Barbara C. Gelpi. Chicago: University of Chicago Press, 1982. 77–98.

Elrod, P. N. *Bloodlist*. New York: Ace, 1990.

Ewen, Stuart. *All-Consuming Images: The Politics of Style in Contemporary Culture*. New York: Basic Books, 1988.

———. *Captains of Consciousness: Advertising and the Social Roots of the Consumer Culture*. New York: McGraw-Hill, 1976.

Ewen, Stuart and Elizabeth Ewen. *Channels of Desire: Mass Images and the Shaping of American Consciousness*. New York: McGraw-Hill, 1982.

Fairchild Market Research Division. *Market Pacesetters (Young Adults)*, ed. Audrey S. Balchen. New York: Fairchild/Capital Cities Media, 1981.

Faust, Christa. "Cherry." *Love in Vein: Twenty Original Tales of Vampiric Erotica*, ed. Poppy Z. Brite. New York: HarperCollins, 1994. 123–38.

Featherstone, Mike. "The Body in Consumer Culture." *Theory, Culture, and Society* 1, 2 (1982): 18–33.

Fiske, John. *Reading the Popular*. Boston: Unwin Hyman, 1989.

Florescu, Radu R., and Raymond T. McNally. *Dracula, Prince of Many Faces: His Life and Times*. Boston: Little Brown, 1989.

Fontana, Ernest. "Lombroso's Criminal Man and Stoker's *Dracula*." *Victorian Newsletter* 66 (1984). *Dracula: The Vampire and the Critics*, ed. Margaret L. Carter. Ann Arbor, MI: UMI Research Press, 1988. 159–65.

Forrest, Katherine V. "O Captain, My Captain." *Daughters of Darkness: Lesbian Vampire Stories*, ed. Pam Keesey. Pittsburgh: Cleis, 1993. 185–227.

Foucault, Michel. *Discipline and Punish: The Birth of the Prison*. 1977. Trans. Alan Sheridan. New York: Vintage-Random House, 1979.

Foust, R.E. "Monstrous Image: Theory of Fantasy Antagonists." *Genre* 13 (1980): 441–53.

Fox, Richard Wrightman and T. J. Jackson Lears. *The Culture of Consumption: Critical Essays in American History, 1880–1980*. New York: Pantheon, 1983.

Fox, Stephen. *The Mirror Makers: A History of American Advertising and Its Creators*. New York: Morrow, 1984.

Friedberg, Anne. *Window Shopping: Cinema and the Postmodern*. Berkeley: University of California Press, 1993.

Fuss, Diana. *Essentially Speaking: Feminism, Nature and Difference*. New York: Routledge, 1989.

Garber, Eric, ed. *Embracing the Dark*. Boston: Alyson, 1991.

Gaskell, Jane. *The Shiny Narrow Grin*. London: Hodder and Stoughton, 1964.

Gautier, Théophile. *La Morte amoureuse* ["Clarimonde"]. 1836. *One of Cleopatra's Nights*, ed. and trans. Lafcadio Hearn. New York: Worthington, 1882. 81–152.

Gelder, Ken. *Reading the Vampire*. New York: Routledge, 1994.

Gibian, Peter. "The Art of Being Off-Center: Shopping Center Spaces and Spectacles." *Tabloid: A Review of Mass Culture and Everyday Life* 5 (1982): 44–64.

Giddings, Paula. *When and Where I Enter: The Impact of Black Women on Race and Sex in America*. New York: Morrow, 1984.

Gilden, Mel. *How to Be a Vampire in One Easy Lesson*. New York: Avon, 1988.

Gilman, Sander. "AIDS and Syphilis: The Iconography of Disease." *AIDS: Cultural Analysis/Cultural Activism*, ed. Douglas Crimp. Cambridge, MA: MIT Press, 1988. 87–107.

Goethe, Johann Wolfgang von. *Faust*. 1790. Trans. Walter Kaufmann. New York: Anchor, 1963.

Gomez, Jewelle. *The Gilda Stories*. Ithaca, NY: Firebrand, 1991.

———. Panelist. Sessions: "Are Gay Villains Politically Correct?" and "Vampires and Homoeroticism." Gaylaxicon IV. Philadelphia, PA, 17–19 July 1992.

———. "Retta's House." *Village Voice* 39, 7 (15 February 1994): 3.

Goodwin, Andrew. *Dancing in the Distraction Factory: Music Television and Popular Culture*. Minneapolis: University of Minnesota Press, 1992.

Gordon, Joan. "Rehabilitating Revenants, or Sympathetic Vampires in Recent Fiction." *Extrapolation* 29 (Fall 1988): 227–34.

———. "Tiny Baby Bite: Vampirism and Breastfeeding." *HOT WIRE: The Journal of Women's Music and Culture* 4, 1 (1987): 44–45, 59.

Goulart, Ron. *The Assault on Childhood*. 1969. London: Gollancz, 1970.

Graham, John. *Amusement Machines: Dependency and Delinquency*. Home Office Research Study No. 101. London: Her Majesty's Stationery Office, 1988.

Graham, Lawrence and Lawrence Hamdan. *Youthtrends: Capturing the $200 Billion Youth Market*. New York: St. Martin's Press, 1987.

Greenfield, Patricia Marks. *Mind and Media: The Effects of Television, Video Games, and Computers*. Cambridge, MA: Harvard University Press, 1984.

Griffin, Gail B. "'Your Girls That You All Love Are Mine': *Dracula* and the Victorian Male Sexual Imagination." *International Journal of Women's Studies* 3 (1980). *Dracula: The Vampire and the Critics*, ed. Margaret L. Carter. Ann Arbor, MI: UMI Research Press, 1988. 137–48.

Grossberg, Lawrence. *We Gotta Get Out of This Place: Popular Conservatism and Postmodern Culture*. New York: Routledge, 1992.

Grover, Jan Zita. "AIDS: Keywords." *AIDS: Cultural Analysis/Cultural Activism*, ed. Douglas Crimp. Cambridge, MA: MIT Press, 1988. 17–30.

Hagio, Moto. *The Clan of Poe*. Tokyo: Shogakkan, 1974–1977.

Haining, Peter. "Introduction to 'A True Story of a Vampire.'" *The Vampire Omnibus*, ed. Haining. London: Orion, 1995. 117–18.

Halberstam, Judith. "Sucking Blood: Why We Love Vampires." *On Our Backs* 9 (March/April 1993): 10–11, 41.

Hall, Stuart and Tony Jefferson, eds. *Resistance Through Rituals: Youth Subcultures in Post-War Britain*. London: HarperCollins, 1976.

Hambly, Barbara. *Those Who Hunt the Night*. New York: Ballantine, 1988.

Hammura, Ryo. *The Blood Vessel of Stone*. [*Ishi-no-Ketsumyaku*]. Tokyo: Hayakawa, 1971.

Hand, Elizabeth. "The Investiture." Excerpted from *Aestival Tide*. New York: Bantam Books, 1992. 90–123. *Techno-Gothic*, special issue of *Hayakawa's SF Magazine* 443, 34/10 (September 1993).

Hanson, Ellis. "Undead." *AIDS: Cultural Analysis/Cultural Activism*, ed. Douglas Crimp. Cambridge, MA: MIT Press, 1988. 324–40.

Haraway, Donna. "A Cyborg Manifesto: Science, Technology, and Socialist Feminism in the Late Twentieth Century." 1985. *Simians, Cyborgs, and Women: The Reinvention of Nature*. New York: Routledge, 1991. 149–81.

Hatlen, Burton. "The Return of the Repressed/Oppressed in Bram Stoker's *Dracula*." *Minnesota Review* 15 (Fall 1980). *Dracula: The Vampire and the Critics*, ed. Margaret L. Carter. Ann Arbor, MI: UMI Research Press, 1988. 117–36.

Haug, Wolfgang Fritz. *Critique of Commodity Aesthetics: Appearance, Sexuality and Advertising in Capitalist Society*. 1971. Trans. Robert Bock. Minneapolis: University of Minnesota Press, 1986.

Hebdige, Dick. *Subculture: The Meaning of Style*. New York: Methuen, 1979.

Hechinger, Grace and Fred M. Hechinger. *Teenage Tyranny*. New York: Morrow, 1963.

Helitzer, Melvin and Carl Heyel. *The Youth Market: Its Dimensions, Influence and Opportunities for You*. New York: Media Books, 1970.

Higashi, Masao, ed. *The Literature of Dracula: A Reader's Guide to Vampire Fiction*. Tokyo: Genso-Bungaku, 1993.

Higashi, Masao and Aoi Ishido, eds. *An Encyclopedia of Japanese Fantasy Writers*. Tokyo: Genso-Bungaku, 1991.

Hinatsu, Konosuke. "On Vampire Narrative." [Kyu-ketsu-ki-dan]. *Chu-ou-kouron* (1931).

———, ed. and trans. *The Vampire: His Kith and Kin* [Kyu ketsu-ki Youmikou]. By Montague Summers. Tokyo: Bukyo-sha, 1931.

Hodge, Brian. "Alchemy of the Throat." *Love in Vein: Twenty Original Tales of Vampiric Erotica*, ed. Poppy Z. Brite. New York: HarperCollins, 1994. 261–92.

Hodgman, Ann. *There's a Batwing in My Lunchbox*. New York: Avon, 1988.

Hoggart, Richard. *The Uses of Literacy*. London: Chatto and Windus, 1957.

Hollander, Stanley C. and Richard Germain. *Was There a Pepsi Generation Before Pepsi Discovered It? Youth-Based Segmentation in Marketing*. Lincolnwood, IL: NTC Business Books, 1992.

Hollinger, Veronica. "The Vampire and the Alien: Variations on the Outsider." *Science-Fiction Studies* 16 (July 1989): 145–60.

Hoyt, Olga. *Lust for Blood: The Consuming Story of Vampires.* Chelsea, MI: Scarborough, 1984.

Huff, Tanya. *Blood Debt.* New York: Daw, 1997.

——. *Blood Lines.* New York: Daw, 1993.

——. *Blood Pact.* New York: Daw, 1993.

——. *Blood Price.* New York: Daw, 1991.

——. *Blood Trail.* New York: Daw, 1992.

Hutcheon, Linda. *A Theory of Parody: The Teachings of Twentieth-Century Art Forms.* New York: Routledge, 1985.

Irigaray, Luce. *This Sex Which Is Not One.* 1977. Trans. Catherine Porter. Ithaca, NY: Cornell University Press, 1985.

Jackson, Rosemary. *Fantasy: The Literature of Subversion.* New York: Methuen, 1981.

Jacobs, Jerry. *The Mall: An Attempted Escape from Everyday Life.* Prospect Heights, IL: Waveland, 1984.

Jakobson, Roman and Morris Halle. "Two Aspects of Language and Two Types of Aphasic Disturbances." *Fundamentals of Language.* The Hague: Mouton, 1956. 53–82.

Jameson, Fredric. "Pleasure: A Political Issue." *Formations of Pleasure,* ed. Tony Bennett et al. London: Routledge and Kegan Paul, 1983. 1–14.

——. *The Political Unconscious: Narrative as a Socially Symbolic Act.* Ithaca, NY: Cornell University Press, 1981.

——. "Reification and Utopia in Mass Culture." *Social Text* 1 (1979): 135–48.

Jenkins, Henry. "*Star Trek* Rerun, Reread, Rewritten: Fan Writing as Textual Poaching." *Close Encounters: Film, Feminism and Science Fiction,* ed. Constance Penley, Elisabeth Lyon, Lynn Spigal, and Janet Bergstrom. Minneapolis: University of Minnesota Press, 1991. 171–203.

——. *Textual Poachers: Television Fans and Participatory Culture.* New York: Routledge, 1992.

Jhally, Sut. *The Codes of Advertising: Fetishism and the Political Economy of Meaning in the Consumer Society.* New York: Routledge, 1990.

Jo, Masayuki. "Vampire" [Kyu-Ketsu-ki]. *Shin-Seinen* (January 1930).

Johnston, Nancy. "Kirk Loves Spock: 'Homosexual' Confession, Repression, and Orgasm." Presented at the 22nd Annual Popular Culture Association Meeting, Louisville, KY, 18 March 1992.

Jones, Ernest. *On the Nightmare.* 1931. New York: Liveright, 1971.

Jones, Landon Y. *Great Expectations: America and the Baby Boom Generation.* New York: Coward, McCann and Geoghegan, 1980.

Kael, Pauline. *5001 Nights at the Movies.* New York: Holt, 1991.

Kafka, Franz. *The Trial.* 1937. Trans. Willa Muir and Edwin Muir. New York: Schocken Books, 1988.

Kaplan, E. Ann. *Rocking Around the Clock: Music Television, Postmodernism, and Consumer Culture.* New York: Methuen, 1987.

Kasai, Kiyoshi. *Vampire Wars.* Tokyo: Kadokawa, 1982–1992.

Kast, Pierre. *Les Vampires d'Alfama*. Paris: Olivier Orban, 1985; London: W. H. Allen, 1976.

Katz, Jonathan. *The Invention of Heterosexuality*. New York: Dutton, 1995.

Keats, John. "Lamia." *Lamia, Isabella, The Eve of St Agnes and Other Poems*. London: Taylor and Hessey, 1820.

Keesey, Pam, ed. *Dark Angels: Lesbian Vampire Stories*. Pittsburgh: Cleis, 1995.

———, ed. *Daughters of Darkness: Lesbian Vampire Stories*. Pittsburgh: Cleis, 1993.

Kikuchi, Hideyuki. *Vampire Hunter-D*. Tokyo: Asahi Sonorama, 1983–.

Kincaid, James R. *Child-Loving: The Erotic Child and Victorian Culture*. New York: Routledge, 1992.

Kinder, Marsha. *Playing with Power in Movies, Television and Video Games: From Muppet Babies to Teenage Mutant Ninja Turtles*. Berkeley: University of California Press, 1991.

King, Stephen. *'Salem's Lot*. New York: Doubleday, 1975.

Klause, Annette Curtis. *The Silver Kiss*. New York: Dell, 1990.

Klein, Martin M. "The Bite of Pac-Man." *Journal of Psychohistory* 2, 3 (1984): 395–401.

Klein, Melanie. *The Psycho-Analysis of Children*. Trans. Alix Strachey. London: Hogarth, 1937.

Koestenbaum, Wayne. "The Queen's Throat: (Homo)sexuality and the Art of Singing." *Inside/Out: Lesbian Theories, Gay Theories*, ed. Diana Fuss. New York: Routledge, 1991. 205–34.

Kotani, Mari. "Techno-Gothic: An Introduction." *Hayakawa's SF Magazine* 443, 34/10 (September 1993). 10–13.

Kowinski, William Severini. *The Malling of America: An Inside Look at the Great Consumer Paradise*. New York: Morrow, 1985.

Krafft-Ebing, Richard. *Psychopathia Sexualis*. 1886. Ed. F. J. Rebman. New York: Special Books, 1965.

Krantz, Judith. *Scruples*. 1978. New York: Warner, 1979.

Kristeva, Julia. *Powers of Horror: An Essay on Abjection*. 1980. Trans. Leon S. Roudiez. New York: Columbia University Press, 1982.

Krzywinska, Tanya. "La Belle Dame Sans Merci?" *A Queer Romance: Lesbians, Gay Men and Popular Culture*, ed. Paul Burston and Colin Richardson. New York: Routledge, 1995. 99–110.

Kubey, Robert and Reed Larson. "The Use and Experience of the New Video Media Among Children and Young Adolescents." *Communication Research* 17, 1 (1990): 107–30.

Kuhn, Annette. *The Power of the Image: Essays on Representation and Sexuality*. London: Routledge and Kegan Paul, 1985.

Langman, Lauren. "Neon Cages: Shopping for Subjectivity." *Lifestyle Shopping: The Subject of Consumption*, ed. Rob Shields. New York: Routledge, 1992. 40–82.

Lardner, James. *Fast Forward: Hollywood, the Japanese, and the Onslaught of the VCR*. New York: Norton, 1987.

Lasch, Christopher. *The Culture of Narcissism: American Life in an Age of Diminishing Expectations*. New York: Norton, 1978.

Latham, Rob. "Dark Historical Science Fantasy." Review of Brian Stableford's *The Empire of Fear* and *The Werewolves of London. Necrofile* 2 (Fall 1991): 8–10.

Lears, Jackson. *No Place of Grace: Antimodernism and the Transformation of American Culture, 1880–1920.* New York: Pantheon, 1981.

Lear's Magazine. Interview with Anne Rice. 2, 7 (Oct. 1989): 88.

Lee, Martyn J. *Consumer Culture Reborn: The Cultural Politics of Consumption.* New York: Routledge, 1993.

Lee, Tanith. *Sabella, or the Blood Stone.* New York: Daw, 1980.

Lee, Vernon. "Amour Dure." *Hauntings.* London: Heinemann, 1890. 1–58.

———. "Prince Alberic and the Snake Lady." 1896. *Pope Jacynth and Other Fantastic Tales.* London: Grant Richards, 1904. 21–114.

Le Fanu, J. Sheridan. *Carmilla.* 1872. *Vampires: Two Centuries of Great Vampire Stories,* ed. Alan Ryan. Garden City, NY: Doubleday, 1987. 71–137.

Le Guin, Ursula K. *The Left Hand of Darkness.* New York: Ace, 1969.

Leman, Bob. "The Pilgrimage of Clifford M." *Magazine of Fantasy and Science Fiction* 66 (May 1984): 8–30.

Levy, Mark R., ed. *The VCR Age: Home Video and Mass Communication.* Newbury Park, CA: Sage, 1989.

Lichtenberg, Jacqueline. *Those of My Blood.* New York: St. Martin's Press, 1988.

———. "Vampire with Muddy Boots." *Onyx* 1 (February 1992): 4–6.

Lorrain, Jean. "The Glass of Blood." 1893. Trans. Brian Stableford. *The Dedalus Book of Decadence,* ed. Brian Stableford. Sawtry, Cambridgeshire: Dedalus, 1991. 86–94.

Lott, Eric. "Whiteness: A Glossary." *Village Voice* 38, 20 (18 May 1993): 38–39.

Lovell, Terry. *Consuming Fiction.* London: Verso, 1987.

Lyotard, Jean-François. *The Postmodern Condition: A Report on Knowledge.* Trans. Geoff Bennington and Brian Massumi. Minneapolis: Minnesota University Press, 1984.

Maas, Peter. *The Valachi Papers.* New York: Putnam, 1968.

MacDonald, Ingrid. "The Catherine Trilogy." *Catherine, Catherine: Lesbian Short Stories.* Toronto: Women's Press, 1991. 29–90.

Macdonald, Lorne. *Poor Polidori: A Critical Biography of the Author of The Vampire.* Toronto: University of Toronto Press, 1991.

Maltin, Leonard. *Leonard Maltin's Movie and Video Guide 1992.* New York: Signet, 1993.

Mark, Marsha, ed. *Disorderly Conduct: The VLS Fiction Reader.* New York: Serpent's Tail, 1991.

Martin, Anya. "A Conversation with Anne Rice." *Cemetery Dance* 3 (Summer 1991): 34–39.

Martin, George R. R. *Fevre Dream.* New York: Simon and Schuster, 1982.

Marx, Karl. *Capital.* Vol. 1. 1867. Trans. Ben Fowkes. New York: Penguin, 1976.

Mascetti, Manuella Dunn. *Vampire: The Complete Guide to the World of the Undead.* New York: Viking, 1992.

McCammon, Robert R. *They Thirst.* 1981. New York: Pocket Books, 1988.

———, ed. *Under the Fang.* New York: Pocket Books, 1991.

McDowell, Ian. "Geraldine." *Love in Vein: Twenty Original Tales of Vampiric Erotica,* ed. Poppy Z. Brite. New York: HarperCollins, 1994. 25–56.

McMahan, Jeffrey N. *Somewhere in the Night*. Boston: Alyson Publications, 1989.
———. *Vampires Anonymous*. Boston: Alyson Publications, 1991.
McNeal, James U. *Children as Consumers: Insights and Implications*. Lexington, MA: Lexington Books, 1987.
McRobbie, Angela. *Feminism and Youth Culture: From "Jackie" to "Just Seventeen."* London: Macmillan, 1991.
Melton, J. Gordon. *The Vampire Book: The Encyclopedia of the Undead*. Washington, DC: Visible Ink, 1994.
Mercer, Kobena. "Black Hair/Style Politics." *New Formations* 3 (Winter 1987): 33–54.
Meyer, Moe. "Introduction: Reclaiming the Discourses of Camp." *The Politics and Poetics of Camp*, ed. Meyer. New York: Routledge, 1994. 1–22.
Meyerowitz, Joshua. "The Adultlike Child and the Childlike Adult: Socialization in an Electronic Age." *Deadalus* 113 (1984): 19–48.
Milbank, Caroline Rennolds. *New York Fashion: The Evolution in American Style*. New York: Harry N. Abrams, 1989.
Miner, Madonne M. *Insatiable Appetites: Twentieth-Century Women's Bestsellers*. Westport, CT: Greenwood Press, 1984.
Moretti, Franco. *Signs Taken for Wonders: Essays in the Sociology of Literary Forms*. Rev. ed. 1987. Trans. Susan Fischer, David Forgacs, and David Miller. New York: Verso, 1988.
Moschis, George P. *Acquisition of the Consumer Role by Adolescents*. Atlanta: Public Services Division, College of Business Administration, Georgia State University, 1978.
Nagakawa, Yoichi. "Vampire" [Kyu-ketsu-ki]. *Nakagawa Yoichi Zenshu No.2*. Tanpen Shousetsu-shuu, 1931; Tokyo: Kadokawa-shoten, 1967.
Nasaw, David. *Children of the City: At Work and at Play*. New York: Oxford University Press, 1985.
Naylor, Gloria, ed. *Children of the Night: Best Short Stories by Black Writers, 1967 to the Present*. Boston: Little Brown, 1996.
Ohara, Mariko. "Girl." 1984. *Monkey Brain Sushi: New Tastes in Japanese Fiction*, ed. and trans. Alfred Birnbaum. Tokyo: Kodansha International, 1991.
———. "Mental Female." 1985. Trans. Kazuko Behrens and Gene Van Troyer. *Avant-Pop Japan*, ed. Takayuki Tatsumi and Larry McCaffery. Tokyo: Hayakawa, forthcoming.
———. *Hybrid Child*. Tokyo: Hayakawa, 1990.
———. *Ephemera the Vampire*. Tokyo: Hayakawa, 1992.
Olsen, Lance. *Ellipse of Uncertainty: An Introduction to Postmodern Fantasy*. Westport, CT: Greenwood Press, 1987.
Paglia, Camille. *Sexual Personae: Art and Decadence from Nefertiti to Emily Dickinson*. New York: Vintage, 1990.
Pantaleone, Michele. *The Mafia and Politics*. London: Chatto and Windus, 1966.
Peiss, Kathy. *Cheap Amusements: Working Women and Leisure in Turn-of-the-Century New York*. Philadelphia: Temple University Press, 1986.
———. "Commercial Leisure and the 'Woman Question'." *For Fun and Profit: The Transformation of Leisure into Consumption*, ed. Richard Butsch. Philadelphia: Temple University Press, 1990. 105–17.

Penley, Constance. "Brownian Motion: Women, Tactics, and Technology." *Techno-culture*, ed. Penley and Andrew Ross. Minneapolis: University of Minnesota Press, 1991. 135–61.

Petrey, Susan. *Gifts of Blood.* New York: Baen, 1992.

Polidori, John. *The Vampyre; A Tale.* 1819. *The Vampyre; and Ernestus Berchtold, or, The Modern Oedipus. Collected Fiction of John William Polidori.* Ed. D. L. Macdonald and Kathleen Scherf. Toronto: University of Toronto Press, 1994.

Pope, Daniel. *The Making of Modern Advertising.* New York: Basic Books, 1983.

Postman, Neil. *The Disappearance of Childhood.* New York: Delacorte, 1982.

Prawer, S. S. *Caligari's Children: The Film as Tale of Terror.* New York: Da Capo, 1980.

Puzo, Mario. *The Godfather.* New York: Putnam, 1969.

Rabkin, Eric S. *The Fantastic in Literature.* Princeton, NJ: Princeton University Press, 1986.

Ramsland, Katherine. *Prism of the Night: A Biography of Anne Rice.* 1991. New York: Plume-Penguin, 1992.

Reynolds, Simon. *Manchester Guardian*, 19 March 1992: 26.

Riccardo, Martin V. *Vampires Unearthed: The Complete Multi-Media Vampire and Dracula Bibliography.* New York: Garland, 1983.

Rice, Anne. *Interview with the Vampire.* 1976. New York: Ballantine, 1977.

———. *Memnoch the Devil.* New York: Knopf, 1995.

———. *The Mummy, or Ramses the Damned.* New York: Ballantine, 1989.

———. *The Queen of the Damned.* 1988. New York: Ballantine, 1989.

———. *The Tale of the Body Thief.* 1992. New York: Ballantine, 1993.

———. *The Vampire Lestat.* 1985. New York: Ballantine, 1986.

Roddick, Ellen. "Dieter's Notebook: Metabolism Demystified." *Cosmopolitan* (March 1976): 40.

Roof, Judith. *A Lure of Knowledge: Lesbian Sexuality and Theory.* New York: Columbia University Press, 1991.

Roth, Phyllis A. "Suddenly Sexual Women in Bram Stoker's *Dracula*." *Literature and Psychology* 27 (1977). *Dracula: The Vampire and the Critics*, ed. Margaret L. Carter. Ann Arbor, MI: UMI Research Press, 1988. 57–67.

Rowe, Michael and Thomas S. Roche, eds. *Sons of Darkness: Tales of Men, Blood and Immortality.* Pittsburgh: Cleis Press, 1996.

———. "Introduction." *Sons of Darkness: Tales of Men, Blood and Immortality*, ed. Rowe and Roche. 9–13.

Russ, Joanna. *The Female Man.* New York: Bantam, 1975.

Russell, Louise B. *The Baby Boom Generation and the Economy.* Washington, D.C.: Brookings Institution, 1982.

Rymer, James Malcolm. *Varney the Vampyre; or, The Feast of Blood.* 1847. Ed. Devendra P. Varma. New York: Arno Press 1970.

Saberhagen, Fred. *The Dracula Tape.* New York: Warner, 1975.

———. *The Holmes-Dracula File.* New York: Ace, 1978.

———. *An Old Friend of the Family.* New York: Ace, 1979.

Salah, Pat. "The Perfect Form." *Blood Kiss: Vampire Erotica*, ed. Cecilia Tan. Boston: Circlet Press, 1994. 1–18.

Sapir, David. "The Anatomy of Metaphor." *The Social Use of Metaphor: Essays on the Anthropology of Rhetoric*, ed. David Sapir and J. C. Crocker. Philadelphia: University of Pennsylvania Press, 1977. 3–32.

Schiavo, Giovanni E. *The Truth About the Mafia and Organized Crime in America*. New York: Vigo, 1962.

Schwartz, Hillel. *Never Satisfied: A Cultural History of Diets, Fantasies and Fat*. New York: Free Press-Macmillan, 1986.

Scott, Jody. *I, Vampire*. 1984. London: Women's Press, 1986.

Sedgwick, Eve Kosofsky. *Between Men: English Literature and Male Homosocial Desire*. New York: Columbia University Press, 1985.

———. *Epistemology of the Closet*. Berkeley and Los Angeles: University of California Press, 1990.

Seid, Roberta Pollack. *Never Too Thin: Why Women Are at War with Their Bodies*. Englewood Cliffs, NJ: Prentice Hall, 1989.

Senf, Carol A. *The Vampire in Nineteenth-Century English Literature*. Bowling Green, OH: Bowling Green State University Popular Press, 1988.

Shilts, Randy. *And the Band Played On: Politics, People, and the AIDS Epidemic*. New York: Viking, 1987.

Siebers, Tobin. *The Romantic Fantastic*. Ithaca, NY: Cornell University Press, 1984.

Simmons, Dan. *Children of the Night*. New York: Warner, 1992.

Skal, David. *Hollywood Gothic: The Tangled Web of Dracula from Novel to Stage to Screen*. New York: Norton, 1991.

———. *The Monster Show: A Cultural History of Horror*. New York: Norton, 1993.

Skipp, John and Craig Spector. *The Light at the End*. New York: Bantam, 1986.

Slater, Don. "Going Shopping: Markets, Crowds and Consumption." *Cultural Reproduction*, ed. Chris Jenks. New York: Routledge, 1993. 188–209.

Smith, Billy G. "Black Women Who Stole Themselves in 18th-Century America." Presented at the Berkshire Conference on the History of Women, Vassar College, 11 June 1993.

Somtow, S.P. [Somtow Sucharitkul]. *Valentine*. New York: Tor Books, 1992.

———. *Vampire Junction*. 1984. New York: Tor Books, 1991.

Spivak, Gayatri Chakravorty. *In Other Worlds: Essays in Cultural Politics*. New York: Routledge, 1988.

Stableford, Brian. *The Angel of Pain*. London: Simon and Schuster (UK), 1991.

———. *The Empire of Fear*. London: Simon and Schuster (UK), 1988.

———. "Eroticism in Supernatural Literature." *Survey of Modern Fantasy Literature*, ed. Frank N. Magill. Englewood Cliffs, NJ: Salem Press, 1983. 2331–49.

———. "Immortality." *The Encyclopedia of Science Fiction*, ed. John Clute and Peter Nicholls. London: Orbit, 1993. 615–16.

———. "The Man Who Loved the Vampire Lady." *Magazine of Fantasy and Science Fiction* (August 1988): 6–28.

———. "The Profession of Science Fiction, No. 42: A Long and Winding Road." *Foundation* 50 (Autumn 1990): 28–51.

———. *Young Blood*. London: Simon and Schuster (UK), 1992.

Steele, Bruce C. "Poppy Art: Horror Novelist Poppy Z. Brite Turns Stomachs and Opens Eyes." *Out* 36 (September 1995): 50.

Stenbock, Eric. "A True Story of a Vampire." 1894. *The Vampire Omnibus*, ed. Peter Haining. London: Orion, 1995. 118–25.

Stevenson, John Allan. "A Vampire in the Mirror: The Sexuality of Dracula." *PMLA* 103 (February 1988): 139–49.

Stoker, Bram. *Dracula.* 1897. New York: Dell, 1965.

Stone, Allucquère Rosanne. *The War of Desire and Technology at the Close of the Mechanical Age.* Cambridge, MA: MIT Press, 1996.

Strasser, Susan. *Satisfaction Guaranteed: The Making of the American Mass Market.* New York: Pantheon, 1989.

Streiber, Whitley. *Communion: A True Story.* New York: Beech Tree Books, 1987.

———. *The Hunger.* New York: William Morrow, 1981.

———. *Transformation: The Breakthrough.* New York: Beech Tree Books, 1988.

———. *The Wolfen.* New York: William Morrow, 1978.

Sturgeon, Theodore. *Some of Your Blood.* New York: Ballantine, 1961.

Sucharitkul, Somtow. *Mallworld.* 1981. New York: Tor Books 1984.

Sudnow, David. *Pilgrim in the Microworld.* New York: Warner, 1983.

Summers, Montague. *The Vampire: His Kith and Kin.* 1928. New York: University Books, 1960.

Sunaga, Asahiko, ed. *Bloody Arabesque: A Vampire Reader.* Tokyo: Pyotol, 1993.

———. *A History of Japanese Fantasy Literature.* Tokyo: Hakusuisha, 1993.

Suvin, Darko. *Metamorphoses of Science Fiction: On the Poetics and History of a Literary Genre.* New Haven, CT: Yale University Press, 1979.

Tan, Cecilia, ed. *Blood Kiss: Vampire Erotica.* Boston: Circlet Press, 1994.

Tieck, Johann Ludwig (attributed to). "Wake Not the Dead" ["The Bride of the Grave"]. c. 1810. *Vampyres: Lord Byron to Count Dracula.* Christopher Frayling. London: Faber and Faber, 1991. 165–89.

Tiptree, James, Jr. "And I Awoke and Found Me Here on the Cold Hill's Side." 1971. *Ten Thousand Light Years from Home.* New York: Ace, 1973. 1–13.

Treichler, Paula A. "AIDS, Homophobia, and Biomedical Discourse: An Epidemic of Signification." *AIDS: Cultural Analysis/Cultural Activism,* ed. Douglas Crimp. Cambridge, MA: MIT Press, 1988. 31–70.

Triggs, J. A. "A Mirror for Mankind: The Pose of Hamlet with the Skull of Yorick." *New Orleans Review* 17 (Fall 1990): 71–79.

Twitchell, James B. *The Living Dead: A Study of the Vampire in Romantic Literature.* Durham, NC: Duke University Press, 1981.

Waddell, Martin. *Little Dracula Goes to School.* Cambridge, MA: Candlewick Press, 1992.

Walker, Alice. *The Color Purple.* New York: Harcourt Brace, 1982.

Ward, Scott, Daniel B. Wackman, and Ellen Wartella. *How Children Learn to Buy: The Development of Consumer Information-Processing Skills.* Beverly Hills, CA: Sage, 1977.

Watney, Simon. *Policing Desire: Pornography, AIDS, and the Media.* 2nd. edition. Minneapolis: University of Minnesota Press, 1989.

Weber, Jean-Jacques. "The Foreground-Background Distinction: A Survey of Its Definitions and Distinctions." *Linguistics in Literature* 8 (1983): 1–16.

Weiner, Lynn. "Sisters of the Road: Women Transients and Tramps." *Waiting for Work: Tramps in America, 1790–1935,* ed. Eric Monkkonen. Lincoln: University of Nebraska Press, 1984. 171–88.

Weiss, Andrea. *Vampires and Violets: Lesbians in the Cinema*. London: Jonathan Cape, 1992.

Wertham, Frederick. *Seduction of the Innocent*. New York: Rinehart, 1954.

Wheelwright, Julie. *Amazons and Military Maids: Women Who Dressed as Men in Pursuit of Life, Liberty and Happiness*. London: Pandora, 1989.

Wilde, Alan. *Horizons of Assent: Modernism, Postmodernism, and the Ironic Imagination*. Baltimore: Johns Hopkins University Press, 1981.

Williams, Raymond. "Advertising: The Magic System." 1969. *Problems in Materialism and Culture: Selected Essays*. London: Verso, 1980. 170–95.

Williams, Rosalind. *Dream Worlds: Mass Consumption in Late Nineteenth-Century France*. Berkeley: University of California Press, 1982.

Williamson, Jack. *Darker Than You Think*. 1948. Reprinted New York: Dell, 1979.

Williamson, Judith. *Decoding Advertisements*. London: Boyars, 1978.

Willis, Connie. "Jack." 1991. *Impossible Things*. New York: Bantam, 1993. 372–432.

Wilson, Elizabeth. *Adorned in Dreams: Fashion and Modernity*. London: Virago, 1985.

———. *The Sphinx in the City: Urban Life, the Control of Disorder, and Women*. Berkeley: University of California Press, 1991.

Wolf, Leonard, ed. *The Annotated Dracula*, by Bram Stoker. New York: Ballantine, 1975.

———. *A Dream of Dracula: In Search of the Living Dead*. New York: Popular Library, 1972.

Wolff, Janet. "The Invisible Flaneuse: Women and the Literature of Modernity." *Theory, Culture and Society* 2, 3 (1985): 37–46.

Woodward, Kathleen. "Youthfulness as a Masquerade." *Discourse* 11, 1 (1988–89): 119–42.

Worley, Lloyd. "The Prenatal and Natal Foundations of the Vampire Myth." Paper presented at the International Conference for the Fantastic in the Arts, Fort Lauderdale, Florida, 1991.

Wright, Dudley. *The Book of Vampires*. New York: Dorset Press, 1987.

Yarbro, Chelsea Quinn. *A Flame in Byzantium*. New York: Tor Books, 1987.

———. *Hotel Transylvania*. New York: St. Martin's Press, 1978.

———. *Path of the Eclipse*. 1981. New York: Tor Books, 1989.

Yokomizo, Seishi. *Dokuro-Kengyo* (The Death's-Head Stranger). Tokyo: Fujimi, 1939.

zana. "dracula retold." *Daughters of Darkness: Lesbian Vampire Stories*, ed. Pam Keesey. Pittsburgh: Cleis, 1993. 19–22.

Zimmerman, Bonnie. "Daughters of Darkness: The Lesbian Vampire in Film." *Planks of Reason: Essays on the Horror Film*, ed. Barry Keith Grant. Metuchen, NJ: Scarecrow Press, 1984. 153–63.

Films Cited

After Hours. Martin Scorsese. 1985.
Alien. Ridley Scott. 1979.
The Big Chill. Lawrence Kasdan. 1983.
Blacula. William Crain. 1972.
Blade Runner. Ridley Scott. 1981.
Blood and Roses. Roger Vadim. 1961.
Bram Stoker's Dracula. Francis Ford Coppola. 1992.
Buffy the Vampire Slayer. Fran Rubel Kuzui. 1992.
Carmilla. Gabrielle Beaumont. 1989.
Communion. Philippe Mora. 1989.
Count Dracula and His Vampire Bride. Alan Gibson. 1973.
The Crow. Alex Proyas. 1994.
The Crow: City of Angels. Tim Pope. 1996.
The Crying Game. Neil Jordan. 1992.
Daughters of Darkness. Harry Kumel. 1971.
Dawn of the Dead. George Romero. 1979.
Dracula. Tod Browning. 1931.
Dracula. John Badham. 1979.
Dracula A.D. 1972. Alan Gibson. 1972.
Dracula: Dead and Loving It. Mel Brooks. 1995.
Dracula Has Risen from the Grave. Freddie Francis. 1968.
*Dracula—Prince of Darkness.*Terence Fisher. 1966.
Dracula Rising. Fred Gallo. 1992.
Dry Kisses Only. Kaucyila Boole, Jane Curtis. 1990.
Fatal Attraction. Adrian Lyne. 1987.
Flashdance. Adrian Lyne. 1983.
Frankenstein. James Whale. 1931.
Les Frissons des Vampires (Sex and the Vampire). Jean Rollin. 1970.
Ganja and Hess. Quentin Kelly, Jack Jordan. 1973.
The Godfather. Francis Ford Coppola. 1972.
Godfather 3. Francis Ford Coppola. 1971.
The Hidden. Jack Sholder. 1987.
Horror of Dracula. Terence Fisher. 1958.
The Hunger. Tony Scott. 1983.
The Incredible Shrinking Woman. Joel Schumacher. 1981.
Innocent Blood. John Landis. 1992.

Interview with the Vampire. Neil Jordan. 1994.
King Kong. Merian C. Cooper, Ernest B. Schoedsack. 1933.
The Lost Boys. Joel Schumacher. 1987.
Love at First Bite. Stan Dragoti. 1979.
Mr. Mom. Stan Dragoti. 1983.
Near Dark. Kathryn Bigelow. 1987.
Pets or Meat: The Return to Flint. Michael Moore. 1992.
Return of the Jedi. Richard Marquand. 1983.
Robocop. Paul Verhoeven. 1987.
Roger and Me. Michael Moore. 1989.
Scars of Dracula. Roy Ward Baker. 1970.
Scream, Blacula, Scream! Robert Kelljan. 1973.
The Seven Brothers Meet Dracula. Roy Ward Baker. 1974.
Sundown: The Vampire in Retreat. Anthony Kickox. 1991.
Taste the Blood of Dracula. Peter Sasdy. 1970.
Terms of Endearment. James L. Brooks. 1983.
The Thing. John Carpenter. 1982.
To Love a Vampire. Jimmy Sangster. 1970.
To Sleep with a Vampire. Adam Friedman. 1992.
Twins of Evil. John Hough. 1971.
The Vamp. Richard Wenk. 1986.
A Vampire in Brooklyn. Eddie Murphy. 1994.
The Vampire Lovers. Roy Ward Baker. 1971.
Vampire's Kiss. Robert Bierman. 1989.
Vampyr. Carl Theodor Dreyer. 1931.
Wolfen. Michael Wadleigh. 1981.

Index

Contributors

BRIAN ALDISS has had a book published every year since 1958. He writes novels and short stories, mainly within the SF orbit. His science-fiction criticism, including *Trillion Year Spree: The History of Science Fiction* (1986), has won many awards. He is also a poet, and he recently illustrated one of his own collections of short stories. His autobiography, *Twinkling of an Eye*, will appear in 1997.

NINA AUERBACH read *Dracula* surreptitiously when she was seven and has identified with vampires since then. She is now the John Welsh Centennnial Professor of History and Literature at the University of Pennsylvania. Her six books include *Woman and the Demon*; *Ellen Terry, Player in her Time*; and, most recently, *Our Vampires, Ourselves*. Her Norton Critical Edition of *Dracula*, co-edited with David Skal, appears in 1997.

MARGARET L. CARTER is a native of Norfolk, Virginia, and earned her Ph.D. in English Literature at the University of California, Irvine. She works part-time as a legislative proofreader for the State of Maryland. Her recent publications include *Dracula: The Vampire and the Critics*, a critical anthology, and *The Vampire in Literature: A Critical Bibliography*. Her short story, "Voice from the Void," is collected in *The Time of the Vampires* (1996), and she is currently writing a monograph on "The Vampire as Alien." She has four children and two grandchildren.

SUZY MCKEE CHARNAS is a born-and-bred New Yorker who has lived in New Mexico with her lawyer husband since 1969. She writes fantasy and science fiction for both adult and young adult readers, has recently become involved in playwriting and writing lyrics for a musical version of *Nosferatu*, and occasionally teaches writing courses and workshops. She is currently working on the fourth and final volume of a futuristic feminist epic that began with her first novel, *Walk to the End of the World*, in 1974 (recently available again through the Women's Press in London). Other of her award-winning titles in fantasy and science fiction include "Boobs," *Motherlines*, and *The Furies*.

JEWELLE GOMEZ is the author of *The Gilda Stories*, winner of two Lambda Literary Awards, and its adaptation for the stage, *Bones and Ash: A Gilda Story*, performed by Urban Bush Women. She is also the author of a collection of essays, *Forty-Three Septembers*, and three collections of poetry, the most recent of which is *Oral Tradition*. She is Executive Director of the Poetry Center and American Poetry Archives at San Francisco State University.

JOAN GORDON received her Ph.D. from the University of Iowa and is Associate Professor of English at Nassau Community College. She has published Starmont Readers' Guides to the writing of Joe Haldeman and Gene Wolfe, as well as scholarly articles on these authors, on feminist science fiction, and on the vampire as metaphor.

VERONICA HOLLINGER is Associate Professor in the Cultural Studies Program at Trent University in Ontario. She is a co-editor of *Science-Fiction Studies* and has published articles on feminist science fiction, cyberpunk, vampires, and postmodern theatre. She won the Science Fiction Research Association's Pioneer Award for her essay on vampires in science fiction.

TREVOR HOLMES is a doctoral student in English at York University in Toronto, where he teaches one section of a course in Gender Studies. When a colleague started a dissertation on vampires in literature, Trevor decided to return to his goth/punk roots and unearthed the idea for a dissertation on goth subjectivity. He has presented papers on *Buffy the Vampire Slayer* and on politeness in Canadian vampire fiction, as well as having invented the character of "Jerry Springer's Undead Nephew" for a special screening of Abel Ferrara's vampire-flick *The Addiction* in Ottawa.

MIRIAM JONES is a doctoral candidate in English at York University, where she is writing about women and violence in British popular literature of the nineteenth century. She is interested in popular, women's, and working-people's culture and has published and delivered papers about vampires in literature and film, ballads, broadsides, eighteenth- and nineteenth-century crime literature, and kung-fu movies.

MARI KOTANI is a science-fiction critic. She is the author of *Techno-Gynesis: The Political Unconscious of Feminist Science Fiction* (Tokyo: Keiso-shobo, 1994), and winner of the 15th Japan SF Award. Her translation from English to Japanese of Donna Haraway's "A Manifesto for Cyborgs" won the 2nd Japan Translation Award: Philosophy Section. Her writings have appeared in many Japanese newspapers and magazines such as *Hayakawa's Science Fiction Magazine* and her most recent study, *Alien Bedfellows*, is forthcoming from Chikuma-shobo, Tokyo.

ROB LATHAM is Assistant Professor of English at the University of Iowa, where he has taught a survey class on "The Vampire in Anglo-American Literature and Film." He is the co-editor of the first four volumes of the *Science Fiction and Fantasy Book Review Annual*, and of *Modes of the Fantastic*, a collection of critical essays on fantastic literature, art, and popular culture. He has published articles in *Science-Fiction Studies*, *Journal of the Fantastic in the Arts*, and *Vanishing Point: Studies in Comparative Literature*, and his book reviews appear regularly in *New York Review of Science Fiction* and *Necrofile: The Review of Horror Literature*. He is currently completing a book-length manuscript entitled "Consuming Hungers: Vampires, Cyborgs, and the Culture of Information."

NICOLA NIXON is an Assistant Professor of English at Concordia University in Montreal. Although her primary area of research is nineteenth-century American literature, especially the writings of Herman Melville and Henry James, she has also published articles on detective fiction and science fiction, and has an article forthcoming on serial killers and late twentieth-century American gothic.

BRIAN STABLEFORD, who holds graduate degrees in both biology and sociology, has published more than forty science-fiction novels and has written a great deal of non-fiction as well, mostly about the history of imaginative literature with occasional diversions into futurology and the popularization of science. He has written game tie-in fantasy novels as Brian Craig and translates French Decadent texts as Francis Amery. In order to get out of the house occasionally, he teaches the "Science Fiction" module of the degree in "Science, Society, and the Media" for the University of the West of England, and an extra-mural course in "Writing Fiction" for the University of Reading. He worked as Contributing Editor on the 1993 edition of *The Encyclopedia of Science Fiction*.

SANDRA TOMC is an Assistant Professor of English at the University of British Columbia in Vancouver. She works on nineteenth- and twentieth-century American popular culture and is completing a book on antebellum literary idleness.

JULES ZANGER retired several years ago from Southern Illinois University, where he was Professor of American Literature and American

Studies. His articles and essays have appeared in *American Literature*, *American Studies*, *Modern Philology*, *Literature in Translation*, *NEQ*, and elsewhere. He has been a Fulbright Scholar in Brazil and Czechoslovakia, and a Visiting Professor in France. At present he lives in Frankfurt and teaches at the University of Frankfurt and the University of Mainz. It remains fun.